55048819

CARMEL CLAY PUBLIC LIBRARY

D0105974

WITHDRAWN FROM
CARMEL CLAY PUBLIC LIBRARY

AUSTRIA'S
BEST-LOVED
DRIVING
TOURS

CARMEL CLAY PUBLIC LIBRARY
55 4th Avenue SE
Carmel, IN 46032
(317) 844-3361
Renewal Line: (317) 814-3936
www.carmel.lib.in.us

#64123 Highsmith® Inc. 2003

⊛Wiley Publishing, Inc.

Touring Club Italiano
Chairman: Roberto Ruozi
General director: Guido Venturini
Touring Editore
Managing director: Guido Venturini
General director: Alfieri Lorenzon
Editorial director: Michele D'Innella
Editorial production and layout: Studio editoriale Selmi
Written by: Orietta Colombai
Translated by: Barbara Fisher
Picture research: Mattia Goffetti
Maps: Graffito-Cusano Milanino; Revised maps: Sergio Seveso

© 2004 Touring Editore
Management and editorial office: Via Adamello, 10 - Milano

© Concept and design The Automobile Association Developments Limited

This Best Drives guidebook was produced by Touring Club Italiano in agreement with The Automobile Association Developments Limited, owner of the 'Best Drives' series

© English translation: The Automobile Association Developments Limited 2004

All rights reserved. No part of this publication may be reproduced, stored in a retrieval system, or transmitted in any form or by any means – electronic, photocopying, recording or otherwise – unless the permission of the publishers has been obtained beforehand.
This book may not be sold, resold, hired out or otherwise disposed of by way of trade in any form of binding or cover other than that in which it is published, without the prior consent of the publisher.

The contents of this publication are believed correct at the time of printing. Nevertheless, the publishers cannot accept responsibility for errors or omissions or for changes in details given in this guide or for the consequences of any reliance on the information provided by the same. Assessments of attractions and so forth are based upon the author's own experience and, therefore, descriptions in this guide necessarily contain an element of subjective opinion which may not reflect the publisher's opinion or dictate a reader's own experience on another occasion.

Published by AA Publishing

Published in the United States by
John Wiley & Sons, Inc.
111 River Street, Hoboken, NJ 07030

Find us online at Frommers.com

ISBN 0-7645-4326-1
ISSN Pending

Photolito and photocomposition: APV Vaccani, Milano
Printed and bound: G. Canale & C. S.p.a., Torino, Italy

A01525

CONTENTS

ROUTE MAP OF AUSTRIA inside front and back covers

ABOUT THIS BOOK 4 – 5

TIROL & VORARLBERG 6 – 47
Tour 1 Glaciers & Green Pastures 8 – 14
Tour 2 The Oberland & South Tirol 15 – 22
Tour 3 The Outer Tirol 23 – 26
Tour 4 Innsbruck 27 – 31
Tour 5 Innsbruck to East Tirol 32 – 39
Tour 6 The Lower Tirol 40 – 45
The Food & Wine of Austria 46 – 47

CARINTHIA & STYRIA 48 – 87
Tour 7 The Dolomites to Millstätter See 50 – 53
Tour 8 The Lakes of Southern Carinthia 54 – 60
Tour 9 From Alps to Spas 61 – 67
Tour 10 Famous Abbeys & Ancient Castles 68 – 76
Tour 11 The Green Lands of Styria 77 – 83
Hot Water Spas 84 – 85
Tour 12 Medieval Towns & Fortresses 86 – 89

NORTHERN SALZBURG & UPPER AUSTRIA 90 – 119
Tour 13 Salzburg 92 – 97
Austria's Tradition of Music 98 – 99
Tour 14 Salzburg & the Salzkammergut 100 – 107
Tour 15 Mühlviertel's Forests & Meadows 108 – 112
Tour 16 Famous Abbeys 113 – 116
Tour 17 South of the Danube 117 – 119

VIENNA, LOWER AUSTRIA & THE BURGENLAND 120 – 157
Tour 18 History & Nature 122 – 125
Tour 19 North of the Danube 126 – 130
Tour 20 Vienna 131 – 137
The Habsburgs 138 – 139
Tour 21 The Forests North of Vienna 140 – 144
Tour 22 The Wine District 145 – 147
Tour 23 The Danube & Neusiedler See 148 – 151
Tour 24 The Southern Vienna Woods 152 – 154
Tour 25 Castles of the Burgenland 155 – 157

PRACTICAL INFORMATION 158 – 173

INDEX & ACKNOWLEDGEMENTS 174 – 176

ABOUT THIS BOOK

This book is not only a practical touring guide for independent travellers, but it is also invaluable for those who would like to know more about Austria.

The country is divided into 4 geographical areas, with town visits and itineraries for each one, starting from places particularly suited as bases for exploring the area. There are also specific city tours from Innsbruck, Salzburg and Vienna.

Each tour has details of the most interesting places to visit en route. Boxes catering for special interests follow some of the main entries – for those whose interest is in history or walking or those who have children. There are also boxes which highlight scenic stretches of road and which give details of the natural environment, local traditions and gastronomy. Special features cover food and wine, spas, music and the Habsburgs.

The simple route directions are accompanied by an easy-to-use map at the beginning of each tour, along with a chart showing how far it is from one town to the next in kilometres and miles. This can help you decide where to take a break and stop overnight. (All distances quoted are approximate.)

Before setting off it is advisable to check with the information centre listed at the start of the tour for recommendations on where to break your journey, and for additional information on what to see and do, and when best to visit.

Tour Information
See pages 163–173 for the addresses, telephone numbers and opening times of the attractions mentioned in the tours, including the telephone numbers of tourist information centres.

Accommodation and restaurants
Pages 159–162 list hotels and campsites along the route of each tour. Also listed are restaurants where you may like to stop for a meal. There are, of course, other possibilities to be found along the way. Tourist offices may be able to help you find hotel accommodation.

Credit Cards
All the leading credit cards are usually accepted in hotels, restaurants and shops; it is wise, none the less, to check for the card symbol. Cash withdrawals can be made using authorised cards at banks and automatic dispensers. Take a note of the card number and emergency number to report any theft or loss.

Currency
Since 1 January, 2002 the Euro (€) has been the official currency of Austria. Euro bank notes are in denominations of €5, €10, €20, €50, €100, €200 and €500; coins are in denominations of 1, 2, 10, 20 and 50 cents and €1 and €2.

Credit and bankcards can be used to withdraw cash from automatic bank dispensers 24 hours a day.

Customs
Purchases for personal use are not subject to customs charges. There are limits for tobacco (800 cigarettes or 400 cigarillos or 200 cigars or 1kg/2lb of tobacco) and alcohol (60 litres/16 gallons of wine or 10 litres/2.6 gallons of spirits or 110 litres/29 gallons of beer). For detailed information on customs matters contact the Zollamt (customs head office) in Vienna, tel: 01 795900.

Pets (dogs and cats) entering require a valid anti-rabies certificate, with authenticated German translation, and an international health card. The vaccination must have been given at least 30 days but no more than a year before entering Austria. There are no formalities for guide dogs.

Discounts
The regional tourist offices sell inclusive cards supplied by some *Länder* and regions offering discounts on transport and at tourist attractions.

These include Inclusive-Card Vorarlberg, valid for 3–10 days (www.vorarlberg-tourism.at); Tirol Card, valid for 15 days (www.tirolcard.com); Kärnten Webung, valid for three weeks (www.kaernten.at); Salzburger Sommer Joker Card, valid for 16 days (www.salzburgerland.com). City cards can also be bought in Vienna, Innsbruck and Salzburg.

Electricity
The current is 220 volts AC, 50 hertz.

Electrical sockets take plugs with two round pins. US appliances will also require a trasformer if they do not have dual voltage facility.

Embassies and Consulates
UK
Jauresgasse 12
A-1030 Vienna,
tel: 01 71613 5151
(consular section)

US
Boltzmanngasse 16,
A-1090 Vienna,
tel: 01 31339-0.

Emergencies
In the event of an emergency you should dial one of the nationwide emergency numbers listed below.
General emergency 112
Police (Polizei, Gendarmerie) 133
Fire Service (Feuerwehr) 122

Ambulance (Rettungswagen) 144
Doctor (Notartzt; only in Vienna and major cities) 141
Roadside assistance (Pannen-hilfe): ÖAMTC 120, ARBÖ 123
Tourist information 21 11 42 22
Lost property 31 34 40 or 7 90 90

Entrance Formalities

On arrival in Austria travellers from EU countries are not subject to any passport checks at airports or border crossings. You must, however, carry valid identification papers (ID card or passport; minors must have a personal document or be registered on a parent's passport).

Hospitality

Austrian hotels are usually modern and offer excellent standards. Specialist hotel chains promote specific forms of tourism: Kinderhotels in Österreich is a chain specialising in families with children (www.kindershotels.com); Urlaub am Bauernhof has farm holidays (www.farmholidays.com); Landidyll has country holidays (www.landidyll.at).

As well as traditional hotels, there are many *Gasthöfe*, simple hotels outside the city centre, and *Gästehaus*, offering bed and breakfast. Lists are available from tourist offices.

Language

Except among small minorities in border regions, German is spoken in Austria. Those who work for tourist services usually speak English, French and Italian.

Medical Assistance

European citizens are entitled to Austrian health service assistance on presentation of form E111. To obtain medical assistance present form E111 to the local health board responsible (Gebietskrankenkasse), which will issue a form valid for Austria. Insurance cover can be taken out to cover all risks of accident or illness during the trip.

Motoring

For information on driving in Austria see pages 158–159.

The Schönbrunn Palace in Vienna was once the summer residence of the Habsburgs

Opening Times

Banks are usually open on weekdays 8–12.30, 1.30–3, (5.30 on Thursdays).

Post offices are usually open Mon–Fri 8–12, 2–6; the cash desk closes at 5. Post offices in railway stations of major cities are also open lunchtime, at night and Sundays. To collect post, which must bear the wording *Poste Restante*, present ID at a main post office. Stamps are also sold by tobacconists (*Tabak Trafik*). Post-boxes are yellow and orange.

Shops are usually open Mon–Fri 6am–7.30pm, Sat 6–5; some shops close for an hour or two for lunch.

Public Holidays

The following days are public holidays (shops, public offices and museums closed):
1 January – New Year
6 January – Epiphany
Easter Monday
1 May – Labour Day
Ascension Day
Whit Monday
Corpus Christi
15 August – Assumption
26 October
1 November – All Saints
8 December – Immaculate Conception
25 December – Christmas
26 December – St Stephen's Day

Telephones

The international dialling code for Austria is 43.

To call Austria from Britain dial 0043, followed by the local dialling code minus the initial zero.

To call Austria from the US or Canada dial 011 43 followed by the local dialling code minus the initial zero.

The code is not required for local calls in Austria.

Public telephone boxes take coins or cards.

All places in Austrian have direct international dialling with 3 or 4 number codes.

Time

Austria lies within the central European time zone and is one hour ahead of Greenwich Mean Time (GMT) in winter and two hours in summer.

Tourist Information

Österreich Werbung/Urlaubs-information Österreich
(Austrian National Tourist Office)
Margaretenstrasse 1
A-1040 Vienna
tel: 01 587 20 00
fax: 01 588 66 48

TIROL & VORARLBERG

A series of high mountain ranges, following one another almost without interruption, dominates the landscape of Tirol and Vorarlberg, Austria's two westernmost *Länder* (provinces). For centuries people have struggled to overcome these natural obstacles to exploit this geographical link between north and south, between the Germanic world and the Latin and Slav nations.

Routes of communication were established across the mountain passes and settlements grew up in the folds between slopes – beyond the barrier of the Arlberg, on the rolling Bregenzerwald hills and on the Bodensee (Lake Constance) plain, in the valleys of the River Inn, and to the west (Oberinntal) and east (Unterinntal) of the Innsbruck-Brenner watershed.

For many hundreds of years, the inhabitants of these valleys and slopes have lived off agriculture and stockbreeding or mining. These days summer and winter tourism are the mainstay of the economy – fortunately without disastrous consequences for the environment and local lifestyles. This area has been protected with the creation of vast nature reserves (particularly the Hohe Tauern park), and you can easily find wild and unspoilt areas in the remote transversal valleys. Traditions and age-old customs are proudly preserved in virtually all parts of this western corner of Austria, from religious and secular celebrations in costume to late summer festivities, when herds descending from the Alpine pastures are decked out with garlands and bells, as well as fantastic carnival parades and charming Christmas markets.

Due to its importance as a link across the Alps between the north and southwest of Europe, history has left its mark in the form of many churches, abbeys and castles – proof of an eventful past.

A suggestion: tours 2 and 4, part of which are in Alto Adige, can be seen as a way of entering Austria directly from Italy (via Bolzano-Merano in the first case and Bolzano-Bressanone in the second) or through Engadine.

Taking a well-earned rest in the Vorarlberg mountains

A refreshment post at the Fernpass in Tirol; the pass leads to the Ausserfern region

Tour 1

Vorarlberg – 'the land before the Arlberg' – reveals its many faces in this tour. It sets off from Bregenz, the capital of the Vorarlberg, on the shores of the Bodensee (Lake Constance) for the gentle rolling hills and woods of the Bregenzerwald before climbing to the breathtaking Arlberg peaks and the Montafon region, on the border with Tirol. The Bielerhöhe Pass (2,036m/6,680 feet), which has fine views over the Silvretta Stausee, marks the turning point of the vaguely triangular route. Here you descend quickly to the Rhine plain and its Bodensee delta via the regions of Bludenz and Bodensee-Alpenrhein, crossed by splendid valleys.

Tour 2

This tour explores the valleys of the Tirolese Oberland and descends the Arlberg into Italy's Alto Adige along the course of the River Inn, towards its source in Engadine. At the Passo di Resia (Resia Pass or Reschenpass), the impenetrable Ötztaleralpen massif forces the route on to Italian territory, taking you along the splendid aperture of Val Venosta. You

climb back to Austria along Val Passiria and, beyond the Passo del Rombo (Rombo Pass), follow the entire length of the Ötztal (Ötz Valley) back to the River Inn. Remember to carry valid passports for the two border crossings.

Tour 3

The starting point for this route is the well-known summer and winter resort of Seefeld in Tirol. At first the tour explores the regions to the extreme northwest of Tirol and enters Germany for a short stretch. After travelling through the charming Leutasch valley, dotted with villages, you cross the Fernpass at 1,216m (3,989 feet), the gateway to the Ausserfern region since Roman times. After passing the main towns of Ehrwald and Reutte, the tour descends to Imst over a far more demanding pass, the Hahntennjoch (1,894m/6,214 feet), along a road of bends and precipices that's a motorcyclists' favourite.

Tour 4

Innsbruck is a combination of history, culture and nature. Despite its impressive title 'capital of the Alps', this is a reassuringly approachable and compact place. You can take in the delights of the old centre on one lovely, unhurried walk, and it's conveniently placed for no

fewer than 15 holiday resorts, so there's a wide choice of mountain excursions, all reached from the old city in a matter of minutes.

Tour 5

This spectacular tour offers views of one of the most beautiful mountain zones in the Alpine region, winding through southeast Tirol and visiting Alto Adige, Osttirol and Salzburg. After following the course of the Sill in the Wipptal, it enters Italy via the Passo del Brenner or Brenner Pass (1,375m/4,508 feet) and the Isarco valley (the river rises near the pass) to reach Bressanone (Brixen). There's a short but enjoyable drive through Val Pusteria, on the edge of the Dolomites, before turning, beyond Brunico (Bruneck), into the Anterselva valley, setting of the splendid Vedrette di Gries nature reserve. After going back across the border at the Passo Stalle (Stalle Pass), you cross the Hohe Tauern and the largest nature park in central Europe, travelling first along the Tauerntal, with views of the Grossglockner and Gross-venediger peaks, then along Salzburg's Oberpinzgau, before eventually returning to Innsbruck. Remember to take valid passports for the crossing into Italy.

Tour 6

The rivers that mark sections of this tour – the Inn and the Saalach in particular – flow here through the wider valleys that open between the mountain ranges of the Tirolese Unterland: the Karwendel, Rofan, Wilder Kaiser, Zahmer Kaiser and, to the south, Kitzbüheler Alpen. The journey begins with typical Tirol features – broad mountain pastures, wooden farmhouses and a carpet of geraniums. You then visit Kitzbühel, one of the most exclusive tourist resorts in the country, before climbing further north to the border with Bavaria and back to discover the history and romance of Kufstein.

Glaciers &
Green Pastures

Vorarlberg crams a great variety of features into its surface
area of just over 2,600sq km (1,000 square miles).
A perfect blend of man and nature, modernity and
tradition gives this 'land before the Arlberg' a special
character and a
distinctive
charm.

4 DAYS • 313KM • 192 MILES

ITINERARY	
BREGENZ	▶ **Dornbirn (13km-8m)**
DORNBIRN	▶ **Schwarzenberg (14km-9m)**
SCHWARZENBERG	▶ **Bezau (7km-4m)**
BEZAU	▶ **Lech (44km-27m)**
LECH	▶ **Sankt Anton am Arlberg (21km-13m)**
SANKT ANTON AM ARLBERG	▶ **Bielerhöhe (65km-40m)**
BIELERHÖHE	▶ **Schruns (33km-20m)**
SCHRUNS	▶ **Bludenz (12km-7m)**
BLUDENZ	▶ **Damüls (30km-19m)**
DAMÜLS	▶ **Rankweil (29km-18m)**
RANKWEIL	▶ **Feldkirch (7km-4m)**
FELDKIRCH	▶ **Hohenems (18km-11m)**
HOHENEMS	▶ **Bregenz (20km-12m)**

❶ Bregenz, Vorarlberg
The capital of Vorarlberg overlooks the eastern tip of Lake Constance (Bodensee), which Austria shares with Germany and Switzerland. A well-equipped tourist resort, Bregenz owes much of its charm to the lake, which can be seen in various splendid aspects from Seepromenade and the top of Pfänder, the mountain that dominates the town. The Oberstadt (Upper Town) occupies the site of the Roman fort that was built here in AD 15. Here you can climb the cobbled Maurachgasse and admire the mighty Martinsturm, with its distinctive onion dome (the town's symbol and all that

---
BACK TO NATURE

You can climb to the Pfänder peak (1,063m/3,487 feet), the mountain that dominates Bregenz, by cableway or by road (7km/4 miles). Near the refuge hut is the Alpenwildpark, an educational wildlife park where hares, goats and wild boar roam. There are two daily exhibitions of birds of prey in free flight (May–early September).

---

remains of its medieval walls), and the 18th-century Deuring Schlösse (castle), today home to an elegant hotel-restaurant. On its left, a shaded flight of steps leads back to the lower town, where more recent buildings include the futuristic Kunsthaus (1994–7), an art gallery showing contemporary work, and the Festspiel und Kongresshaus, an open-air theatre with a delightful stage set on the water.

[i] *Bahnhofstrasse 14*

▶ *Travel south on the 190.*

❷ Dornbirn, Vorarlberg
Founded in the 6th century AD, Dornbirn is the largest town in Vorarlberg and an important textile centre. In the heart of the town is Marktplatz, where a cluster of old buildings includes the imposing neo-classical parish church of St Martin (1839–40); the Rotes Haus (Red House), a traditional Rhine valley building of brick and wood (1634), originally painted red with ox blood; and the Luger Haus, altered in the early 20th century in 'altdeutsch' (old German) style, with typical projecting tower and tympanum.

The open-air Festspiel und Kongresshaus in Bregenz; Lake Constance is in the background

The well-known Vorarlberger Naturschau (the region's biggest natural history museum) has been revamped with interactive exhibitions and hands-on attractions, and the Rolls-Royce Museum has the largest collection of Phantoms in the world.

Take a break at Bödele, about 10km (6 miles) from Dornbirn. The Fohramoos (high peat-bogs and marshes), meadows, woods and protected natural area offer splendid views of nearby Switzerland, Lake Constance and the Allgäu Alps in Germany.

[i] *Kulturhaus*

▶ *From Bödele proceed eastwards on the 48.*

❸ Schwarzenberg, Vorarlberg
This is a resort and typical Bregenzerwald village with traditional wooden peasant dwellings. The Dreifaltigkeitskirche (church) was restored after a fire in 1757 and contains

an altarpiece by Angelika Kauffmann (1741–1807), a painter who lived many years in

SPECIAL TO...

Alpine summer pastures, mountain dairies, specialised restaurants, craft workshops and regional delicatessens are encountered along the Käse Strasse, the 'cheese trail'. On the Bregenzerwald roads, following a route that passes Schwarzenberg, Schwarzach, Langen, Hittisau, Sibratsgfäll and Egg among others, signs indicate shops taking part in the initiative. Here milk and all its by-products reign supreme – from more than 30 types of cheese to Topfen (yoghurt and unpasteurised milk), Gsig (the original Bregenzerwald chocolate) and desserts made of caramelised whey. At Hittisau, visit the Alpensennereimuseum, dedicated to the methods and traditional tools used in cheese-making.

Rome and was one of the founders of London's Royal Academy of Arts.

⊡ *Hof 454*

▶ *Continue along the **48** southbound; turn right on to the **200** and then left on to the local road to Bezau.*

4 Bezau, Vorarlberg

Lying in a sunny position sheltered from the wind, Bezau is now a renowned summer and winter holiday resort, regarded as the capital of Bregenzerwald and the stronghold of its traditions. Women can often still be seen wearing the Juppe, a long, black pinafore dress with a fine embroidered bodice. Until 1982 this was the terminal of the narrow-gauge railway line from Bregenz. Today, the Wälderbähnle runs only 6km (4 miles), to Bersbuch, with period steam or diesel locomotives operating from May to October.

From Bezau, a cableway climbs to the Sonderdach and

Schwarzenberg's Schubertiade, a great *Lieder* and chamber music festival held in June and August to September

Baumgartenhöhe (1,631m/5,351 feet), starting points for hiking expeditions and parascending jumps.

⊡ *Platz 39*

▶ *Retrace your steps to the **200** and take this southeast over the Hochtambergpass; at Warth turn right on to the **198** (stretch of road prohibited to caravans).*

5 Lech, Vorarlberg

Lech village lies in a hollow between vast slopes that in summer become a paradise for hiking expeditions (250km/155 miles of paths, also reached by cableway and chair-lift). Despite its fame as an exclusive skiing resort, Lech has managed to preserve its character. Between the roofs of its houses rises the bell-tower of the lovely

FOR HISTORY BUFFS

On the extreme limit of their migration westwards, the Valais Walsers, a race of mountain valley-dwellers, found a new home in the Vorarlberg mountains among woods and meadows. That was in the early 14th century and their history and culture continue to form an integral part of the region's social fabric, as demonstrated by the traditional costumes and the Grosses Walsertal dialect of Lech and Damüls.

A three-hour hike from Oberlech (reached from Lech by cable-car) to the Gasthaus Bodenalpe (on the main road to Lech) makes a fine excursion exploring Walser country, via the Auenfelder Alpe model alpine summer pasture and Bürstegg.

Pfarrkirche St Nikolaus, built in 1390 on the site of a Romanesque building (of which some frescoes were recently found). The square tower, 33m (108 feet) high, and the apse are the only survivors of the Gothic church; most of the rest is rococo restoration dating from 1791.

Continue along the 198 road. After 5km (3 miles) you reach Zürs, a splendidly positioned mountain resort. Not far away, to the northeast, is the small but lovely Zürsersee. Travelling south, the road goes over the Flexenpass (1,784m/5,853 feet) and starts its panoramic descent along the steep slopes of the Arlberg.

ℹ️ *Dorf 2*

▶ *Continue east on the 197 Arlbergpass (stretch of road prohibited to caravans) or, if weather conditions permit, after 10km (6 miles) turn right for Langen and take the Arlbergtunnel.*

6 St Anton am Arlberg, Tirol
The undisputed Mecca of winter sports, with 260km (160

miles) of downhill pistes and 30km (18 miles) of cross-country circuits, St Anton owes the second part of its name (as do many other places in Vorarlberg and Tirol) to its position on the slopes of the Arlberg. A spectacular cableway climbs in three sections to the Valluga peak (2,809m/9,216 feet), which offers a fine view. In town, visit the Ski und Heimatmuseum of alpine sporting history.

ℹ️ *Alberhaus*

▶ *Take the 316 dual carriageway and exit at Pians; continue southwest on the 188.*

7 Bielerhöhe, Vorarlberg
Just outside Galtür is the starting point of the winding toll road known as the Silvretta Hochalpenstrasse (22.3km/14

A chair-lift in the Arlberg skiing area, near Lech

miles to Partenen; maximum gradient 10 per cent; closed in winter; no caravans). This leads to the Bielerhöhe Pass (2,036m/ 6,680 feet) in the Silvretta and Verwall ranges, on the border between Vorarlberg and Tirol. For a while, the road flanks the Silvretta Stausee, the highest artificial basin in Europe, which in summer offers fishing and boat excursions, as well as

SCENIC ROUTES

Along the Silvretta Hochalpenstrasse, just past Galtür, there's an interesting detour along a steep road towards Zeinisjochhaus. After meeting the road to the Zeinis Pass (Zeinisjoch, 1,842m /6,043 feet), carry on to skirt the artificial lake of Kaps before returning to the Silvretta Hochalpenstrasse on the pass road. This circular tour has magnificent views.

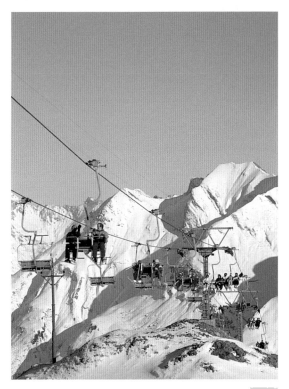

unequalled views of Hohes Rad (2,934m/9,626 feet) and Piz Buin, at 3,312m (10,866 feet) the highest mountain in Vorarlberg.

After this taxing stretch of mountain road, the Balbier falls,

short story. Today's visitors are no less enthusiastic about the Schruns/Tschagguns ski slopes, and can enjoy the beautiful scenery in summer as well. A winding path between the

although the first record of Villa Pludono, as it was then called, dates from 830. In 1228, Bludenz belonged to the counts of Montafon, whose castle, Schloss Gayenhofen, passed to

Schruns, in the Montafon high-mountain valley

about 10km (6 miles) from Partenen at Gortipohl, offer an inviting rest, complete with barbecue areas and the Aktivpark Montafon, a partly indoor recreational park with play and sports activities for adults and children.

▶ *Continue northwest on the 188 at Tschagguns, then turn right on to the local road to Silbertal.*

8 **Schruns,** Vorarlberg
American novelist Ernest Hemingway was a great fan of Montafon, the beautiful valley that winds for 40km (25 miles) through the Silvretta and Verwall ranges. He spent the winter of 1925–26 with his family in Schruns, and later described his skiing exploits in a

nearby villages of Silbertal and Bartholomäberg explores the Montafon mines and leads to an old mining shaft, a miners' chapel and a museum.

ⓘ *Silvrettastrasse 6*

▶ *Return to the 188 at Tschagguns and continue northwest.*

9 **Bludenz,** Vorarlberg
Bludenz is an important cultural and economic centre and home of the world-famous Suchard chocolate. It stands at the centre of a star formed by five splendid valleys: Montafon, Brandner Tal, Klostertal, Grosses Walsertal and Wallgau. Not surprisingly, Bludenz is renowned as an ideal base for skiing excursions in winter and for hiking in summer.

Remains from the Bronze Age indicate the existence of an ancient human settlement here,

the Habsburgs in 1394. In the 15th and 17th centuries three fires devastated the town. The only buildings spared were the castle, almost entirely rebuilt in

FOR CHILDREN

Travelling along the scenic Brandner Tal road, 12km (7 miles) southwest of Bludenz, you encounter the picturesque village of Brand. A 2km (1-mile) trail with an agricultural theme gives children the chance to try their hands at rural work and to play with the farm animals in the mini-zoo. This is just one of more than a hundred attractions and events for children in the Vorarlberger Kinderzauber, a programme promoted by Vorarlberg Tourismus and featured in a brochure available from local tourist offices.

baroque style in the 18th century and now the seat of administrative offices, and the church of St Laurentius (1514), both in a dominant position over the picturesque Altstadt (the Old Town) and reached by a long covered flight of steps. Two of the gates in the original ring of 15th-century walls remain: Mühlertor (lower gate) and Oberes Tor (upper gate), which today houses the Stadtmuseum of local history, art and folklore.

Below: Damüls
Bottom: Vorarlberg mountain cheeses left to ripen in a cellar

ℹ️ *Werdenbergerstrasse 42*

▶ *Take the 193 to Faschina and then Damüls.*

🔟 Damüls, Vorarlberg
Originally settled by the Walser mountain people, Damüls was once an isolated mountain village (1,500m/4,920 feet), and is still remembered as such by its oldest inhabitants, though new roads have now opened it up to the winter sports trade. In the central church, Pfarrkirche St Nikolaus (1484), there's a fine cycle of late-Gothic frescoes found in the 1950s and known as the 'Bible of the Poor'.

A chair-lift climbs to Uga-Alp (1,810m/5,938 feet), from where you can walk (about 45 minutes) to the top of Mittagspitze (2,097m/6,880 feet), a peak in the Bregenzerwald. The view more than rewards the effort.

i *Kirchdorf 138*

▶ *Continue west on the 51.*

① Rankweil, Vorarlberg
On a rocky spur overlooking the Rhine valley is the village of Rankweil, which still attracts pilgrims to the Wallfahrtskirche Unsere Liebe Frau, a fortified Marian sanctuary (1470). Of note inside are a Romanesque crucifix (1233) in silver and precious stones and a venerated wooden statue of the Madonna.

South of Rankweil (about 5km/3 miles) you climb to the village of Übersaxen, in a splendid position, with a pretty 14th-century church.

i *Rathaus am Marktplatz*

▶ *Take the 64 southbound and then turn on to the 190, again southbound.*

② Feldkirch, Vorarlberg
This is the town of the counts of Montfort, who governed the area in the 13th and 14th centuries from Schattenburg, Feldkirch's castle. Feldkirch also has other claims to fame. It's known as the town of four nations, enclosed as it is between Austria, Germany, Switzerland and Liechtenstein; and it has associations with many literary figures, including the writers Hermann Hesse, Thomas Mann, James Joyce and Sir Arthur Conan Doyle. All this apart, Feldkirch is a handsome and relaxed medieval town with narrow streets, porticoes and gardens.

Following the Hirschgraben (graben – 'ditch' – refers to the medieval moat) you pass in front of the mighty Katsenturm ('tower of the cats'), the best known of several towers and gates in the old ring of walls. Carry on along Neustadt, which circumscribes the old centre to the west, to reach the church, Domkirche St Nikolaus (1478), an interesting example of the

A concert on the stage of the Renaissance Palast Hohenems

transition from late Gothic to Renaissance style, with fine works in wrought iron and paintings by the Danube School. Next take Burggasse, climbing to the imposing castle-fortress, which today contains the Heimatmuseum (collection of weapons, tools and everyday objects) and a restaurant (with annexed miniature golf course).

Just outside the town centre a trail leads to the Wildpark Ardetzenberg, a large wildlife park open every day, all year round.

i *Herrengasse 12*

▶ *Follow the 190 northeast to Hohenems.*

③ Hohenems, Vorarlberg
The counts of Ems play a pivotal role in the history of this town set in a strategic position between the Unterland and the Oberland of the Rhine valley. The counts had close economic ties with Italy, further consolidated by the marriage of Wolf Dietrich von Ems (1507–38) to Clara de' Medici,

sister of Pope Pius IV. Their palace, the Palast Hohenems (not open to visitors), still dominates the Stadtplatz. It was erected in pure Renaissance style (1562–67) . Another Ems, Count Kaspar, was a great book-lover who started a library here, later found to contain two of the three existing manuscripts of the *Nibelungenlied*, the first masterpiece of German poetry which inspired Wagner's operatic cycle, the *Ring of the Nibelung*.

Passing through a covered passageway to the left of the palace you come to the Pfarrkirche (1581, altered in 1797), the parish church, devoted to San Carlo Borromeo, bishop of Milan and yet another relation of the Ems. Its 16th-century altarpiece is the most notable example of Renaissance art in Vorarlberg. The Stoffels Säge-Mühle open-air museum has a sawmill in operation.

i *Schweizer Strasse 10*

▶ *Return to Bregenz on the 203 through Lustenau or on the A14.*

The Oberland
& South Tirol

5/6 DAYS • 428KM • 266 MILES From the extremes of Arlberg's mountain country you head south towards Italy, exploring gentler, more Mediterranean-style valleys, passing vineyards and orchards. A visit to the historic towns of South Tirol reveals their cultural and historical links with Austria.

ITINERARY

ST ANTON AM ARLBERG	▶ Landeck (29km-18m)
LANDECK	▶ Fliess (11km-7m)
FLIESS	▶ Ladis (14km-9m)
LADIS	▶ Serfaus (8km-5m)
SERFAUS	▶ Nauders (37km-23m)
NAUDERS	▶ Passo di Resia (6km-4m)
PASSO DI RESIA	▶ Malles Venosta (22km-14m)
MALLES VENOSTA	▶ Silandro (23km-14m)
SILANDRO	▶ Merano (33km-20m)
MERANO	▶ Obergurgl (64km-39m)
OBERGURGL	▶ Sölden (14km-9m)
SÖLDEN	▶ Umhausen (23km-14m)
UMHAUSEN	▶ Pitztal (62km-38m)
PITZTAL	▶ St Anton am Arlberg (82km-51m)

Carnival time in Fliess

architecture in Oberland. Its greatest treasure is the main altarpiece, the Schrofenstein (Adoration of the Magi, 1513). A cable car climbs from near by Zams (3km/2 miles northeast) to Mount Venet (2,513m/8,245 feet), a skiing and summer hiking destination.

ⓘ *Malserstrasse 10*

▶ *Head southeast along the 315 to the turning on the left for Fliess (17).*

2 Fliess, Tirol

The pretty village of Fliess has a long and fascinating history. Long before the Romans came to these parts on Via Claudia Augusta, the Piller Sattel rise was a holy site used for sacrificial rites (ashes found here date from the Bronze Age, c1500 BC). As well as these discoveries and evidence of the Roman settlement, the Archäologisches Museum houses the remarkable 'bronze treasure' of the Hallstatt

era (7th–6th century BC). A circular path leads around Piller Moor, a marshy area above the village.

SCENIC ROUTES

Just before the turning for Ladis, at Prutz, turn left on to the Kaunertal road. From Feichten (the largest town in the valley) this toll road (closed in winter from the mouth of the lake) is called Kaunertaler Gletscher-Panoramastrasse ('road of the glaciers') and runs for 26km (16 miles). It climbs first to the Stausee Gepatsch, a lovely artificial lake, and then, ever steeper, through splendid old cembran pine-woods and meadows to the 2,750m (9,022-foot) spurs of the Weissee Spitze glacier, where skiing is possible in summer.

ⓘ *Dorf 89*

▶ *Go back along the same road to the 315 and follow this to the sign for Fiss and Serfaus*

ⓘ Alberhaus, St Anton am Arlberg,

▶ *Take the 316 eastbound to Landeck.*

1 Landeck, Tirol

Travelling along the beautiful valley that opens to the east of St Anton, shortly before Strengen on the right, you'll see the soaring outline of the Trisannabrücke, a railway viaduct dramatically straddling the River Sanna. Equally remarkable, on the outskirts of Landeck, is the sight of the castle above the town. Schloss Landeck has watched over the busy trade routes of Val Venosta and Engadine since the 13th century, and there's a sweeping view of the valley from the top of its tower. Since 1973 the castle has been the home of the Bezirksmuseum, a regional museum of sacred and secular art.

The parish church of Mariä Himmelfahrt, first recorded in 1270 and altered in the 15th and 16th centuries, remains one of the finest examples of Gothic

The great Schloss Landeck, now the home of the Bezirksmuseum

Touring by mountain bike near Nauders, in the Tirolese Oberland

(19); turn right and, after less than 1km (0.6 mile), take the 286 to Ladis.

3 Ladis, Tirol

'Refreshing' is the most fitting description of Ladis and of Obladis, above it, both renowned for their waters and therapeutic spa treatments. Visitors can use a hydro-massage plant, 10 minutes' walk from

Lader Weiher, Ladis' lake, or enjoy the waters of the Sauerbrunn-Quelle (spring).

In the village, delicate frescoes adorn the façades of several houses (Rechelerhaus at No 3, Stockerhaus at No 6, both 16th- to 17th-century). The mighty Burg Laudegg (fort) rises above a sheer drop northeast of the village, with a 13th-century watchtower and 16th-century ring of walls.

i No 27

▶ *Return southwest on the 286 and take the 19 to Fiss and Serfaus.*

4 Serfaus, Tirol

Leave your car on the outskirts of Serfaus, take the Dorffbahn (underground pneumatic railway) to the lifts and set off to explore the Sammnaungruppe, skis on your feet or rucksack on your back, depending on the

season. In the village itself, two parish churches known as 'old' and 'new' are, in fact, part of a single complex.

The 'old' sanctuary of Unsere Liebe Frau im Walde is a simple Gothic 14th-century hall with a superb altar painting, Virgin and Child, dated 1300. Next door, the Pfarrkirche Mariä Himmelfahrt dates from 1497 to 1516. A pleasant hour and a half's walk leads to the solitary church of St Georg ob Tösens, a place of pilgrimage in the Middle Ages (ask at the inn near the church for the keys). This was originally the setting for the Tirol's oldest panel painting, executed in 1250 and now kept in the Tiroler Landesmuseum Ferdinandeum in Innsbruck; a copy is on display here.

i Untere Dorfstrasse 13

RECOMMENDED TRIPS

Every village between Landeck and Merano sits on the route of the old Via Claudia Augusta, which in Roman times linked the Adriatic Sea with the River Danube, via the Alps. A network of cycle and hiking routes runs all along the original road and is marked with information boards in several languages. The Fliess archaeological museum organises themed tours.

▶ *Return along the 19 to the 315, and take this southwest to Nauders.*

5 Nauders, Tirol

Climbing between the Finstermünz and Resia passes, 5km (3 miles) before the Italian border, you pass the resort of Nauders, settled by the ancient Romans as Inutrium and annexed to the county of Venosta in the 10th century. Its fort, Burg Naudersberg, is clearly visible from the road in a dominant position south of Nauders.

Built in the early 14th century as a fortress, it was converted for the border garrison in 1510 by Emperor Maximilian I, and eventually rebuilt in the early 1800s. From 1300 to 1919 the castle was used as a law court; the museum on the second and top floors is partly devoted to the judicial system and its history.

The oldest church in Tirol, the Leonardskapelle, stands near by (ask at the castle restaurant, in the old stables, for the keys). This classic example of a 12th-century Romanesque chapel, with square nave, semicircular apse and bell tower, has some original and late-Gothic frescoes (c1460).

ℹ️ *Dr-Tschiggfrey-Strasse 66*

▶ *Continue along the 315 to the Passo di Resia.*

6 Passo di Resia/ Reschenpass, Tirol-Alto Adige

During their military campaigns of AD 16, Roman commanders Tiberius and Drusus re-discovered the importance of this mountain pass, which had

---

FOR CHILDREN

From early July to mid-September, Nauders offers a host of adventurous attractions for children, such as a visit to the mines of Zibern. Young participants are even allowed to take home the odd specimen of 'precious' stone as a souvenir.

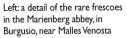

Left: a detail of the rare frescoes in the Marienberg abbey, in Burgusio, near Malles Venosta

been in use during the Bronze Age. Today its strategic position in Dreiländerechk (the 'corner of the three nations', Italy, Austria and Switzerland) ensures its continuing role as a border pass and as the hub of a 'border-free' tourist zone that comprises more than 2,000km (1,240 miles) of hiking paths and 1,500km (930 miles) of mountain-bike tracks.

On the Italian side, the road skirts the artificial basin formed by the Adige close to its source. This man-made lake was created between 1949 and 1950 by submerging the two villages of Curon/Graun and Resia/Reschen, which were then rebuilt on its shores. The 14th-century bell tower of the church of Curon Vecchia still rises from the waters.

☐ *Via Principale 22, Resia*

▷ *On entering Italy, the 315 becomes the SS40, which you follow to Malles Venosta.*

7 Malles Venosta/Mals in Vinschgau, Alto Adige
On a slope on the southernmost tip of upper Val Venosta, Malles first comes into view as an unmistakable silhouette. Making up its distinctive skyline are the castle tower of Castel Frölich (now in ruins) and the bell towers of four churches, one Gothic and the others Romanesque. St Benedetto (St Benedikt) church is of particular historical interest, built in the early 9th century and decorated with rare frescoes and stuccowork. Among its treasures are the fine ornamental motifs decorating one of the columns and, across the two apses, a full-length portrait of a proud Frankish nobleman.

The imposing white outline of the Benedictine abbey of Monte Maria (Marienberg) rises

against dark green woodland 5km (3 miles) northwest of Malles, above Burgusio/Burgeis. The church and crypt, famous for its splendid Romanesque frescoes (1160), are open to visitors.

On the road back to Burgusio you can admire the Castello del Principe (Fürstenburg), erected in 1280 by the bishops of Chur. Continuing along the main road to Silandro/Schlanders, you'll pass Sluderno/Schluderns, dominated by Castel Coira (Churburg, 1253), today seen in the form of a splendid Renaissance palace and housing an impressive collection of arms and armour.

☐ *Piazza Glückh 3*

▷ *From Spondigna, follow the left fork on the SS40 (SS38) to Silandro.*

8 Silandro/Schlanders, Alto Adige
Picturesque Silandro, Val Venosta's main town, boasts a wonderful climate and an enviable position (near the famous Venosta skiing resorts, among others). It has 300 days of sunshine a year and varied natural surroundings – thick woods alternating with fields on the slopes of Monte Tramontana, and chestnut groves and vineyards on the slopes of Monte Mezzodì. Between them, on the valley floor, extensive orchards grow apricots and apples.

The pointed bell tower of the parish church of St Maria Assunta – the town's symbol – is the tallest in South Tirol at 97m (318 feet). Built in the 16th century, it tilts to the west to resist the winds blowing from the Lasa plain. Among the orchards on the edge of town stands the delightful Castel Silandro (Schlandersburg), an exceptionally fine examples of a

The turreted profile of Castel Coira, a spectacular palace in Val Venosta

Lombard Renaissance residence. The keep dates from the 13th century and the living quarters from the 16th century.

i *Via Capuccini 10*

▶ *Continue along the SS38 to Merano.*

🅷 Merano/Meran, Alto Adige

People have settled at the confluence of the Adige and Passirio rivers since prehistoric times, and since then Merano has had a turbulent history. It served as an essential road junction during the Roman era and as a fortified town in the early Middle Ages. It then became the prestigious capital of the county of Tirol, the boundaries of which went far beyond those of today's Land. In 1420, when power passed into the hands of the Habsburgs, administrative offices were transferred to Innsbruck and the mint to Hall. From then on, a slow decline reduced Merano to a 'cattle town' (Kuhstadt) in the

Right: the symbol of Merano
Below: a view of the winter sports resort of Sölden

1700s, when livestock was driven beneath the old porticoes of the town centre. A revival in its fortunes started in 1838, with the publication of an essay on the curative powers of Merano's climate, written by a doctor of the Viennese court. Since then the nobility of Europe have been flocking to what is now an elegant, busy holiday and spa resort, to enjoy its extremely temperate climate.

Most of Merano's monuments are concentrated in the old centre, which features three gates and a street flanked by the Gwölben (porticoes).

FOR HISTORY BUFFS

On the way through Val Passiria, between San Martino and San Leonardo, you come across Maso della Rena (Sandwirt), where Andreas Hofer was born in 1767. This champion of the Tyrolean peasants fiercely resisted annexation of the region by Napoleonic Bavaria. He was eventually abandoned by his Habsburg supporters and shot by the French in Mantua in 1810. His remains were subsequently re-interred in the Hofkirche in Innsbruck.

The Gothic cathedral is worth a visit, as is the Castello Principesco (Landesfürstliche), a miniature medieval fortress, once a ducal residence and now housing a collection of Gothic and Renaissance furnishings and art. Near by is the Museo Civico, displaying archaeological finds, paintings and sculptures of various periods as well as exhibits on local art and folk culture.

From nearby Tirolo/Dorf Tirol (4km/2.5 miles northwest), a pleasant and scenic 1km (0.6-

mile) walk ends at Castel Tirolo, the residence of the counts who governed this region until the 15th century. It was begun in 1120 as a symbol of lordly power, but suffered from repeated bouts of subsidence. Only the entrances of the palace and chapel remain of the original castle, plus the two-storey chapel, with precious frescoes and ornamental motifs.

i *Corso della Libertà 45*

▶ *Travel north on the **SS44** to San Leonardo in Passiria. Here take the **SS44bis** northwest. Once back on Austrian soil after the Rombo Pass, the **SS44bis** becomes the 186. Take this to the turning south for Obergurgl (15). No caravans are allowed on the road from Moso in Passiria/Moos in Passeiertal to the local road to Obergurgl, and this part of the route is closed in winter. There is a toll section from the Rombo pass to Hochgurgl.*

10 Obergurgl, Tirol

Cross the Rombo Pass into Austrian territory, then continue along the scenic Timmelsjoch-strasse, which winds through the Gurgler Tal with splendid views of the southern slopes of the Stubaier Alpen and the Ötztaler Alpen.

At the end of the valley, closed off by a spectacular amphitheatre of mountains, is the famous skiing resort of Obergurgl, the highest-lying village in Austria (1,910m/6,266 feet).

Cable-cars and chair-lifts climb to the Hohe Mut (2,670m/8,760 feet) and Festkogel (3,038m/9,967 feet), where you can admire the glaciers of the surrounding peaks as far as the distant Schalf-kogel (3,540m/11,614 feet).

i *Hauptstrasse 108*

▶ *Return to the 186 along the same road and continue north to Sölden.*

11 Sölden, Tirol

Zwieselstein marks the southernmost tip of the Ötztal, which extends about 50km (31 miles) north as far as the main Inn valley. The first major centre along its descending, winding and busy road is Sölden, an ideal resort for anyone who loves sports and action holidays. You can ski and snowboard here in summer on the Tiefenbachferner (2,796m/ 9,173 feet) and Rettenbach

Skiers at Obergurgl, the highest village in Austria

(2,684m/8,806 feet) glaciers, linked by a tunnel and also reached by car along a 13km (8-mile) stretch of road, which has a splendid view of the peaks and glaciers.

i *Rettenbach 466*

▶ *The 186 continues to Umhausen.*

🄓 Umhausen, Tirol

An 8km (5-mile) detour to the right from Umhausen, on the road to Oetz, leads to the Stuibenfall, the highest waterfall in Tirol (150m/492 feet), formed after the course of the Horlachbach river was changed by a landslide.

As an alternative to the car, a marked path leads from Umhausen to the waterfall in a circular tour of average difficulty. Night excursions by lantern-light (the falls are fully illuminated on Wednesday evenings) are particularly delightful.

A snowy scene in Tirol showing some of the many rural wooden buildings found in the Kaunertal

---

SPECIAL TO...

An easy path at the bottom of the picturesque Ventertal (15km/9 miles southwest of Zwieselstein) climbs to Italian territory and the Similaun refuge hut. Near here, in the autumn of 1991, the 5,000-year-old mummified remains of a man were found. Now on display in the Bolzano civic museum, the man has been given the affectionate nickname Ötzi, after the Ötztal.
In Umhausen an archeologically themed park called Ötzidorf features an interactive walk designed to give visitors a glimpse of neolithic life.

---

road, you come to Mittelberg, a holiday resort and starting point for the Pitzexpress, an underground railway that takes tourists and summer skiers to the Mittelskigel (3,159m/10,364 feet). The Pitz-Panoramabahn, Austria's highest cableway, climbs to the Hinterer Brunnekogel (3,440m/11,286 feet), which has a beautiful view of the ski runs on the glacier and the Wildspitze (3,774m/12,382 feet), the highest point in the Tirol.

> ℹ️ *Ortsinformationsstelle, St Leonhard im Pitztal*

> ▶ *Follow the 16 to Ims; from here the 316/E60 takes you back to St Anton.*

> ℹ️ *Dorf 3*

> ▶ *Continue along the 186 via Oetz to the junction with the 171; take this westbound to Imst, then south on the Pitztal road (16).*

🄔 Pitztal, Tirol

As you turn left to enter the Pitztal, you encounter the village of Arzl, where a lovely path leads to the Pitzenklamm, a gorge crossed by a bridge. At 94m (308 feet) this is the highest

pedestrian bridge in Europe, and people flock here to practise bungy-jumping. The next village, Wenns, perched on a high terrace, deserves a stop to admire the rococo interior of the parish church of St Johannes and the Platzhaus, now the Stern Inn, with late 16th-century frescoes on the façade combining biblical and secular themes.

After passing through Jerzens and St Leonard im Pitztal, at the end of the valley

---

BACK TO NATURE

Several parts of Pitztal and Kaunertal of particular environmental importance were made protected areas in 1999 with the institution of the Kaunergrat Park. Of note among the proposed guided hikes are those that follow the ibex and observe the 1,300 species of moths and butterflies in the meadows above Fliess.

The Outer
Tirol

After a breath of mountain air at Seefeld in Tirol, where golf and skiing enthusiasts from all over Europe meet up, comes a touch of wilderness on a tour of the secluded Leutasch valley and the Ausserfern, whose name means 'beyond the far-off'.

2/3 DAYS • 243KM • 151 MILES

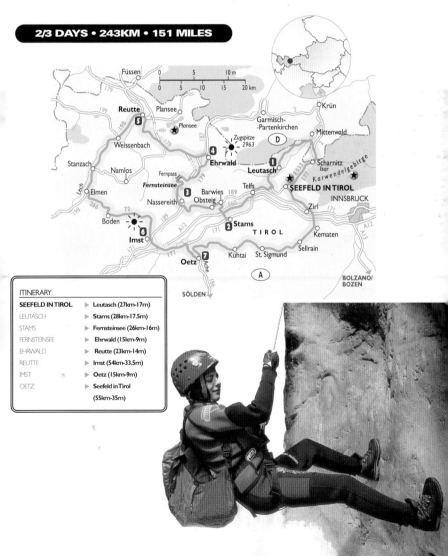

ITINERARY		
SEEFELD IN TIROL	▶	Leutasch (27km-17m)
LEUTASCH	▶	Stams (28km-17.5m)
STAMS	▶	Fernsteinsee (26km-16m)
FERNSTEINSEE	▶	Ehrwald (15km-9m)
EHRWALD	▶	Reutte (23km-14m)
REUTTE	▶	Imst (54km-33.5m)
IMST	▶	Oetz (15km-9m)
OETZ	▶	Seefeld in Tirol
		(55km-35m)

BACK TO NATURE

Scharnitz (8km/5 miles north of Seefeld) provides access to the Alpenpark Karwendel, a protected area of 900sq km (347 square miles) that encompasses this range of calcareous mountains blanketed with ancient larch forests. The tourist office provides information on hikes in the park, ranging from one-hour trails to the four-day Grand Tour.

The lovely façade of a house in Seefeld in Tirol on a snowy night

Klosterstrasse 43, Seefeld in Tirol

▶ *From Seefeld take the 1771 E533 to Scharnitz, which continues in Germany as the 2. Before Mittenwald turn left, then left again on the Leutascher Strasse which, back in Austria, becomes the 14.*

❶ Leutasch, Tirol

Pretty, tranquil villages are scattered along the 16km (10 miles) of the Leutascher Ache river valley, an area popular with tourists, who come to appreciate the scenic beauty of the Wettersteingebirge massif, on the border with Germany. On the opposite side is the well-known Garmisch-Partenkirchen. Wonderful hikes are possible in the transversal valleys, especially in the lush Gaistal.

Kirchplatzl 128a

▶ *Follow the 35 southbound and at Bairbach turn right on to the 36. At Telfs take the A12/E60 (enter at Telfs Ost) to the Mötz exit; from here the 171 leads to Stams.*

❷ Stams, Tirol

The Zisterzienserstift (Cistercian abbey) of Stams was built in 1273 by Mainardo II of Tirol as a burial place for members of his family. He passed responsibility for its maintenance to the Cistercian monks, who, over time, made it one of the country's main cultural and religious centres. Little remains of the original building, which underwent frequent baroque alterations from the 1600s on.

To the right of the entrance to the abbey church (restored between 1729 and 1732) is the Heiligenblutkapelle (Chapel of the Holy Blood), whose splendid 1716 'rose' grille is a masterpiece of gilded wrought iron. The tombs of the Tirol princes are in the crypt, reached from the near end of the nave. Today the abbey palace is home to a wintersports school.

Bahnhofstrasse 1

▶ *Take the 236 northbound to Barwies, where you turn left (west) on to the 189; from*

FOR CHILDREN

North of Seefeld, on the 177, is the new PlayCastle Tirol games park, designed as a giant medieval castle. Inside children can try out a wide range of interactive attractions, skate on a three-level rink and enjoy 'multi-sense' films, among countless other activities.

Dormitz continue northbound on the 179 Fernpass.

8 Fernsteinsee, Tirol
A little before the Fernpass (5km/3 miles) take a break at the lovely alpine lake of Fernstein, dominated by the castle of the same name (1519; not open to visitors). If you hire a rowing boat you can reach the ruins of Sigmundsburg, an old hunting lodge built on an islet in 1478. Alternatively, follow the track on a 40-minute or so circuit of the lake. Its crystal-clear waters make Fernsteinsee particularly well suited to underwater photographic expeditions.

Karl-Mayr-Strasse 116a, Nassereith

▶ *Along the 179, just past the Fernpass, turn right on to the 171 for Lermoos and right again, after Biberwier, on to the 391 to Ehrwald.*

4 Ehrwald, Tirol
After crossing the Fernpass (1,216m/3,990 feet), a convenient mountain pass, and skirting the Blindsee you come to Ehrwald, a charming tourist resort overshadowed by the solitary Zugspitze (2,963m/ 9,721 feet). To climb to the top head 3km (2 miles) northeast of the village to Obermoos, departure point of the Tiroler Zugspitzbahn, a cable-car originally installed in 1924–26 and replaced in 1990. This is one of the most dramatic cableways in the Alps, ascending 1,717m (5,633 feet) in three sections and carrying 100 people at a time to the peak in just seven minutes.

Kirchplatz 1

▶ *Turn left on to the 187. At Lermoos continue on the 179 to Reutte.*

5 Reutte, Tirol
The Zeiller dynasty of painters, active between the late 17th and late 18th century, is closely linked to that of Reutte, their place of birth, where vivid frescoes decorate the houses along the Obermarkt. These

Detail of the 17th-century altar in the abbey church at Stams

include, in order, the Grünes Haus (No 25), seat of the Heimatmuseum of local history and folklore, and, opposite, the Gasthof zur Goldene Krone (No 46, an excellent family-run restaurant) and Zum Schwarzen Adler (No 75).

Just outside Reutte, a cableway climbs from the village of Höfen to the Alpenblumen-garten, an alpine flower garden run by the local mountain rescue service at a height of 1,700m (5,577 feet). Between June and August there's a magnificent display of blooms.

RECOMMENDED WALK

A path leads to the Plansee, the second largest lake in Tirol, from the village of Mühl, just outside Reutte to the northeast. About an hour and a half's walk takes you via the Stuibenfall waterfall. Ferries operate on the lake between May and October.

SCENIC ROUTES

The mountains provide a very impressive backdrop on either side of the Leutasch valley. The scenic mountain road of Hahntennjoch is dominated on the right by the imposing, bare rock Muttekopf amphitheatre (2,774m/9,101 feet). On reaching the pass park your car and walk along one of the many paths that explore the surrounding mountains. The subsequent descent to the valley is along a giddy road winding among looming mountains and slopes through the gorge that ends at Imst.

i *Untermarkt 34*

▶ *Take the 198 Lechtalin road southwest and at Elmen turn left on to the 266. At Boden transfer on to the 72 dell'Hahnternnjoch. No caravans are allowed on the road between Elmen and Imst; it is closed in winter from Boden to Imst.*

6 Imst, Tirol

Imst is inextricably associated with water. The original Roman settlement that stood here was called *Hoppidum Humiste*, or 'gushing spring', and in the old centre there are no fewer than 21 elaborate fountains, installed as a precaution after a devastating fire in 1822.

The famous Rosengarten-schlucht is a breathtaking gorge, just a few minutes from the centre, formed by the raging waters that pour down to the valley from the spurs of the surrounding Lechtaler Alpen (recommended walk on the well-maintained track).

Hauptstrasse climbs past fine old houses with baroque façades in the upper part of the centre, overlooked by the parish church of Mariä Himmelfahrt (14th to 15th century) and the

SPECIAL TO...

Carnival parades are a tradition of the upper Inn valley, held in the same place every four to five years. The most important is the famous Schemenlaufen di Imst, which alternates with similar celebrations at Wenns, Nassereith and Telfs. Some of the carved masks used for these events are on display in a special museum in Imst, the Imster Fasnachtshaus.

A picture of the Fernsteinsee, a lovely alpine lake close to the Fernpass

tallest bell tower in Tirol (85m/279 feet).

i *Johannesplatz 4*

▶ *From Imst follow the 171 southbound and then continue east to the beginning of the 186 Öetztal, which heads southeast to Oetz.*

7 Oetz, Tirol

Oetz, a tourist resort that gives its name to the long valley winding to the south, has great views from the church of St Georg und Nikolaus, which also boasts a handsome bell tower and Gothic crypt dating from 1398. A 20-minute walk leads to the Piburger See, a small, limpid lake reflecting the conifers of the surrounding woodland. Its warm waters are very enticing in summer.

i *Hauptstrasse 66*

▶ *Take the 237/13, and follow it through Kühtai and Gries im Sellrain until you pass the A12, then continue north on the 177 to Seefeld.*

Innsbruck

A stroll through the cobbled streets of the old centre of Innsbruck is a real delight. With its unbroken line of ancient buildings, the town is steeped in atmosphere, and if you have time to spare it's well worth discovering the unexpected treasures concealed behind façades and in the museums.

2 DAYS

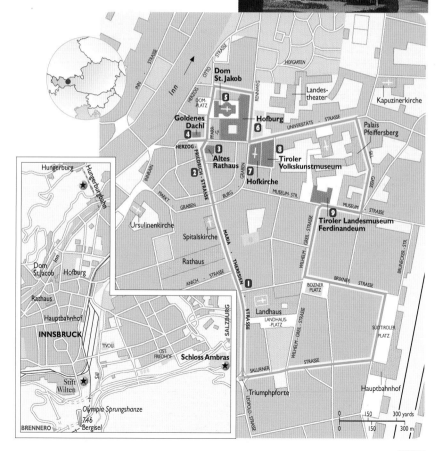

ⓘ *Burggraben 3*

▶ *Park in the central Kurzpark-
zonen or in one of the many
private covered car parks. An
Innsbruck Card gives you
unlimited use of the public
transport system. The tour
starts from the Hauptbahnhof
(railway station). Follow
Salurner Strasse to Maria-
Theresien-Strasse, which leads
to a partly pedestrianized
zone.*

Herzog-Friedrich-Strasse, the
main axis of the old town

Bavarian invaders in 1703. The
statuette on top is splendidly set
against the backdrop of the
Nordkette mountains.

▶ *Cross the junction with Markt-
Graben and Burg-Graben,
which marks the beginning
of the old centre.*

❷ Herzog-Friedrich-Strasse

Since the 13th century this
street has been the main axis of
the old city, widening as it
winds into the heart of the old
centre before eventually bearing

> ### RECOMMENDED WALK
>
> The Hafelekar peak
> (2,334m/7,657 feet), backdrop
> to Maria-Theresien-Strasse, is
> easily reached using the
> Hungerburg cableway and two
> sections of the Nordkette
> cableway. A high-altitude path
> starts from the upper station
> and, after climbing to the
> summit, descends to the
> Pfeishütte refuge hut which
> offers an unparalleled view of
> the city and surroundings.

❶ Maria-Theresien-Strasse

The wide street that leads to the
old centre starts, to the south,
with the Triumphpforte (1765),
a triumphal arch erected to mark
the marriage of the future
Leopold II, son of Maria
Theresa. The untimely death of
his father, Franz of Lorraine,
during the wedding festivities is
recalled on the north side of the
arch.

In the centre of the street,
flanked by elegant baroque
buildings, is the Annasäule,
the column of St Anne, which
commemorates liberation from

left towards the River Inn.
Exclusive shops and elegant
cafés are tucked beneath the
porticoes and charming 16th-
century houses are decorated
with elaborate loggias, frescoes
and coats of arms. The side
streets branching off Herzog-
Friedrich-Strasse are paved with
porphyry from Trentino and
conceal fascinating surprises –
such as the 'crossroads of the
four animals', between Seiler-
Gasse and Kiebach-Gasse,
named after the creatures
depicted in the wrought-iron inn
signs near by.

❸ Altes Rathaus and Stadtturm

The Altes Rathaus, the old city
hall dating from 1358, stands at
No 21, at the point where
Herzog-Friedrich-Strasse
widens into a triangle. Its red-
painted façade bears the arms of
Innsbruck in stone, representing
the city's name, which means
'the bridge over the Inn'. The
building is dominated by the
Stadtturm (Civic Tower,
1442–50), with its onion dome
and 1603 clock. Climb the 148
steps for a sweeping 360-degree
view.

The famous Goldenes Dachl balcony in Innsbruck, with a gilded roof, built for Maximilian I in the Neuer Hof

4 Goldenes Dachl and Maximilianeum

Blocking the street at No 15 and forcing it to bear left is the Neuer Hof (1420), the former residence of the dukes of Tirol. Its façade features the Goldenes Dachl ('golden roof') loggia (1494–96), covered with 2,657 gilded copper tiles, now used as the town's symbol. (The most popular souvenirs are delicious, tile-shaped chocolates sold by the famous Munding cake shop, Kiebachgasse 16.)

From the balcony here, Emperor Maximilian I, who commissioned the loggia, would watch games and tournaments, as reproduced in the bas-reliefs of the contemporary Katzunghaus (No 16), near by. At 11.30am on summer Sundays musicians in period costume play Renaissance arias on his balcony. More about this Tirolean sovereign can be discovered at the Maximilianeum museum, on the second floor of the Neuer Hof.

▶ *To the right of the Goldenes Dachl, take Pfarr-Gasse to the cathedral square.*

5 Dom St Jakob

Overlooking the quiet Domplatz are the concave façade and two symmetrical towers of the Cathedral of St Jakob, reworked in baroque style by J J Herkommer and J G Fischer (1717–24) on the site of a 13th-century church. Inside, in a dazzle of polychrome marble, the eye is immediately drawn to the main altar and the Madonna by Lucas Cranach the Elder (1520), venerated by Innsbruck residents and reproduced in medallions on many city-centre houses.

▶ *Turn right at the end of a passage left of the cathedral into Herren-Gasse and then right again into Rennweg.*

6 Hofburg

After Innsbruck consolidated its status as capital of the powerful Tirol in the 15th century, Maximilian I decided to enlarge the imperial residence and seat of central government, the Hofburg. Three centuries later Empress Maria Theresa ordered a complete overhaul in her attempt to establish a visible Habsburg stronghold in the decentralised Tirol. As a result, only the foundations and cellars (not open to visitors) of the original Gothic palace remain. About 15 rooms on the second floor, now housing state offices, are open to visitors, including the sumptuous reception hall that, in Maximilian's time, was

FOR HISTORY BUFFS

A Bronze Age settlement at the confluence of the Sill and Inn rivers formed the nucleus of the 3rd-century AD Roman community, Veldidena. The town of Innsprukke was founded in 1180 by Count Berthold von Andechs and given trading privileges in 1239. It passed into Habsburg control in 1363 and became their capital in 1420, enjoying a golden period during the reign of Maximilian I (1493–1519) and Ferdinand II (1529–95), before being incorporated into the Viennese administration in 1665.

The Stadtturm rising above the roofs of the Hofburg

it becomes apparent that this imperial church is more of a remarkable historical monument than a place of worship. The nave is entirely taken up by the cenotaph of Maximilian I, his great sarcophagus protected by a gilded wrought-iron gate. Lined up to guard it are 28 impressive bronze statues portraying his ancestors. These Schwarz-männer ('black fellows'), as the townspeople affectionately call the statues blackened by time, were cast between 1511 and 1533 and represent one of the most vivid examples of sculptural art of the period. They include the figures of Albrecht of Habsburg and King Arthur, copied from a drawing by Dürer, which are simpler but more animated than their companions. This spectacular scene was never actually completed, but was inspected as work progressed by the Emperor himself, eager to arrange a worthy burial. Ironically, his remains were laid not in the Hofkirche but in the Wiener Neustadt, in Lower Austria.

Across the way from the tomb of Andreas Hofer, a Tirolean hero, you can climb to the Silberne Kapelle ('silver chapel'). Archduke Ferdinand II (1529–95) and his beloved wife Philippine Welser were laid to rest here.

decorated with figures of mythical Tirolean giants. Nowadays the walls are covered in portraits of Maria Theresa, Franz of Lorraine and their 16 children, who included the ill-fated Marie Antoniette. On your way out you might be tempted by the delicacies of the Café Sacher, which has tables in the palace courtyard.

▶ *Turn into Universitäts-Strasse; on the right is the entrance to the Volkskunstmuseum and the Hofkirche.*

7 Hofkirche

The serene, timeless air of the cloisters in the old Franciscan convent (Neues Stift) makes a fitting prelude to a visit to the Hofkirche. As soon as you enter,

8 Tiroler Volkskunstmuseum

During the 19th century, faced with the loss of their customs

---

SPECIAL TO...

In the southern district of Welten is a Premonstratensian abbey of the same name, founded in 1138 and given baroque additions in the 1600s. Of note are the church of St Laurentius, the library and the Gothic art collection.

BACK TO NATURE

A nature trail winds around the Patscherkofel (2,247m/7,372 feet), the mountain that dominates Innsbruck to the south. With the aid of 15 information posts, this two-hour walk provides an introduction to the ecosystem of the mountain area.

and crafts to encroaching industrialisation, the Tiroleans set up a folk art museum, the Volkskunstmuseum. In the wide corridors and old cells on the ground and first floors of the Neues Stift you can admire exhibitions devoted to the life, culture and handicrafts of the Tirolean area (including Trentino Alto Adige and the Ladin valleys around the Dolomites). There are remarkable reconstructions of the traditional *Stuben* ('living rooms' of the peasant homes), as well as exhibitions of traditional costumes and crib scenes.

▶ *Continue to the end of Universitäts-Strasse; turn right into Sill-Gasse, then right at the junction with Museum-Strasse.*

9 Tiroler Landesmuseum Ferdinandeum

A major refurbishment of the Ferdinandeum art museum was completed in 2003, improving the display space for its collections, which range from prehistoric times to the 19th century and include master-pieces by Cranach the Elder, Rembrandt and Dürer. The new Art Box is a venue for special exhibitions.

▶ *Return to Hauptbahnhof by following Wilhelm-Greil-Strasse to Bozner Platz and Brixner Strasse.*

EXCURSION

▶ *A shuttle service to Ambras (4km/2.5 miles from the centre) departs from Maria-Theresien-Strasse. Alternatively you can reach the castle on trams 3 and 6. By car, follow the signs from the railway station for Amras-Igls.*

10 Schloss Ambras

Between 1563 and 1566, Ferdinand II extended the 10th-century fortress that stood on the slopes of the Patchberg, south of Innsbruck, and had it remodelled in Renaissance style.

The Hochschloss (upper castle) contained the residential quarters of the Archduke's wife, Philippine Welser, who was unwelcome at court because of her bourgeois background. The Unterschloss (lower castle) was designed to house the Archduke's rich collections, forming the basis of one of the first modern museums.

Here you can visit the Waffensammlung, a collection of weapons and armour, the fascinating Kunst-und Wunderkammer, or 'cabinet of art and curiosities', and the Spanish Room, a splendid reception hall 43m (141 feet) long. Today the upper part of the castle houses a vast portrait gallery dedicated to the House of Austria. There are hundreds of paintings, including works by

FOR CHILDREN

If you alight at the intermediary station on the Hungerburg cableway you can visit the Alpenzoo, where more than 2,000 animals from 150 different species indigenous to the alpine area, inhabit a broad, sunny slope. Among other attractions, the amusement park has a mysterious 'bear's den'.

Lukas Cranach the Younger, Giuseppe Arcimboldo and Diego Velázquez.

A room in Schloss Ambras' Waffensammlung, the famous armour and sword collection that belonged to Friedrich II

Innsbruck to East Tirol

4 DAYS • 356KM • 221 MILES

The largest nature park, the most majestic waterfalls, the two highest peaks as a backdrop – a clutch of superlatives marks this tour through mountain and valley, with the added bonus of art and culture in Alto Adige.

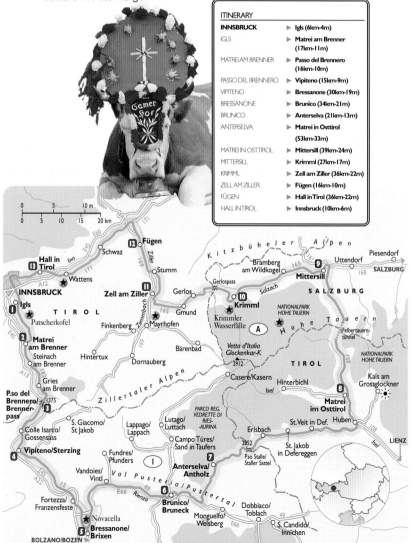

ITINERARY	
INNSBRUCK	▶ **Igls (6km-4m)**
IGLS	▶ **Matrei am Brenner (17km-11m)**
MATREI AM BRENNER	▶ **Passo del Brennero (16km-10m)**
PASSO DEL BRENNERO	▶ **Vipiteno (15km-9m)**
VIPITENO	▶ **Bressanone (30km-19m)**
BRESSANONE	▶ **Brunico (34km-21m)**
BRUNICO	▶ **Anterselva (21km-13m)**
ANTERSELVA	▶ **Matrei in Osttirol (53km-33m)**
MATREI IN OSTTIROL	▶ **Mittersill (39km-24m)**
MITTERSILL	▶ **Krimml (27km-17m)**
KRIMML	▶ **Zell am Ziller (36km-22m)**
ZELL AM ZILLER	▶ **Fügen (16km-10m)**
FÜGEN	▶ **Hall in Tirol (36km-22m)**
HALL IN TIROL	▶ **Innsbruck (10km-6m)**

Mountains and valleys in Tirol –
in the Innsbruck region

ⅈ *Burggraben 3, Innsbruck*

▶ *Head south to Igls on the **33**
(Igler Strasse).*

🄋 **Igls,** Tirol
Igls is an elegant mountain
resort with a distinctly Tirolean
character. It is situated on a
sunny plateau south of
Innsbruck and can be reached in
an hour on a No 6 tram, passing
meadows and woods. A former
Winter Olympics venue (1964
and 1976), it maintains its
sporting reputation with
everything from golf to summer

RECOMMENDED WALK

The Zirbenweg 'pine trail' starts
at the Patscherkofel cableway
station (Igls) and crosses a
splendid protected area.
Running halfway up the
mountainside, it leads to
Tulfeinalm and from here you
can descend to the valley on
the Tulfes lifts. A shuttle bus
returns to Igls (in all about two
and a half hours).

---

bobsleigh rides (whizzing down
the Olympic run on a wheeled
bobsleigh).
A cableway takes 20 minutes
to reach the Patscherkofel
(2,247m/7,372 feet), with views
over the Dolomites, the
Ötztaleralpen, the Stubaier
Alpen and Zugspitze. You can
also visit the highest Alpine
garden in Europe, with 400
different alpine plant species.

ⅈ *Piazza Principale*

▶ *Continue south on the **33**
then turn right on to the **38**
and pass through Patsch, St
Peter and Pfons.*

🄌 **Matrei am Brenner,** Tirol
The Brenner road is lined with
16th-century village houses,
featuring characteristic sloping
roofs and frescoed façades; of
note, among others, is the
Gasthof zur Uhr, still operating
as a restaurant. Several different
day excursions are possible in
the surrounding countryside, an
area admired by the German
writer Goethe as he passed en
route to Italy. They include trips

to the nearby Wipptal valleys,
from the Mühlbachl suburb to
the sanctuary of Maria Waldrast,
or the two-hour hike to Europe's
highest Klostergasthaus
(convent offering refreshments).

ⅈ *Brenner Strasse 104*

▶ *Take the **182** for the Passo
del Brenner/Brennerpass.*

🄏 **Passo del Brenner/
Brennerpass,** Tirol-Alto
Adige
Since 1919 the Brenner Pass has
marked the road and rail border
between Austria and Italy. As
one of the lowest passes in the
Alpine range (1,375m/4,508
feet), it was extensively
exploited in Roman times –
remains of the old road can be
found near the lake of the same
name. Today it carries much of
the traffic between Italy and
Germany.

▶ *Take the **SS12** southwest to
Vipiteno (Italy).*

4 Vipiteno/Sterzing, Alto Adige

The first town of importance on Italian soil could not have a more Tirolean appearance and atmosphere. A stroll down the only main street (divided into Via Città Vecchia to the north and Via Città Nuova to the south) reveals typical late-Gothic houses and geraniums adorning the bow windows. Stop in one of the many *Gasthäuser* (inns) to admire the fine wooden cladding and beamed or vaulted ceilings, signs of a wealthy town that was already flourishing in the Middle Ages, due first to its wine trade and later to its silver mining.

In the courtyard of the Palazzo Comunale (Rathaus) is a famous Mithraic stone, thought to have served as a Roman sacrificial altar. Opposite the 1470 Torre delle Dodici (Zwölferturm), the tower that separates the old and new districts, is the church of Spirito Santo. Unremarkable on the outside, it has a rich interior, where paintings and ornamental motifs come together to form a

single gigantic fresco by Giovanni da Brunico (1415).

South of Vipiteno, on a lone rock, stands Castel Tasso (Schloss Reifenstein), an old fortified castle with fairy-tale towers, crenellation, creaking drawbridges, stairs and galleries. Built in 1100, it owes its appearance and what remains of the furnishings to a 16th-century restoration carried out for the Knights of the Teutonic Order.

[i] *Piazza Città 3*

▶ *Continue southeast along the SS12.*

5 Bressanone/Brixen, Alto Adige

Bressanone lies in a green hollow at the point where the Isarco valley and Val Pusteria meet. Surrounded by hillside vineyards and dominated to the east by the Cima di Plose (2,486m/8,156 feet), it was for centuries a powerful bishopric and the political capital of Alto Adige. Today it's a pretty tourist and spa resort. The town started to develop in the 10th century

Vipiteno's main street, with the city tower in the background

around the Episcopal church and gained importance when, in the following century, Emperor Corrado II gave the bishop the status of prince, allowing him to oversee the counties of the Inn valley, the Isarco valley and the Brenner Pass – a situation that lasted until 1803. In the old centre, to the right of the confluence of the Isarco and Riese rivers, you can still see the middle-class districts of the ecclesiastic area around the cathedral, a baroque masterpiece. The cloister remains of the original Romanesque-Gothic building and bright Gothic frescoes create an enchanting atmosphere. Palazzo dei Principi Vescovi, reconstructed in Renaissance style but preserving the four corner towers of the 13th-century structure, houses the Museo Diocesano, with the cathedral treasure and a rich collection of carved crib scenes.

Several paths start from Valcroce (2,050m/6,726 feet),

Pacher (1435–98) was born and worked. This late-Gothic master combined the styles and forms of the southern Germanic area in his great altarpieces, adding the new techniques of perspective introduced in the Italian Renaissance. An ascent starting from the east gate leads to the castle, where the fortifications and frescoed inner courtyard can be visited.

The open-air Museo Etno-grafico in the Teodone suburb provides an insight into southern Tirolean vernacular architecture and farming life. About 20 rural buildings have been transferred to the lands around the Mair am Hof residence, along with exhibitions of everyday implements and objects.

ℹ️ *Via Europa 24*

▶ *About 8.5km (5 miles) along the SS49, turn left on to the Anterselva provincial road.*

7 Anterselva/Antholz, Alto Adige

The Anterselva valley runs for 20km (12 miles) in the shadow of the Vedrette di Ries (along with the peaks of Collalto, 3,436m/11,273 feet, and Collaspro, 3,273m/10,738 feet), a superb mountain area protected as a nature park offering guided excursions (contact Anterselva di Mezzo tourist office).

Beyond the three villages that share their name with the valley – Anterselva di Sotto, Anterselva di Mezzo and Anterselva di Sopra – you reach the lake of the same name, in a splendid position at 1,640m (5,380 feet). Negotiate the hairpin bends to the Stalle Pass, which gives access to Defereggen Tal in Eastern Tirol.

ℹ️ *No 81, Anterselva di Mezzo*

▶ *The provincial road from Anterserva di Mezzo to the*

above the Plose cableway, offering views of the town and the Dolomites.

ℹ️ *Viale Stazione 9*

▶ *Climb Val Pusteria northbound on the SS49.*

6 Brunico/Bruneck, Alto Adige

In 1251 Bruno of Bullenstätten and Kirchberg, the bishop of Bressanone, built the castle that still dominates the town. The houses squeezed between the riverside fortress and the Rienza river were surrounded by walls, sections of which are now incorporated into other constructions. Brunico clusters around the old street that crosses it from gate to gate and which, despite a few concessions to modernity, has managed to maintain its relaxed atmosphere.

On Via Centrale (now a pedestrian and shopping area) No 29 is the house where sculptor and painter Michael

The two tall bell towers of Bressanone's baroque cathedral

BACK TO NATURE

The roof of Austria is shared by Grossglockner, Eastern Tirol Salzburg and Carinthia, as is the Hohe Tauern National Park, a vast tract of 1,787sq km (690 square miles), of which 610sq km (235 square miles) are in Tirol. Central Europe's biggest nature reserve features the characteristic alpine landscape of the Alte Tauren, with peaks rising to above 3,000m (9,842 feet), large glaciers, beautiful valleys and a wide variety of indigenous wildlife (ibex, golden eagles, lynxes) and flora. There are numerous organised excursions, popular treks to Grossglockner and special activities for children.

Stalle Pass is closed in winter. From the pass, continue into Austria on the 25 Defereggental road to Huben, where you bear left on the 108.

8 Matrei in Osttirol, Osttirol

At the junction between the upper Isel valley to the south and Tauerntal to the north, on the Felbertauern road, Matrei in Osttirol stands beneath the glaciers of Austria's two highest peaks: Grossglockner (3,798m/ 12,461 feet) to the east and Grossvenediger (3,666m/12,028 feet) to the west. This pretty mountain resort provides incomparable natural and sports attractions, as well as cultural highlights such as the baroque-style parish church of St Alban, with frescoes by Franz Anton Zeiller (1716–93) and a fine organ, and, in the opposite hamlet of Ganz, the late-Romanesque church of St Nikolaus (14th- to 15th-century, keys at the farm next door), with a two-tiered choir – both frescoed.

The Goldried cableway climbs to the Europa Panoramaweg, a high-altitude path with a view of about 60 peaks higher than 3,000m (9,842 feet). Above the village is the Zedlacher Paradies, an ancient larch wood, containing trees up to 600 years old. This can be reached on foot directly from Matrei (quite a demanding hike) or from Zedlach (6km/4 miles to the west).

[i] *Rauterplatz 1*

▶ *Continue along the 108 (Felbertauernstrasse), passing through a toll tunnel (5km/ 3 miles). Beyond Matrei and*

Burg Weissenstein, a medieval fortress dominating the road to the left, continue along the scenic Felbertauernstrasse (toll) and enter the Salzburg province of Pinzgau.

9 Mittersill, Salzburg

The Salzach forms the axis of this province and, south of the river, comprises the Alte Tauern park. Mittersill is one of its main centres, situated where the north–south and east–west roads cross.

Schloss Mittersill was reconstructed in its present form in 1532, having been set alight

SCENIC ROUTES

From Huben, travel northeast on the Kalser Tal road, which enters the Alte Tauern National Park, with fine views of the Schober, Granatspits ranges and Glockner. From Kals you can continue along Kalser Glocknerstrasse, an alpine road (toll) that, after 7km (4 miles) of breathtaking views, reaches the Lucknerhaus refuge hut. From the car park, if you wish to stretch your legs, you can follow the circular Glocknerspur nature trail, with interactive posts identifying local flora, fauna and geology.

during a peasant revolt. There's a fine triptych in the Gothic chapel of the Hexenturm (tower).

In the town, the Felberturm (medieval tower) houses a museum with various exhibits (minerals, folklore, mountaineering) linked to the region. In winter, skiing enthusiasts can test their skills on 150km (93 miles) of pistes and, passing from one lift to another (there are 60 in the area), travel as far as Kitzbühel.

[i] *Marktplatz 4*

▶ *Take the 165 to Krimml and Gerlos.*

10 Krimml, Salzburg
Krimml is famous for the Krimmler Wasserfälle, one of the

Landing in the countryside near Kirchberg

highest waterfalls in Europe, which in three stages makes a descent of 380m (1,247 feet). A 5km (3-mile) path begins from the car park south of the village and skirts the three stages in succession. It's a 15-minute walk to the first and an hour to the third, where the path continues into the wild Krimmler Achental, a narrow valley formed by the tumultuous river that creates the waterfalls. Before undertaking the walk, preferably mid-morning when light conditions are most suitable, you can buy a combined ticket and visit the WasserWunderWelt ('wonderful world of water') theme park, with interactive exhibitions and audiovisuals.

If you can't reach the falls, you can enjoy a view of them from the Gerlos-Alpenstrasse, a splendid stretch of scenic road between Krimml and Gerlos that crosses the regional border between Salzburg and Tirol.

A wild mountain landscape near Matrei in Osttirol

FOR CHILDREN

From May to September and Christmas to March, a steam train puffs through Zillertal three times a day along the 35km (22 miles) that separate Mayrhofen from Jenbach. There are traditional carriages with wooden seats and if you like the wind in your hair you can ride in the open-top goods wagon. It's even possible to drive the locomotive by prior arrangement with the Mayrhofen station master.

[i] *Oberkrimml 37*

▶ *Continue along the 165 to Zell (the Krimml-Gerlospass stretch is a toll section).*

⓫ Zell am Ziller, Tirol

Zell am Ziller occupies a wide plateau where the Gerlos valley and Zillertal meet. An interesting guided walk to the Hainzenberg area (south of the resort) starts from the Goldschauberwerk, a disused goldmine where tunnels have been opened to visitors. It also has an interesting museum (Erlebniswanderung

Goldebergau). Next comes a visit to the Hochzeller Käsealm, a dairy, and the nearby Tierpark Heinzberg, a small wildlife park that's home to alpine artiodactyls. Continue along the Wallfahrtskirche Maria Rast (1739), a pilgrim route, before reaching the Knappensäule, a column donated by miners in 1832 to thank the Virgin Mary for her protection.

[i] *Dorfplatz 3a*

▶ *Take the 169 Zillertal road northwards.*

⓬ Fügen, Tirol

Sun-kissed Fügen lies at the point where Zillertal widens and the Ziller river is about to flow into the Inn. The surrounding slopes once yielded copper, iron and silver but today attract skiers and mountain-lovers. Bubenburg is a 16th-century castle refashioned in baroque form, now a boarding school. The parish church of Mariä Himmelfahrt (1494) has 14th-century frescoes, late-Gothic reliefs and baroque sculptures by Franz Xaver Nissl (1731–1804), a local artist.

Bird-watchers will enjoy the Vogel-Lehrpfad, a nature-trail

The old centre of Hall in Tirol, full of monuments and atmosphere

that circles through the woods of Hart, a village on the opposite side of the valley (2km/1 mile from the centre of Fügen). A two-hour walk with information boards gives you the opportunity to identify various local bird species and their nests.

FOR HISTORY BUFFS

In 1818, when the craftsman Mauracher of Fügen was asked to repair the Oberndorf organ in Salzburg, he happened to hear a Christmas song composed a year earlier by Franz Xaver Gruber. When he returned home he took the music and text with him and offered them to the well-established local singers, the Rainer Sänger family. This was the start of the successs of *Stille Nacht* (*Silent Night*), which thanks partly to international tours made by the Rainer family, remains the most popular Christmas carol in the world. One of the exhibitions in the Heimatmuseum in Fügen focuses on the history of *Stille Nacht* and its singers.

SPECIAL TO...

The most popular tourist attraction in Austria after Schönbrunn Castle in Vienna is the Swarovski Kristallwelten Museum ('world of crystal') in Wattens, 7km (4 miles) east on the 171. The building, designed to celebrate the centenary of the famous crystal works (1995), nestles in a hillside and resembles the head of a giant covered in vegetation, with glittering eyes and a fountain for a mouth. Inside, seven large underground chambers contain highly original displays of crystal in all shapes and sizes, variously interpreted by famous artists.

i No 300

▶ Continue along the **B169** to the junction with the **B171**, which you follow southwest through Schwaz and Wattens.

13 Hall in Tirol, Tirol
Along the course of the Inn river, on the outskirts of Innsbruck (less than 10km/6 miles) and at the foot of the Bettelwurf (2,726m/8,944 feet), you encounter the delightful town of Hall, linked since the Roman era with the mining of rock-salt. In 1477 Archduke Sigismund transferred the Tirol mint here from Merano, providing the town's other speciality.

Munzgasse leads from Unterer Stadtplatz, a tree-lined square in the lower town, to the castle, Burg Hasegg, built in 1489 and featuring the mighty Münzturm, where, in 1494, the marriage of Emperor Maximilian I and Bianca Maria Sforza was celebrated. The courtyard leads to the Museum der Stadt, tracing the town's history, and the Alte Münze, the old mint. Here you'll be told the history of the Hall *taler* – said to be the forerunner of the

American silver dollar – and you can even create a coin of your own on the spot. Back in the elongated central square, there's an intriguing view of tympanums and bell towers among the roofs of the Obere Stadt, the medieval upper town. To get there climb Langer Graben, flanked by narrow and atmospheric paved streets with beautiful 15th-century houses. On Oberer Stadtplaz are the Gothic Town Hall (Rathaus), with decorated crenellation, and the late-Gothic parish church of St Nikolaus, with twin aisles, rich baroque frescoes (1752) and a bell tower.

Nearby Thaur (3km/2 miles northwest) is known as the 'crib village' for its locally made statuettes and compositions, many of which are now on display at the Tiroler Volkskunstmuseum in Innsbruck.

i *Wallpachgasse 5*

▶ *Return to Innsbruck on the A12.*

Hall in Tirol's 15th-century Münzerturm

The Lower
Tirol

2/3 DAYS • 270KM • 168 MILES

Kufstein is the cultural and economic hub of the Unterinntal, for centuries contested by Bavaria and Tirol under the watchful eye of its invincible Burg (fort). It's also the starting point for a tour that passes through airy valleys before visiting the queen of skiing resorts, Kitzbühel.

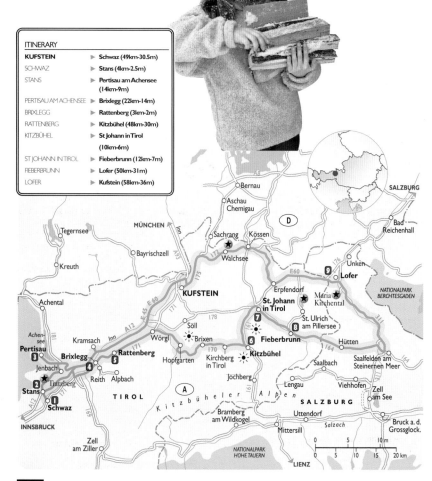

ITINERARY

KUFSTEIN	▶ **Schwaz (49km-30.5m)**
SCHWAZ	▶ **Stans (4km-2.5m)**
STANS	▶ **Pertisau am Achensee (14km-9m)**
PERTISAU AM ACHENSEE	▶ **Brixlegg (22km-14m)**
BRIXLEGG	▶ **Rattenberg (3km-2m)**
RATTENBERG	▶ **Kitzbühel (48km-30m)**
KITZBÜHEL	▶ **St Johann in Tirol (10km-6m)**
ST JOHANN IN TIROL	▶ **Fieberbrunn (12km-7m)**
FIEBERBRUNN	▶ **Lofer (50km-31m)**
LOFER	▶ **Kufstein (58km-36m)**

[i] *Unterer Stadtplatz 8, Kufstein*

▶ *Go to Schwaz on the A12.*

1 Schwaz, Tirol

Lying between the spurs of the Tuxer pre-Alps and the right bank of the Inn river, opposite the Karwendel peaks, Schwaz is today a bustling little town with a population of just over 12,000. Yet strolling along the medieval Franz-Josef-Strasse, it's not hard to imagine the town known as the Mutter aller Bergwerke ('the mother of all mines') in the 15th and 16th centuries. Then, at the height of its splendour as the silver and copper mining capital of Tirol, the miners alone numbered 12,000.

Across one end of the central street is the impressive Gothic parish church of Unsere Lieben Frau, remodelled in 1490–1502, its roof covered with 15,000 copper tiles. At the opposite end of Franz-Josef-Strasse, Burg Gasse leads to the Franziscanerkirche (1508–15), the church of the Franciscan monastery, with a splendid interior in which a soaring Gothic structure is combined with delicate baroque decoration. Watching over the town from on high is Schloss Freundsberg, a castle erected in the 12th century and converted to a residence for the dukes of Tirol in 1472–76. Its mighty keep houses the Museum der Stadt, with five floors of local art and artefacts.

[i] *Franz-Josef-Strasse 2*

▶ *Turn off the 171, which crosses Schwaz to the north, on to the 215 (Unterinntal Strasse).*

2 Stans, Tirol

Along the upper road to Stans you can stop near Vomp and visit the Stift Fiecht, a baroque Benedictine convent with a fine abbey church frescoed in pale colours and adorned with stuccowork. The statue of the Blessed Virgin used to adorn the Annasäule in Innsbruck.

The Renaissance courtyard of Tratzberg castle, near Stans

At the northermost tip of Stans is the start of a well-maintained path to the romantic Wolfsklamm. Along this, an hour and a half's walk leads through woods and across a breathtaking gorge to the convent of St Georgensberg (today in part a restaurant with accommodation), founded in 1138 but reconstructed five times, the last in 1868.

Continuing towards Jenbach, 2km (1 mile) from Stans, you can ascend (on the miniature train or 15 minutes on foot) to Schloss Tratzberg, built in Renaissance style at the time of Emperor Maximilian (1500–15) over the ruins of a 13th-century castle. Impeccably preserved, thanks to the counts of Enzenberg, who have lived here for 150 years, it contains an impressive courtyard with decorated arches. Other interesting features are the Habsburg room, which has a remarkable family tree that unfolds along the walls (1508), and the Königstube, with precious Renaissance carvings and original furnishings.

[i] *Unterdorf 62*

> ### SPECIAL TO...
>
> To learn more about the history of mining, visit the Silberbergwerk, on the outskirts of Schwaz (signposted on the 171 from Kufstein). Here you take a miniature train 800m (2,643 feet) underground into the galleries used by miners in medieval times.

▶ Continue along the 215 northeast to Jenbach, where you turn left for Maurach and then Pertisau (220).

3 Pertisau am Achensee, Tirol

Emperor Maximilian chose the region around the Achensee, enclosed within the Karwendel and Rofan mountains, as his favourite hunting ground. Apart from the game, it had the advantage of a tranquil alpine lake, which today can be admired from the windows of the romantic Achenseebahn and then from the deck of a boat (steam trains from Jenbach to Seespitz and boat services operate mid-May to October). Back on the road, the next stop is Pertisau, a charming resort on the western lake shore. A cable-way travels up to Zwolferkopf and you can stroll through alpine pastures or even float down to the valley on a paraglider.

[i] Hnr 53d

▶ Back in Maurach, follow the 181 to Wiesing and from here the 171 to Brixlegg.

4 Brixlegg, Tirol

On the approach to Brixlegg a sequence of well-preserved castles appears. The first, on the left, is Schloss Lichtwerth (late-12th century, privately owned), followed, on the right, by Schloss Lipperheide (only open to visitors during exhibitions).

A little further ahead, on the outskirts of Brixlegg, is Schloss Matzen, first recorded in 1282 although its courtyard has overlapping arches dating from the early 16th century, surrounded by a splendid 19th-century park with two small artificial lakes and English gardens. Schlossturm houses the Heimatmuseum (local museum) of the nearby village of Reith.

On the opposite bank of the Inn river is Kramsach with its four small lakes (east of the village, swimming permitted). The lake road also leads to the Museum Tiroler Bauernhöfe, the largest open-air Tirolean museum, where 34 historic rural buildings have been reconstructed, complete with furnishings and tools.

[i] Römerstrasse 1

SCENIC ROUTES

On the 171, just before Brixlegg, turn on to the lovely 12km (7-mile) road that follows the Alpbach river valley in the shadow of Wiedersberger Horn (2,127m/6,978 feet). The villages of Reith and Alpbach offer an insight into Tirolean life, with traditional wooden peasant houses and flower-filled balconies.

▶ Continue along the 171.

5 Rattenberg, Tirol

The medieval village of Rattenberg, one of the smallest and best-preserved in Tirol, is surrounded with car parks, offering easy access to the central pedestrian area. The main Südtiroler-Strasse is lined with houses of the 15th and 16th centuries, with fine overhangs and portals. After reaching the eastern end of the street, turn left for the church, Pfarrkirche

Schloss Matzen, near Brixlegg, at the mouth of the Alpbachtal

St Vigil, Gothic in style (two apses, blind façade) but with 18th-century frescoes and altars. If, on the other hand, you turn left into Klostergasse you come to the Klosterkirche St Augustin (1384), the church of the convent of the Servites. Here you can visit the Augustiner-museum, housing the records of 900 years of Tirolean history. Before leaving Rattenberg you might want to browse in one of the famous local crystal works.

A sweeping view of Kitzbühel, showing the Streif, the famous downhill ski slope

⌐i⌐ *Klostergasse 94*

▶ *Take the **A12** and leave it at Wörg; from here continue on the **170** to Kirchberg and Kitzbühel.*

6 Kitzbühel, Tirol

The prosperity of Kitzbühel is nothing new. In medieval times its strategic position on the road between Venice and Bavaria earned it considerable privileges. Later, in the 16th and 17th centuries, huge profits came from the exploitation of the nearby salt mines. Architectural and artistic evidence of its wealth is all around, from Pfeghof, the stately mansion with a 16th-century tower, home of the

---

FOR HISTORY BUFFS

Thanks to the wealth produced by the Kitzbühel mines, Rattenberg and Schwaz became towns of international importance, open to all the latest ideas – including Lutheranism. In the 1500s, Rattenberg was a stronghold of the Anabaptists, who managed to unsettle the Catholics to such a degree that they instituted the 'Rattenberg devil trials'. As recently as the 19th century, Protestants were still banned from the region, as is clearly shown in the picture by Mathias Schmid (1835–1923), *Chasing Protestants from Zillertal* in 1837, displayed in the Tiroler Landesmuseum Fernandeum in Innsbruck.

BACK TO NATURE

A path starts from the top of Kitzbüheler Horn, reached from Kitzbühel by cableway or on a narrow mountain toll road, and crosses the Alpenblumengarten, where 120 species of alpine flora grow. You can take the self-guided educational route or, in July and August, join a guided tour.

Dawn mists over the Walchsee, a small lake near Kufstein

Heimatmuseum (folklore, mining and skiing history, regional painting), to the 15th-century parish church of St Andreas, with rich baroque decorations, an imposing main altar (1663) and works by Veit Rabl.

Nowadays, though, Kitz (as it's affectionatley known) is best known for skiing, a sport 'imported' from Norway in the late 1800s and practised ever since with growing success on the slopes of Hahnenkamm to the southwest (1,668m/5,472 feet) and Kitzbüheler Horn to the northeast (1,996m/6,549 feet). The area now has 60 lifts and 160km (100 miles) of pistes. In winter it is easy to imagine yourself hurtling at full speed, like the World Cup champions, down the legendary Streif, a famous downhill slope – or, in summer, book a free guided excursion to the meadows of this famous piste.

[i] *Hinterstadt 18*

▶ *Drive to St Johann on the 161.*

7 St Johann in Tirol, Tirol
The busy Kaiserstrasse demonstrates this well-established tourist resort's role as an important road junction. St Johann's past is recalled in its Tirolean dwellings with frescoed façades and the two churches of Mariä Himmelfahrt (1723–28) and St Nikolaus, in the Weitau district, erected in 1262 and remodelled in the 18th century, with a precious, rare

glass window dating from 1493 behind the altar.

Sports- and nature-lovers can indulge themselves on the slopes of the northern side of Kitzbüheler Horn in summer and winter (17 lifts, 60km/37 miles of pistes; unfortunately the nature of the mountains prevents a direct link to nearby Kitzbühel).

In summer, you can stop at the intermediary station of the Harschbichl cableway and reach the Bergsee mountain lake and the Angerer Alm, a famous restaurant and starting point for easy hikes down to the valley. The Hochfeld chair-lift climbs to the summer sleigh run, 1km (0.6 mile) long, with a descent of more than 150m (492 feet).

[i] *Poststrasse 2*

▶ *Take the 164 southeast to Fieberbrunn.*

8 Fieberbrunn, Tirol
According to legend, in 1354 the Grand Duchess of Tirol, Margarethe Maultasch, stopped in the village of Pramau after being overcome by a sudden fever. She was suddenly cured when she drank the mineral water from the local spring, and decreed that the village be renamed Fieberbrunn, or 'fever spring'.

Now a tourist and spa resort, Fieberbrunn is regarded as the gateway to the Pillerseetal, which can be explored on a scenic road to the north (26km/ 16 miles to Waidring).

It's worth venturing at least as far as pretty St Ulrich (7km/4 miles), on the southern side of the lake that gives its name to the valley. A path skirts the water to the east (the road passes on the other side) and leads to the fine chapel of St Adolari (1407) and its important cycle of Gothic frescoes of the Virgin Mary.

[i] *Dorfplatz 1*

▶ *The 164 leads to Saalfelden and here you turn left (north) on to the 311 for Weissbach and Lofer.*

FOR CHILDREN

The Familienland Pillerseetal project in the Pillersee valley has more than 40 attractions for the whole family: a miniature train, a waterslide into the lake, raft trips, a mini-zoo, an Indian village, a big dipper and much more.

9 Lofer, Salzburg
The old village of Lofer is set at the point where the Saalach valley widens, dominated by the Stein mountains. Its houses are in the traditional characteristic painted style and the Gothic parish church has interesting 15th-century frescoes. Near by, a series of caves and gorges provide a popular natural spectacle.

Of particular note, near Weissbach (on the route, 10km/6 miles before Lofer), are the Seisenbergklamm gorge, crossed on foot in an hour, and Lamprechtsofenhöhle, a cave with an underground waterfall.

From St Martin take the toll road southwest (6km/4 miles in all from Lofer) to the sanctuary of Maria Kirchental (1693–1701, designed by baroque architect Johann Fischer von Erlach in his youth). One of his earlier works, it shows how brilliantly he solved the problem of setting a church in a landscape surrounded by mountains. From here you can walk in two hours to the Prax-Eishöhle ice cave.

i No 310

▶ *From Lofer, take the 312 to Erpfendorf where you turn right for Kössen on the 39. Then turn left on to the 172 for Walchsee to Sebi and from here south on to the 175 to Ebbs and Kufstein.*

> **RECOMMENDED WALKS**
>
> On the return journey, about 15km (9 miles) before Kufstein, stop at Walchsee, overlooking the lake of the same name. A 5km (3-mile) path leads around the lake in an hour, with views of sailing boats and windsurfers and the Zahmer Kaiser peaks to the south. In winter, the cross-country ski trail follows much the same route.

Flowers and frescoes adorn a house in St Johann in Tirol

THE FOOD & WINE OF AUSTRIA

Several influences have produced the rich, nourishing dishes of Austrian cuisine. They have their roots in peasant culture and the dictates of the climate (especially in Vorarlberg, Tirol, Salzburg and Upper Austria), and have also absorbed elements of Croatian, Bohemian and Hungarian cuisine in the eastern regions.

For low-fat, healthy food, you should seek out the new regional recipes, such as those served up in the 'creative cuisine' restaurants of Vorarlberg and in the hotels with health programmes that are scattered all over the region. And don't forget to try one of the delicious desserts the country is famous for, such as *Strudel* or *Sachertorte*.

Whether you prefer the traditional or the light version, there's nothing to beat an Austrian dish accompanied by one of the fine local wines.

Strudel, the delicious fruit dessert that is the hallmark of Austrian pastry-making

Second meat and fish courses

On the shores of the Bodensee (Lake Constance), perch and whitefish are the speciality, cooked with vegetables and herbs. Alternatively, you can sample the traditional meat dishes of Austrian cuisine virtually everywhere. These range from game, flavoured with juniper, bay leaves and bacon, to boiled beef, the *Tafelspitz* favoured by Franz Joseph, various Hungarian-inspired goulashes and *Schweinsbraten*, roast pork. The famous *Wiener Schnitzel*, a slice of veal, pork or turkey coated in breadcrumbs and fried, is a close relative of the Italian *cotoletta alla Milanese* but is thinner, with no bone, has

Suppen

You could make do with just a snack (*Jause*) on your refreshment stops – for example, the famous bacon, sausage and cheese platters eaten with rye bread. But if you decide to sit down for a complete meal you may well start with the classic *Suppe*, a meat or vegetable soup in one of countless varieties. These include *Rindsuppe*, beef broth with chives; *Frittatensuppe*, with strips of omelette; *Canederli* in broth (balls of hard bread softened in milk and mixed with egg), made with liver for *Leberknödelsuppe*; the Carinthian *Saure Suppe*, sour and coloured with saffron; and *Kürbisgemüse-suppe*, typical of Styria, a smooth, tasty cream of pumpkin soup.

First courses

The generous portions, rich ingredients and green side salad or potato salad make these a meal in their own right. Delicious *Käsespätzle* (cheese dumplings), a speciality served

in Vorarlberg, become *Spinatspatzln* (spinach dumplings) in Tirol. In Carinthia there's no escaping the intriguing taste of *Kärtner Käsnudel*, mint and ricotta cheese ravioli. The essential ingredient in Styrian pumpkin soup is the flesh of the gourd, enhanced with the extracted seeds and oil – the precious *Kernöl*.

flour added to the breadcrumbs and is fried in lard.

Delights and desserts

Strudel and *Sachertorte* are the stars of the Austrian sweet trolley. The traditional strudel is made with an apple filling (*Apfelstrudel*) wrapped in paper-thin pastry, but a good Austrian pastry chef uses only the fruit in season, and plum and apricot strudels are a true revelation. The famous *Sacher* should be tasted in Vienna, in the *Konditorei* of the hotel of the same name (budget permitting). Demel, a rival establishment, is still pursuing a 50-year-old legal dispute to determine the origins of this divine cake!

Above: vineyard in the Burgenland region
Below: drinking a toast

All washed down with...

Austria has been cultivating vines for thousands of years, particularly in Styria, Lower Austria and Burgenland. Listed below are renowned wine-producing areas drawn from the 16 officially recognised zones. As Austria has only a limited red wine production (23 per cent), these refer to white wines unless otherwise specified.

Southeast Styria (1,230 hectares/3,040 acres): this transition zone between the dry Pannonian and the humid

Wine ages in the barrels in a cellar in Krems, in Lower Austria

Mediterranean climate produces fruity white wines.

Southern Styria (1,902 hectares/4,700 acres): the hills of this area are mainly used to grow Welschriesling grapes (delicate apple aroma, light, with a hint of tartness), Sauvignon white and Morillon.

Western Styria (531 hectares/1,312 acres): a small wine-producing zone between Ligist and Eibirwald, renowned for the sharp Schilcher.

Wachau (1,350 hectares/3,335 acres): situated in the part of the Danube valley between Melk and Krems, Wachau produces mainly Grüner Veltliner, spicy, fresh and sparkling with an aromatic bouquet, and Riesling, a delicate and fruity classic.

Weinviertel (16,263 hectares/40,187 acres): the region's name ('wine district') tells it all. This is the home of Vertliner.

Neusiedlersee (8,332 hectares/20,589 acres): the exceptionally good wines of northern Burgenland are a result of the Pannonian climate, which is responsible for the whites such as Ausbruch of Rust and the reds such as Blaufränkisch. The Italian **Alto Adige** and wine-producing regions of **Val Venosta** produce excellent reds (Blauburgunder, Pinot Nero) and whites (Riesling) while from **Valle Isarco** come the white Müller-Thurgau and aromatic Traminer wines.

CARINTHIA & STYRIA

The journey across Styria and Carinthia explores the green heart of Austria. These two *Länder* (provinces), which make up Austria's central belt, face south and east and are therefore open to both Mediterranean and Slav influences. Much of the area is still unspoiled; Carinthia is 78 per cent pasture, meadow and forest, Styria 60 per cent woodland.

In the north, the mighty mountain ranges of the Hohe and Niedere Tauren are dotted with well-established summer and winter resorts. In the south, the Karnische Alpen, shared with Italy, give way to the east to magnificent lakes – no fewer than 1,270 in Carinthia alone – and to the hills of lower Styria, extending as far as the eye can see.

In the southeast, Christendom had to be defended against marauding Magyars and Turks. Abbeys, castles and fortresses have been preserved and bear witness to an uneasy past.

The region's rich mineral deposits have dictated much of its history and economy. Its wealth of art and architecture are the legacy of medieval gold-mining (in southern Salzburg, visited by the tours in this section) and northern Styria's iron mines, still active in the Erzberg area. Another natural source of income are the spa springs, recently revived to attract visitors.

A stay in long-established spa towns such as Badgastein or Badhofgastein (across the Salzburg border) or Villach, in Carinthia, or newcomers such as the Carinthian Bad Kleinkirchheim and Bad Radkersburg, in eastern-most Styria, makes a refreshing break for mind and body.

The two main towns, Klagenfurt and Graz, though quite different in style, character and atmosphere, both testify to the love of local tradition, history and culture that typify southern Austria. This is also reflected in the importance placed on the nation's artistic heritage, which has earned Graz its status as a Unesco-protected site.

Klagenfurt, a nocturnal view of the Wörther See shore

Snow-foxing in Carinthia – anything goes when playing in the snow

mountains, the rugged Dachstein and the Niedere Tauren, recommended in winter for skiing enthusiasts. The tour through breathtaking scenery is interspersed with visits to famous towns such as Friesach, Gurk and Maria Saal.

Tour 11
From Graz, the capital of Styria and Austria's second largest city, this tour sets out to explore the different faces of central Styria, visiting modern industrial centres and old medieval villages on the outward and return journeys and venturing into Upper Austria near the Kalkalpen national park. On the return journey, the road known as the Eisenstrasse, or 'iron route', passes through places associated with iron-mining and processing, scattered around Mount Erzberg.

Tour 12
Starting from 'Carinthia's paradise', as the Lavanttal is known, home of apples and cider, this trip crosses the hilly regions of southern and eastern Styria. The scenery is made up of pumpkin fields (a staple of traditional local cuisine) and vineyards, that stretch endlessly across the slopes on the border with Slovenia and Burgenland. Keeping watch over this countryside are ancient castles and fortified posts.

Tour 7
After starting in (and eventually returning to) the Tirolean enclave of Osttirol (East Tirol), the first Carinthian tour underlines the region's reputation as a land of rivers, lakes and mountains. Valleys created by the Lesach, Gail and Drava are majestically dominated by the Karnische Alpen, on the border with Italy, and the Kreuzeck range, the outpost of the Hohe Tauren. Millstätter See and the other lakes en route provide many opportunities to stop and relax before returning to Lienz.

Tour 8
This journey past one lake after another (more than 10 on this tour) takes you across southern Carinthia almost in one breath, with stunning mountain and hill-country views at every stage. Klagenfurt, capital of the *Land*, and its romantic lake Wörther See are a fitting conclusion for a journey along the water's edge.

Tour 9
This tour climbs from lower Carinthia towards the imposing Grossglockner, Austria's highest mountain and the country's most famous Alpine road. After a glance at the lunar landscape of the calcareous Salzburg Alps, the Kalkhochalpen north of Saalfelden, it returns towards Carinthia, taking in Goldegg – Salzburg's 'sunny terrace' – and the valley of gold and spas, with its exclusive resorts of Bad Hofgastein and Badgastein.

Tour 10
A highland itinerary takes you across the verdant Nockberge

A view of Graz – it once rivalled Vienna for cultural and historical importance

The Dolomites
to Millstätter See

From high-mountain hikes on the Dolomites to the inviting waters of the Millstätter See, in Carinthia, this is a varied and stimulating tour, a treat for nature-lovers in summer, skiers in winter and art-lovers all year round.

ITINERARY	
LIENZ	▶ **Sillian (31km-19m)**
SILLIAN	▶ **Maria Luggau**
	(29km-18m)
MARIA LUGGAU	▶ **Kötschach/Mauthen**
	(27km-17m)
KÖTSCHACH/MAUTHEN	▶ **Hermagor (31km-19m)**
HERMAGOR	▶ **Millstatt (51km-32m)**
MILLSTATT	▶ **Gmünd (20km-12.5m)**
GMÜND	▶ **Greifenburg**
	(41km-25.5m)
GREIFENBURG	▶ **Lavant (33km-20m)**
LAVANT	▶ **Lienz (8km-5m)**

3 DAYS • 271KM • 168 MILES

❶ Lienz, Osttirol

Lying in a fertile hollow between the Hohe Tauern mountains to the north and the northeastern spurs of the Dolomites – the Lienzer Dolomiten – to the south, the capital of East Tirol is a lively town dedicated to tourism.

On its outskirts are two sites of great historical and artistic interest. On the left bank of the Isel river stands the solitary parish church of St Andreas, built in 1457 on early Christian (5th-century) foundations; the nave and aisles are embellished with fine Gothic fresco cycles. further west, the opposite side of the river is dominated by the 13th-century castle of the Görz counts, Schloss Bruck. Here you

SPECIAL TO...

The Schloss Bruck Museum, in Lienz, boasts a rich collection of works by Albin Egger-Linz (1868–1926), who hailed from nearby Dölsach and was considered one of the most important Tirolean painters. His powerfully realistic pictures often portray the peasant life, history and scenery of East Tirol.

SCENIC ROUTES

As an alternative to the 100 road between Lienz and Sillian, on the stretch between Leisach and Strassen (32km/20 miles) you can take the Pustertaler Höhenstrasse. This high panoramic road runs across the slopes of the Villgrater Berge, making the most of the beautiful upper Puster valley. Along the way you can visit Schloss Anras, summer residence of the bishops of Brixen from 1200 to 1809.

can visit the Museum der Stadt, interesting not only for its permanent art, history and folk collections but also for its prestigious temporary exhibitions.

Just outside the village of Leisach (2km/1 mile southwest) is the Wasserschaupfad Galitzenklamm, a trail with walkways and platforms that enable visitors to appreciate the Galitzenbach river gorge in all its wild beauty.

ⓘ *Europaplatz 1*

▶ *Take the 100 road westbound to Sillian.*

Lienz' 13th-century Schloss Bruck

❷ Sillian, Osttirol

The Pustertal, divided between Austria and Italy after World War II, is one of the largest and loveliest valleys in the Eastern Alps. Sillian is the main Austrian town here, famous as a summer and winter resort. Bicycle rides on the banks of the Drau river, along the surfaced Draurandweg, and mountain hikes on the slopes of the Thurntaler (reached by cableway) can be combined with a visit to the ruins of Schloss Heinfels, which dominate the valley. Parts of the keep and original 12th-century palace can be seen.

ⓘ *No 86*

FOR CHILDREN

On the Pustertaler Höhenstrasse, 10km (6 miles) southwest of Lienz, the Wildpark Assling is a refuge for many animal species. Deer, ibex, bison and raccoons are among the inhabitants, and well-maintained paths allow visitors to appreciate them in their natural habitat.

▶ *Go back along the same road (about 4km/2.5 miles) and turn right on to the scenic Karnische Dolomitenstrasse (111), which runs through the Gail river valley.*

8 Maria Luggau, Carinthia
The Lesach valley road, which runs half on Tirolean territory and half in Carinthia, crosses an idyllic valley, unspoiled by tourism and industry, where corn cobs are still hung out in the sun on the wooden balconies of the old farmsteads.

At Maria Luggau, behind the baroque basilica of Maria Schnee, are four old timber mills where, every fortnight in summer, residents still grind grain using the pressure of the river water.

ⓘ *No 29, Liesing*

▶ *Continue along the 111 road.*

4 Kötschach/Mauthen, Carinthia
From the 1st century AD, travellers from *Aquileia* to *Aguntum* (today's Lienz) used the *Iulia Augusta* way, a route which has been reconstructed and signposted along the 52 road in Italy and the 110 in Austria. Standing at the point where this ancient road encounters the Lesach valley is the town of Kötschach-Mauthen, divided in two by the Gail river and still a major road junction. The church of Unsere Liebe Frau (1518–27), which acts as the valley's cathedral, is the late-Gothic work of Bartlmä Firtaler and features fine stucco decorations on vaulted ceilings. A haunting 1915–18 museum displays mementoes and relics from World War I. To round off the visit, head 11km (7 miles) south of Mauthen to the Plöckenpass, where paths wind their way round military posts to create an open-air war museum.

ⓘ *Rathaus, No 390*

▶ *The 111 road leads to Hermagor.*

5 Hermagor, Carinthia
A 10km (6-mile) detour south, 7km (4 miles) before Hermagor in the upper Gail valley, leads to the Sonnenalpe Nassfeld, a 10km (6-mile) skiing area where the Pramollo pass leads into Italy.

Before visiting Hermagor and the Gothic parish church of St Hermagoras und Fortunatus (1485), stretch your legs in the Garnitzenklam (route open Jun–Sep), starting 2km (1 mile) south of nearby Möderndorf. The 6km (4-mile) path crosses a spectacular ravine, leading over sheer drops and waterfalls and across walkways and bridges. The final stretch is not recommended for vertigo sufferers. At Möderndorf, the Gailtal Museum in the castle has a bible that once belonged to Martin Luther.

ⓘ *Gösseringlände 7*

▶ *Follow the 111 road to St Stefan an der Gail, where you turn left (northeast) on to the 33 road to Paternion. Just*
before the junction with the *A10*, turn left for Feistritz an der Gail, cross the Drau river and take the *39* road to Dobriach; here you skirt the northern shore of Millstätter See on the *98* road.

6 Millstatt, Carinthia
Two features dominate the environs of Millstatt: mountain peaks (the immense Millstätter Alpe, rising to 2,091m/6,860 feet) and water, which flows crystal-clear from the springs and down the valley into the second largest lake in Carinthia, the Millstätter See. As well as being the perfect base for water sports and mountain excursions, Millstatt is a centre of culture and art, and hosts a programme of concerts between May and October. These Musikwochen ('music weeks') are held in its famous Benedictine abbey, founded in the 11th century. While enjoying the music you can admire its fine portal with ornamental reliefs (c1170) and the various 15th- and 16th-century frescoes. Further along

A sweeping view of Gmünd, at the foot of the Hohe Tauern

the lake, a right turn at Seeboden leads to Treffling (8km/5 miles from Millstatt) and the Schloss Sommeregg (1237), housing a well-known restaurant and the Folterauskunft, a museum of torture.

☐ *Marktplatz 14*

▶ *Drive to the northern tip of the lake on the same road and take the A10 northbound for Gmünd.*

7 Gmünd, Carinthia
Wedged between the Hohe Tauern and the Nockberge, at the mouth of the Malta valley, is the well-preserved walled town of Gmünd, complete with virtually intact bastions and turreted gates. This stronghold was used by Salzburg's archbishop-princes to control passage along the important Venice-Nuremberg route via Salzburg. Hauptplatz runs from one gate to the other and is

SCENIC ROUTES

One of the most beautiful mountain roads in Austria, the Malta-Hochalm-Erlebnisstrasse (about 20km/12 miles, toll), runs through the Malta valley, which branches off from Gmünd, against the backdrop of the Hohe Tauern mountains and numerous spectacular waterfalls. The dramatic Kölnbrein dam spans the valley; visitors can stroll across its barrage 200m (656 feet) above the ground.

overlooked by the parish church of Mariä Himmelfahrt (1339), with tombs in the aisles and rich baroque altars. The towering Alte Burg, a 13th-century fortress almost entirely in ruins, has a section rebuilt in Renaissance style and now housing an elegant restaurant and hosting temporary exhibitions, concerts and theatrical productions.

The Porsche Automuseum Pfeifhofer has more than 40 original Porsche cars and commemorates the years (1944–50) when Gmünd was the headquarters of the famous car manufacturer.

☐ *Rathaus*

▶ *Return along the A10 and turn right on to the slip road that ends at Lendorf. Continue west on the 100 road.*

8 Greifenburg, Carinthia
As you follow the upper Drau valley, you come across the village of Steinfeld (6km/4 miles before Greifenburg), where a high road leads to nearby Gerlamoos and its famous church (keys at No 15). Fortunately, the Gothic revamp of the original Romanesque building (1516) preserved its precious 14th-century frescoes, on the south front. Inside is a fresco cycle with vivid scenes.

The valley road continues to Greifenburg, where mountain

and lake lie in the shadow of its castle (not open to visitors). A lovely 12km (7-mile) road leads northwest up to the Emberger Alm (1,800m/5,905 feet), where numerous scenic paths cross the slopes of Mount Hochtristen (2,536m/8,320 feet). Weather permitting, you can swim in the local Bad See, or head 10km (6 miles) southeast to the Weissen See, whose clear blue waters, warm in summer, freeze in winter to form the largest permanently iced-over surface in Europe.

☐ *Gemendeamt*

▶ *Remaining on the 100 road, you reach Görtschach, where a short detour to the south leads along the 318 road to Lavant.*

9 Lavant, Osttirol
From the houses on the wooded Kirchhüger, the hill that dominates Lavant, it is a 20-minute walk to the baroque sanctuary of St Ulrich (1770–71) and, slightly further on, the Gothic St Petrus und Paulus Kapelle (1485). In the 3rd century AD this was the seat of the bishopric of *Aguntum*, as confirmed by the remains of early Christian buildings found in both churches. Parts of a castle have also been uncovered.

☐ *No 32*

▶ *Return to the B100 and follow it to Linz.*

FOR HISTORY BUFFS

For a fascinating overview of the Lienz area's history, pay a visit to the Aguntum archaeological park, 4km (2.5 miles) southeast of the capital. Excavations have been under way since 1700 to uncover the remains of the ancient Roman site (1st century AD) and earlier Illyrian and Celtic settlements. Finds are on display in the annexed museum.

The Lakes of
Southern Carinthia

Villach is a well-known spa town at the gateway to Austria, Italy and Slovenia, where the different cultures meet to create a relaxed and romantic atmosphere. It makes an ideal prelude to seductive southern Carinthia and its glittering lakes.

ITINERARY

VILLACH	▶ Faaker See (7km-4m)
FAAKER SEE	▶ Ferlach (36km-22m)
FERLACH	▶ **Bad Eisenkappel** **(33km-20.5m)**
BAD EISENKAPPEL	▶ Eberndorf (15km-9m)
EBERNDORF	▶ Völkermarkt (10km-6m)
VÖLKERMARKT	▶ **Klagenfurt (28km-17m)**
KLAGENFURT	▶ Maria Wörth (15km-9m)
MARIA WÖRTH	▶ **Velden am Wörther See** **(12km-7.5m)**
VELDEN AM WÖRTHER SEE	▶ **Feldkirchen in Kärnten** **(25km-15m.5)**
FELDKIRCHEN IN KÄRNTEN	▶ Ossiach (12km-7.5m)
OSSIACH	▶ Villach (14km-9m)

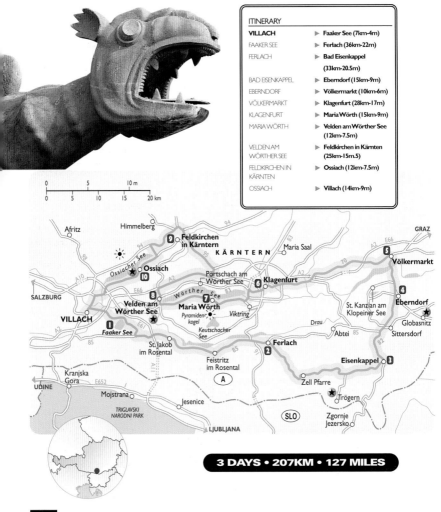

3 DAYS • 207KM • 127 MILES

A view of Villach, an old town on the banks of the Drava

❷ Ferlach, Carinthia

Along the course of the Drau river in the Rosental, just before entering Ferlach, stop at the Kirschentheuer Carnica Bienenmuseum to find out all you need to know about bees and their produce. In contrast, the Büchsenmacher und Jagdmuseum in Ferlach is a gunsmiths' museum: arms have been manufactured in this 'gun town' since 1555.

The Loiblpass and the border with Slovenia are just 13km (8 miles) away. Near Unterloibl (3km/2 miles from Ferlach), on the southward road to the pass, is the Tscheppa ravine (Tscheppaschlucht); a hike of just over 1km (0.6 mile) – possible between May and October – offers spectacles such as the Tschauko waterfall, 26m (85 feet) high, and the 'devil's arch' excavated into the rock. After two hours or so you reach the opposite side, where you can stop in one of the traditional restaurants or take advantage of a free lift back to the car park.

> 🛈 *Kirchgasse 5*

> ▶ *Drive southeast on the **103** road to Zell-Pfarre and turn right on to the **108** Shaidsattel road. Continue east on the **131** to Bad Eisenkappel.*

❸ Bad Eisenkappel, Carinthia

Austria's southernmost resort, at the point where the Rosen and Vellach valleys meet, is renowned for its lithium spa waters (*Bad*); it's also an industrial centre for Lavanttal iron (*Eisen*) and the setting for a chapel (*kappelle*) since 1050.

Conspicuously set on the edge of the town is Schloss Hagenegg, a castle built in 1430 by Wolfgang Hagen and owned by the counts Thurn Valsassina (not open to visitors). A less striking but equally impressive

> 🛈 *Rathausplatz 1, Villach*

> ▶ *Drive to the northern tip of the Faaker See on the **84** road.*

❶ Faaker See, Carinthia

You can travel by car or, more romantically, on a mini-cruise on the River Drau (mid-May to mid-Oct) from Villach to the Faaker See, where the lake's turquoise waters lap around a pretty little island and reflect the distinctive outline of the Mittagskogel (2,145m/7,037 feet). You can stop in one of the lake's charming resorts or water-sports centres, or set off to explore the ruins of Finkenstein castle, which dominate the

landscape from an 850m (2,789-foot) rise 4km (2.5 miles) to the west of Faak am See. In summer the modern Burgarena, among its ruins, is the venue for entertainment and concerts.

The world cycling championship was held in this area in 1987, and cyclists can still enjoy first-class facilities and tracks. If you feel fit enough, park the car at the lake and continue the journey pedalling along the Rosental.

> 🛈 *Dietrichsteiner Strasse 2*

> ▶ *The **B84** circles the east side of the lake to meet the **85** Rosental road, which you follow to the east.*

Klagenfurt's elongated Alter Platz with the 17th-century Pestsäule at its centre

building is the pilgrim church at the cemetery, Wallfahrtskirche Maria Dorn, which has fine 15th-century frescoes depicting scenes from the lives of Jesus and the Virgin Mary.

The spectacular Obir caves (visits May–October), at a height of 1,078m (3,537 feet), are reached by shuttle-bus from the centre of Bad Eisenkappel. Inside are amazing stalactites and stalagmites – a dramatic experience enhanced by background music and lighting.

The southwestern road to Ferlach leads 7km (4 miles) to a left-hand detour, which takes you to another natural wonder, the Trögerner Klamm, a monumental gorge dug into the rock. Now a nature reserve, it provides a habitat for rare plants, and is surrounded by the Potok woods, rich in black pine and flowering ash.

ⓘ *Hauptplatz 7*

▶ *Head north on the 82 road.*

4 Eberndorf, Carinthia
The mighty, four-sided building that dominates Eberndorf may look like a castle but it is, in fact, a Benedictine abbey. Founded in 1149 and originally occupied by the Augustinians, the Stift (abbey) was fortified in the 15th century as a defence against forays by the Turks and Hungarians. Visits are possible all year round but particularly worthwhile in summer, when

---

FOR HISTORY BUFFS

Archaeological excavations of the Hemmaberg hill (842m/2,762 feet), reached along a short stretch of road west of Globasnitz (8km/5 miles southeast of Eberndorf) have shown that, in the 5th and 6th centuries AD, a former Celtic settlement evolved into an important early Christian pilgrimage site. The foundations of five churches and reception halls for the pilgrims have been uncovered. Finds are on display in the Globasnitz archaeological museum.

---

the Südkärntner Sommerspiele music and theatre festival is held in the courtyard surrounded by three tiers of arches.

A series of small, clear lakes, all good for swimming, lies within a radius of just 5km (3 miles) just east of Eberndorf. Secluded Gösselsdorfer See is ideal for families; the shores of the Turner See shelters thousands of birds, either in the Sablatnig marsh nature reserve or in captivity in the Vogelpark; and the Klopeiner See is the site of prehistoric and Roman settlements. You can explore the lakes and local woods, meadows and farms from mid-May to mid-September on board the *Bummelzug* miniature railway.

ⓘ *Kirchplatz 1*

▶ *Continue along the 82 road.*

5 Völkermarkt, Carinthia
Völkermarkt stands on one of the many artificial lakes formed in the upper reaches of the Drau river. Every Wednesday this medieval village clustered around the Hauptplatz fills with stalls in readiness for the Markt

that gave the town its name. At the back of the square is the neo-classical façade of the Neues Rathaus (new town hall), on the site of the 13th-century Burg (fort). On the opposite side, one of the few remains of the original castle is the Rundturm, a round tower with a Renaissance bas-relief. A narrow lane skirting the façade to the right leads to the Bezirks-heimatmuseum, devoted to the Carinthian resistance movement of 1918 and to the 1920 referendum for *Land* unification. The church of St Ruprecht, on the western outskirts of town, has an important Romanesque bell tower. The church was rebuilt in 1857, but the tower dates from the 12th century.

ⓘ *Hauptplatz 1*

▶ *Follow the* **70** *road westwards to Klagenfurt.*

🖪 Klagenfurt, Carinthia
Klagenfurt, capital of Carinthia and 'Rose of the Wörther See' (the nearby lake, linked by a canal), has a mix of strong southern tradition and urbane elegance, best seen in the mansions that overlook the new centre's streets.

Start your visit from Neuer Platz, dominated by the fountain guarded by a dragon, sculpted by Andrä Vogelsang in 1593. According to legend the dragon – Klagenfurt's emblem – lived in the marsh on which the town was built in the 12th century. Kramergasse, a pedestrian street lined with smart shops, leads to the historical core of Klagenfurt, the elongated Alter Platz. Of note among the baroque mansions surrounding it is the yellow façade of the 17th-century Altes Rathaus (old town hall), with its lovely courtyard and tiered arcades. Just a stone's throw from the western tip of the square is the Landhaus, the seat of regional government, a Renaissance building (1574–94) with two towers standing proud of the façade. Here you can visit the elaborately decorated Wappensaal (hall of coats-of-arms), with 665 shields of the provincial states, governors and vice-canons of Carinthia painted on its walls. The 17th-century

FOR CHILDREN

The open-air Minimundus display stands beside Klagenfurt's amusement park, Europapark; here, with the aid of an audio-guide, you can admire more than 150 miniature reproductions (scale 1:25) of famous buildings from all over the world. Every new model is produced using materials as close as possible to the originals and takes up to seven years to complete.

arms and frescoes on the ceiling are the work of J F Fromiller.

Back in Neuer Platz, pass in front of the neo-classical façade of the new town hall and turn into 10-Oktober-Strasse. Turn left into Lidmansky Gasse to reach the cathedral, commissioned by Protestants at the end of the 16th century. Despite considerable damage during World War II, the sumptuous interior was spared

Walls covered with coats-of-arms in the Wappensaal, Klagenfurt

Maria Wörth seen from above, picturesquely extending into the waters of the Wörther See

and is rich in stuccowork and paintings. Leaving the cathedral behind you, turn into Museumgasse, one of the last streets on the right of Lidmansky Gasse, where at No 2 you can visit the Landesmuseum für Kärten. Exhibits include finds from the Hallstatt era (Bronze Age) and the ancient Roman settlement of *Virunum* (2nd century AD). Before completing the circle and returning to Neuer Platz, stop in Lidmansky Gasse at the famous Pumpe restaurant to taste their *Kärntner Käsnudel*, local ravioli filled with ricotta and mint.

As an alternative to the traditional town tour, the local tourist office provides walks around 53 churches and 23 castles, all in Klagenfurt and the immediate environs.

A separate excursion can be made to the Cistercian abbey of

Viktring, 6km (4 miles) southwest of the centre. Founded in 1142, it was almost entirely rebuilt in the 18th century and has a long rococo façade overlooking the park. The abbey church has 15th-century stained glass windows in the choir.

> SPECIAL TO...

Reifnitz, on the Wörther See, marks the beginning of the 'valley of the four lakes' road, the largest lake being the Keutschacher See (2km/1 mile south of Reifnitz). Some of the interesting spots in this area include the Pyramidenkogel, 4km (2 miles) northwest of Keutschach, with a viewing tower on its summit (lift to the platform at 905m/2,969 feet, where the view takes in all Carinthia), and the Zauberwald an 'enchanted forest' for children on the Rauschele See.

☐ *Rathaus, Neuer Platz*

▶ *Follow the southern shore of the Wörther See on the 96 road.*

7 Maria Wörth, Carinthia
'Such melodies fly over the Wörther See that one must take care not to trample them.' This rather florid description was offered by Johannes Brahms (1833–97), who spent years composing on the shores of this emerald-green lake. Scattered along its southern shore, around Maria Wörth, are several secluded and romantic spots, not untouched by tourism but maintaining their serenity none the less. The village of Maria Wörth stands out from the rest because of its position and thousand-year history.

From an islet on the Wörther See, the Bavarian bishop of Freising set about spreading the Christian message through Carinthia. His island church, the Pfarrkirche St Primus und

BACK TO NATURE

More than 350 species of exotic and alpine animals live in the vast park that surrounds Schloss Rosegg (4km/2.5 miles south of Velden), owned by the Liechtenstein family. As well as the wildlife park, you can visit the wax museum inside the castle and the maze in the English garden.

(general layout) and baroque (interior and, above all, main altar) styles. In 1770 an embankment was created, transforming the island into a peninsula and laying the foundations for the success of this 'pearl of the Wörther See'.

[i] *Freisinger Platz*

▶ *The 96 road continues west to Velden am Wörther See.*

8 Velden am Wörther See, Carinthia

Velden has remained true to its role as an exclusive holiday resort since the opening of the first fully equipped lido in 1865 and the conversion of local buildings into Wörthersee-Archiktektur villas after a devastating fire in 1881. A more recent example of this vernacular style is the Casino pavilion, with its lakeside terrace. Inaugurated in 1989, it now hosts more than 300 cultural events a year, including private viewings, concerts and dance festivals.

In keeping with the resort's high society image, the Schloss Velden, a lakeside Renaissance castle, was turned into a top hotel in the 19th century (currently closed). Tourist boats start their journeys across the tranquil waters of the Wörther See to Klagenfurt from here.

[i] *Villacher Strasse 19*

▶ *Follow the A2 eastbound and exit at Pörtschach to continue north, first on the 73 road and then on the 95.*

9 Feldkirchen in Kärntern, Carinthia

As far back as the 9th century, the strategic importance of this site halfway between the

Felician, was first built in the 9th century; the present building incorporates Romanesque (crypt), Gothic

Velden am Wörther See, the late 16th-century Schloss Velden

Klagenfurt plain and the Nockberge was understood. Today it's a lively exhibition and trade centre and a good base for excursions to nearby beauty spots such as the lakes of Flatschach and Maltschach, where swimming is permitted.

The Bamberger Amthof was the administrative seat of the lords of Bamberg from the 16th century, and has recently been restored to house a museum of local history and culture, two art galleries and a conservatory.

i Amthofgasse 3

▶ *Follow the 94 road southwest for about 7km (4 miles), then turn left (south) on to the 50 road and then right (southwest) on to the Ossiacher See road (49).*

⑩ Ossiach, Carinthia
On the southern shore of the fish-filled lake of the same name

Holiday relaxation in Carinthia, near the Ossiach lake and woods

SCENIC ROUTES

For an overview of central Carinthia, follow the lovely Gerlitzen alpine road at Bodensdorf, on the Ossiacher See. At the end of a 1,800m (5,905-foot) ascent, a footpath continues to the summit (1,909m/6,263 feet).

is Ossiach, a holiday resort with a strong artistic and cultural heritage. For a while, in the 16th and 17th centuries, the local Benedictine abbey (Stift) – founded in 1028 – was one of the most important in Austria. Today it has been turned into a hotel, but proof of its ancient splendour can still be seen in the collegiate church of the Assunta. Built in Romanesque style, it has Gothic baroque additions, with fine polychrome stuccowork by the school of Wessobrunn (1740) and frescoes by J F Fromiller (1744). Also of note is the triptych of the Virgin

Mary by Master Lukas (1505) and, against the external wall, the tombstone of the Polish king Boleslaus II (1039–81). In July and August the church hosts the internationally renowned concerts of the Carinthischer Sommer music festival.

i No 8

▶ *The 49 leads back to Villach.*

SPECIAL TO...

The castle of Landskron, which dominates the Ossiacher See from its lofty perch, 7km (4 miles) northeast of Villach, is well known for its training centre for birds of prey. Here you can see displays of eagles in flight. At the 'cavaliers' banquet' in the castle restaurant (reservation required), diners must tackle their food with a knife only, as the fork was considered an instrument of the devil in the Middle Ages.

From Alps to
Spas

3/4 DAYS • 294KM • 183 MILES

At the foot of the scenic Mount Goldeck (2,142m/7,027 feet) and a stone's throw from the romantic Millstätter See, you can find culture and relaxation at Spittal an der Drau, where, on warm midsummer evenings, the Renaissance courtyard of Schloss Porcia (1533–98) is the setting for the great Komoedienspiele theatre festival.

ITINERARY		
SPITTAL AN DER DRAU	▶	Flattach (36km-22m)
FLATTACH	▶	**Grosskirchheim (38km-23m)**
GROSSKIRCHHEIM	▶	**Heiligenblut (11km-7m)**
HEILIGENBLUT	▶	**Grossglockner Hochalpenstrasse (48km-30m)**
GROSSGLOCKNER HOCHALPENSTRASSE/	▶	Zell am See (7km-4m)
ZELL AM SEE	▶	**Saalfelden am Steinernen Meer (14km-9m)**
SAALFELDEN	▶	Goldegg (58km-36m)
GOLDEGG	▶	**Dorfgastein (17km-10m)**
DORFGASTEIN	▶	**Bad Hofgastein (9km-5m)**
BAD HOFGASTEIN	▶	**Badgastein (8km-5m)**
BADGASTEIN	▶	**Mallnitz (6km-4m)**
MALLNITZ	▶	**Spittal an der Drau (42km-26m)**

RECOMMENDED WALKS

Mount St Daniel, named after a church erected on the site of a former Roman temple, is protected as a nature reserve. You can enjoy its beauty on an easy path from Kolbnitz, 19km (12 miles) north of Spittal, to the summit plateau (960m/3,150 feet). Here, you can taste fine local Carinthian dishes at the famous Herkuleshof restaurant (keys to the church), visit the fish pond and, weather permitting, go swimming in the pool. An equally delightful path descends to Penk with information boards explaining the hunting tradition along the way.

high-mountain lifts then climb to Mount Schareck (3,123m/ 10,246 feet), where the gaze sweeps over the Grossglockner, Sonnblick and Dachstein ranges. You can also reach the mouth of the spectacular Ragga river ravine (Raggaschlucht) from Flattach, in the opposite direction (south). The excursion includes a crossing of the ravine, an educational geological path and a return trip through the woods, which takes about an hour and a half.

The Möll river and its subsidiary streams are ideal for rafting enthusiasts.

The Renaissance-style courtyard of Schloss Porcia, at Spittal an der Drau

ⓘ *Burgplatz 1, Spittal an der Drau*

▶ *From Spittal take the 100 and then the 106 northwest before bearing left on to the 106 to Flattach.*

1 Flattach, Carinthia
There is skiing all year round on the Mölltal glacier (Mölltaler Gletscher), at 3,000m (9,843 feet), reached from Flattach on the splendid 18km (11-mile) scenic road (last section toll) that follows the Fragrantbach river, passing its many small lakes. Underground cable-cars and

FOR HISTORY BUFFS

The hill known as St Peter in Holz (standing about 4km/2.5 miles northwest of Spittal) was first inhabited in the 12th century BC. Around AD 50 the ancient Celtic settlement of *Teurnia* was absorbed into a new Roman town, which in turn, in the 5th and 6th centuries, became the fortified capital of the province of *Noricum* and an important bishopric. Fascinating discoveries from different stages of the town's history are displayed in the St Peter Museum.

ⓘ *No 99, Flattach*

▶ *Continue on the 106 road to Winklern, where you turn north on to the 107.*

2 Grosskirchheim, Carinthia
This enchanting holiday resort comprises Döllach and nearby villages along the Möll valley, and is the base for Carinthia's Hohe Tauern National Park information centre, which provides details of excursions, and holds slide shows and exhibitions about the area. The Hohe Tauern mountains are rich

in ore, and the history of mining is traced in the Goldbergbau-und-Heimatmuseum in Schloss Grosskirchheim. Built in 1561, the castle was once the base of the region's gold-mining administration.

[i] Döllach 47

▶ The 107 continues to Heiligenblut.

3 Heiligenblut, Carinthia
Its enviable position on the green slopes of the Möll valley has made Heiligenblut one of the most photographed places in Austria, with the mighty Grossglockner providing a backdrop to the handsome 15th-century church, Wallfahrtskirche St Vinzenz. A reliquary here is said to contain drops of Christ's blood (heiligen Blut means 'holy blood'). According to legend St Briccius was taking it to Denmark when he was struck by an avalanche near by.

St Vinzenz, in Heiligenblut, with Grossglockner in the background

The church is also one of the leading examples of Austrian Gothic style, with an elegant buttressed polygonal apse and a soaring square bell tower. A fresco depicting St Christopher (1460) covers the left side. Inside, the altarpiece features a masterpiece of late Gothic art, the *Coronation of the Virgin* (1520) by the Michael Pacher workshop.

For an extraordinary view of the peaks that crown the Grossglockner, climb by cableway to Mount Schareck (2,604m/8,543 feet), which shares its name with another mountain, reached from Flattach. From here you can either take one of the paths up to the peak or descend to the valley through the meadows.

[i] Hof 4

▶ Continue along the Grossglockner Hochalpenstrasse. The Heiligenblut-Ferleiten stretch is a toll road and subject to winter closure (Dec–Apr).

4 Grossglockner Hochalpenstrasse
Heiligenblut marks the beginning of the real climb along the mountain road considered one of Austria's greatest tourist attractions: the Grossglockner-Hochalpenstrasse. Covering 48km (30 miles) in all, with a gradient of 12 per cent, it leads to Bruck, in Salzburg. As it crosses the Hohe Tauern park, the road reaches its highest point at Mount Hochtor (2,576m/8,451 feet), marking the border between the provinces of Carinthia and Salzburg. From here it descends to the Fuscher Törl pass (2,428m/7,966 feet). At the pass, a road branches off to the left and leads to the Edelweissspitze scenic viewpoint (2,571m/8,435 feet), with a panorama of 37 peaks higher than 3,000m (9,843 feet).

The most interesting and popular detour, branching off just 8km (5 miles) from Heiligenblut, is the Gletscherstrasse, or the glacier road, leading to the incredible

▷ *Drive to Zell am See on the 311 road northbound.*

BACK TO NATURE

Since the Grossglockner road opened in 1935 there have been a large number of complaints about the impact of the bridges (nearly 70), tunnels and asphalt and concrete on the previously unspoiled Hohe Tauern National Park. But efforts have been made to bring visitors' attention to the fragile environment, allowing them, for instance, to observe animals running free on the Grossglockner from a station on the Franz-Josefs-Höhe.

---

5 Zell am See, Salzburg

Zell is an important centre in the southwestern Salzburg district of Pinzgau. It stands on the lake of the same name, which is good for fishing, sailing, windsurfing and water skiing, although the water can be chilly, as it flows from the surrounding glaciers.

Not far from the lakeshore promenade is the central Stadtplatz, where you can visit the four-storey Heimatmuseum (traditional dress, handicrafts, minerals, history of skiing) in the Vogt-Turm, a 13th-century

Pasterze glacier. On the way, where the road ends, is the Franz-Josefs-Höhe (2,422m/ 7,946 feet); from the car park, a cableway descends to the glacier, dominated by the Grossglockner (3,797m/12,457 feet) – Austria's highest peak – the Adlersruhe (3,454m/11,332 feet, left) and the Johannisberg (3,460m/11,352 feet, right).

ⓘ *Grohag, Heiligenblut*

Snowboarding on the powder snow of the Zell am See

BACK TO NATURE

The wildlife park at the Grossglocknerstrasse toll station of Ferleiten is ideal for an educational pause and a little relaxation on the lakeshores. From the observation tower you can spot up to 200 different animal species. Children will enjoy the next-door Kindererlebnisland, an amusement park with games and various attractions.

---

granary tower. Set slightly back from the south of the square is the Romanesque parish church of St Hippolyt (9th to 12th

century), with its great 13th-century bell tower and late-Gothic women's gallery. On the other side of the Brucker Bundesstrasse, which passes through the town, is Schloss Rosenberg, a 16th-century turreted castle now used as the town hall.

Together with Kaprun (7km/4 miles south-west), Zell am See has created the Europa-Sportregion ski area; in winter, this offers more than 130km (80 miles) of ski slopes, and skiing is also possible in summer on the Kitzsteinhorn glacier.

i *Brucker Bundesstrasse 1a*

▶ *Continue to Saalfelden on the 311.*

6 Saalfelden am Steinernen Meer, Salzburg
Saalfelden's geographic position is a complex one – the town sits at the centre of Pinzgau, in the Saalach valley, near the border

with Tirol and not far from Kitzbühel, against the backdrop of the rugged Steinernes Meer to the northeast and the lunar Leoganger Steinberge to the northwest. It's a lively and very popular summer and winter tourist resort, thanks to the

SCENIC ROUTES

Just 10km (6 miles) south of Saalfelden, at Maishofen, you can take the scenic Glemmtal road along the course of the Saalach river through glorious pastureland. At Saalbach a cableway climbs to the summit of the Shattenberg (2,018m/6,620 feet), with beautiful views towards the calcareous peaks of the Loferer Steinberge to the north. In winter, ski enthusiasts can enjoy the Saalbach-Hinterglemm ski area, with its 200km (124 miles) of slopes and 60 ski lifts.

Zell am See, the Kitzsteinhorn peak and glacier, which also offers summer skiing

scenic beauty and the gentle slopes of the Pinzgauer Grasberge, which separate it from the higher mountains.

A chair-lift climbs to the nearby Mount Biberg (1,443m/4,734 feet); from the last station you can stay at the Huggenberg refuge hut in summer and either climb to the top (40 minutes) or experience a breathtaking descent on the longest summer bobsleigh run in Europe.

For historical and cultural background on the region visit Schloss Ritzen, south of town, and its Pinzgauer Heimat-museum, which has a huge collection of cribs.

i *Bahnhofstrasse 10*

▶ *Follow the 164 eastwards past the Salzach and take*

The Gasteiner Ache river
waterfall, Badgastein

⚫ *Hofmark 18*

▶ *Return to the **311** on the
same road and continue
eastwards to the junction with
the **167** Gasteinertal road,
which you take southbound.*

8 **Dorfgastein,** Salzburg

Guarding the mouth of the
valley formed by the Gasteiner
Ache, to the left of the road,
stand the ruins of Klammstein
castle, until the 16th century the
administrative headquarters of
the local gold and silver mines.
Not far away (a 15-minute walk)
is the entrance to the Entrische
Kirche (literally translated as the
'frightening church'), a system
of caves used in the 15th
century by Protestants who
gathered there in secret.

There's a foretaste of the
spa towns along the Gasteiner
valley at the small village of
Dorfgastein, the first important
centre on the valley road. Even
in winter, visitors can plunge
into the steaming waters of the
Felsenbad open-air rock pool.

⚫ *No 11*

▶ *Continue along the **167**.*

9 **Bad Hofgastein,** Salzburg

Given its position halfway along
the valley, Bad Hofgastein is the
ideal place for a stop combining
the pleasures of mountain and
spa. In winter, you can spend
the whole day skiing on the
Dorfgastein-Bad Hofgastein-
Badgastein area, on the slopes of
the Kreuzkogel (2,027m/6,650
feet), Schlossalm (2,050m/6,726
feet) and Stubnerkogel
(2,246m/7,369 feet), before
immersing yourself in the hot
Kurzentrum pools.

The Gothic parish church of
Mariä Himmelfahrt (1498–1507)
is worth a visit at any time of
year. Its sumptuous main altar
was sculpted by P Mödlhammer
and painted by Andrä Eisl
(1738). On the outer walls are
the tombs of the miners (16th

*the **311** south to St Johann
in Pongau and Schwarzach.
After passing Schwarzach,
turn on to the **213** for
Goldegg and Weng.*

7 **Goldegg,** Salzburg

Picturesque Goldegg and its
small lake, in Salzburg's Pongau
district, are dominated by the
impressive silhouette of Schloss
Goldegg, a castle built in 1322
and extended in the 16th
century. Some rooms still have
their original wooden cladding;
the painted panels and
impressive frescoes lining the
walls and ceiling of the
Rittersaal (hall of the Knights)
are Renaissance works. The

Pongau Museum, based here,
displays objects and utensils
illustrating peasant life.

SPECIAL TO...

To the west, running parallel to
the Gasteiner valley, is the
Rauris valley (the mouth is
9km/5 miles from the Klamm
Pass). This is where the 'gold
rush' started during Roman
occupation. Exploitation of the
mines reached its peak in the
Middle Ages, but continued until
1800. Excursions lead to the old
gold mines of Kolm-Saigurn, at
the end of the valley.

to 17th century) who made the town's fortune.

ℹ️ *Tauernplatz 1*

▶ *Continue along the 167 to Badgastein.*

10 Badgastein, Salzburg
Badgastein (or Bad Gastein) is famous for its gold and spa treatments. When Hitler ordered the Austrians to re-open the medieval gold mines of the Hohe Tauern mountains, the workers who ventured into the shafts emerged empty-handed, but cured of their ailments. Scientific studies later showed that the air in the tunnels excavated at Böckstein (4km/2.5 miles south of Badgastein) – which reaches a temperature of 40°C (104°F) and 97 per cent humidity – is rich in radon, a slightly radioactive gas with health benefits. The first person, however, to analyse the benefits of the waters was the physician and researcher

Badgastein, a spa of aristocratic tradition on the two banks of the Gasteiner Ache

Theophrastus Bombastus von Hofenheim (also known as Paracelsus)

Today visitors can partake of professional treatments in the Gasteiner Stollen (Gastein tunnel) and Kurhaus, the spa built in the town centre. Set beside the noisy Gasteiner Ache waterfall, it exploits the curative waters of 18 hot springs, as the Romans did centuries ago. There is a range of sports and entertainments here, including golf, a casino and skiing.

ℹ️ *Kaiser-Franz-Josef-Strasse 27*

▶ *Continue to Böckstein where a shuttle train passes through the tunnel (Tauerntunnel) and links up with the 105 road to Mallnitz.*

11 Mallnitz, Carinthia
Mallnitz, on the edge of the Hohe Tauern National Park, is an excellent base for high-mountain excursions. Two cable-cars climb from the hamlet of Stappitz (2km/1.2 miles north) up the Hannoverhaus, at the foot of the Ankogel glaciers (3,252m/10,670 feet), the

starting point for several well-signposted paths.

Even closer to Mallnitz, towards Obervellach, is a chair-lift that ascends to 1,900m (6,230 feet) and the Häusleralm, on the opposite side of the mountain. Before setting out, you can collect information at the BIOS museum-workshop, where 80 interactive stations introduce natural features of the region arranged under the themes of water, air, earth and fire.

ℹ️ *No 11, Mallnitz*

▶ *The 105 meets the 106 at Obervellach; follow this southeast. Shortly after Möllbrucke turn left on to the 100, which leads back to Spittal.*

FOR CHILDREN

The Mallnitz BIOS houses Bubble World, where children can play with soap bubbles and compete to blow the biggest and most colourful examples.

Famous Abbeys
& Ancient Castles

5/6 DAYS • 473KM • 294 MILES

It's a tough choice: the scenic splendours of nature parks, or the rich history and architecture of medieval villages? Luckily, this tour through Carinthia, Salzburg and Styria gives you the chance to enjoy both options.

ITINERARY		
VILLACH	▶	**Bad Kleinkirchheim** (37km- 23m)
BAD KLEINKIRCHHEIM	▶	**St Michael im Lungau** (69km-43m)
ST MICHAEL IM LUNGAU	▶	**Tamsweg** (16km-10m)
TAMSWEG	▶	**Mauterndorf** (10km-6m)
MAUTERNDORF	▶	**Radstadt** (39km-24m)
RADSTADT	▶	**Schladming** (18km-11m)
SCHLADMING	▶	**Murau** (74km-46m)
MURAU	▶	**St Lambrecht** (18km-11m)
ST LAMBRECHT	▶	**Friesach** (30km-19m)
FRIESACH	▶	**Gurk** (62km-39m)
GURK	▶	**Strassburg** (4km-2.5m)
STRASSBURG	▶	**St Veit an der Glan** (27km-17m)
ST VEIT AN DER GLAN	▶	**St Georgen am Längsee** (7km-4.5m)
ST. GEORGEN AM LÄNGSEE	▶	**Maria Saal** (18km-11m)
MARIA SAAL	▶	**Villach** (44km-27m)

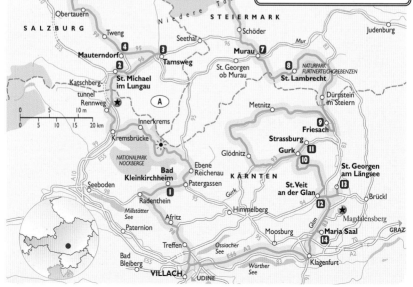

FOR CHILDREN

At Bad Bleiberg, 15km (9 miles) west of Villach, you can enter the tunnel of Terra Mystica and explore the earth and its wonders. A 68m (223-foot) slide takes you into the heart of the mine, where the journey continues on a miniature railway, past multimedia effects. Children can also take part in an exciting treasure hunt.

ℹ️ *Villach, Rathausplatz 1*

▶ *Follow road 94 to the north and take the 98 to Radentheim on the left (northwest); here, turn right (east) on to road 88 for Bad Kleinkirchheim.*

🛈 **Bad Kleinkirchheim,**
Carinthia

Nobody knows how long ago the rumour first spread that the water flowing from the Augenquelle, Bad Kleinkirchheim's 'spring of the

Bad Kleinkirchheim – spa bathing in the snow-clad setting, above; below, the ski school

eyes', was good for the eyesight. Certainly, there was a spa here in 1473 – the present Gothic church of St Kathrein was erected around it in 1492, and the curative waters still flow along a stone channel in its crypt. In the adjacent spa and in the Römerbad, inspired by ancient Rome, the cascades, hydromassage baths and

---

SCENIC ROUTES

A little way past Ebene Reichenau, 47km (29 miles) north of Villach, take the scenic road to Innerkrems known as Nockalmstrasse (35km/22 miles, toll). This leads you through the Nationalpark Nockberge, a protected area of considerable scenic interest. Its distinctive volcanic Nocken mountains, blanketed with vegetation, are lower and more rounded than the alpine reliefs.

RECOMMENDED TRIP

Pölltal nature park, on the border between Carinthia and Salzburg, west of Rennweg, is closed to traffic in the summer months. The 'valley of a thousand orchids' can safely be explored from a miniature railway on its 15-minute journey from Rennweg. It also provides access to various hikes.

children's area make a trip to the spa a treat for everyone.

In winter you can soak in the hot water of the covered pool while watching skiers zigzagging down the slopes of the Kaiserburg (2,055m/6,724 feet) and returning on one of the five

The mighty 13th-century Burg Mauterndorf

lifts operating on two slopes. In summer there are superb views of the surrounding Nockberge region from the station on top of the Kaiserburg and along the numerous paths that start there.

ℹ *Dorfstrasse 30*

▶ *At Wiedweg, road **88** meets road **95**. Follow this north before turning left on to the local Grundtal road to Innerkrems and Kremsbrücke. From the latter resort, take the **A10** to the Rennweg exit and then drive to St Michael im Lungau on road **99**.*

❷ St Michael im Lungau, Salzburg

The point where the scenic road between Rennweg and St Michael reaches its height (1,641m/5,384 feet) – avoiding the stretch of toll motorway – marks the start of the

Katschberg chair-lift to Aineck. From the top, at 2,210m (7,251 feet), you can admire a region renowned for its winter skiing and wooded scenery.

Descend to St Michael and stop at the parish church after which the town is named, to see its fine 13th-century frescoes and parts of the original Romanesque choir (1147). Along the road to Tamsweg, halfway between St Michael and Unternberg, stands Schloss Moosham, a 13th-century stronghold that was for many years the seat of the regional court, notably in the dark era of the witch-hunts. Today it houses a folk and art museum.

ℹ *Raikaplatz 242*

▶ *Drive 4km (2.5 miles) along road **99** and turn right on to road **96**. Near Tamsweg, turn right (south) on to road **95**.*

3 Tamsweg, Salzburg

The main town in Lungau – the wooded region southeast of Salzburg – Tamsweg clusters around the old Marktplatz. On Corpus Christi – and sometimes in summer – the square hosts the popular Samsonumzug, a festival during which one man carries a giant effigy of Samson (6m/20 feet tall) on his shoulders.

In nearby Kirchengasse is the former hospice of St Barbara which houses the Lungauer Heimatmuseum, with displays of Roman finds, ancient weapons and peasant furnishings.

Outside town, on a hill to the south, is the sanctuary of St Leonhard, erected between 1421 and 1433 and fortified a few decades later. The outer windows are Gothic master-pieces, the work of craftsmen from Salzburg and Vienna; of particular note in the choir is the Goldfenster ('gold window').

ⓘ *Marktplatz 134*

▶ *Road **95** to the west leads to Mauterndorf.*

4 Mauterndorf, Salzburg

Visitors come to this small resort for its lovely walks to Trogalm See and for the ski runs from the Grosseck (2,066m/6,778 feet). Its pride is the Burg Mauterndorf (1253), a former customs post and summer residence of the archbishop-princes of Salzburg.

Visits to the castle begin with a self-guided tour through the great complex, where you are invited to imagine yourself in the shoes of the 16th-century archbishop-prince Leonhard von Keutschach. You then visit the rooms of the Lungauer Landschaftmuseum, a museum dedicated to the natural and cultural landscape of Lungau, and finally the castle inn serves snacks and medieval dinners. Meanwhile, younger visitors can pretend to be ladies and noblemen in the courtyard playground.

ⓘ *No 7, Mauterndorf*

▶ *Follow road **99** northwards to Tweng and Radstadt.*

5 Radstadt, Salzburg

Like many of the settlements along the old Roman roads that became major trade routes in the Middle Ages, Radstadt enjoyed considerable privileges during its long history. Records first mention it in 1074; by 1527 it had gained full independence from the archbishopric of Salzburg. The town's former prestige is evident in its mostly intact fortifications: three corner

The gentle view of woods and pastures on the border between Carinthia and Salzburg

towers (1527–35) joined by sections of the 13th-century walls, which allowed access to the centre through six points of passage.

On one of the straight roads that intersect at the central square is the Stadtpfarrkirche Mariä Himmelfahrt, a church with a late-Romanesque nucleus (14th century) and 17th-century alterations by Santino Solari. A lovely 12km (7-mile) road (which can be walked) leads to

SPECIAL TO...

According to legend, around the year 1000 on a farm in Tirol, a length of wool was accidently dropped in boiling water and became matted. The mountain-dwellers, too poor to throw anything away, retrieved the wool and found that it had become strong and waterproof. They had stumbled upon the most popular Austrian innovation: the Loden. Today, Schladming is one of the leading production centres of the famous green fabric.

the Radstadt viewpoint, on Mount Rossbrand (1,770m/5,807 feet). In winter people ski on the slopes of Kemahdhöhe (1,677m/5,502 feet), on the opposite side of the valley, cut by the river Enns.

ℹ️ *Stadtplatz 17*

▶ *Drive to Schladming on the E651/146 eastbound.*

6 Schladming, Styria

Continuing along the Ennstal, just after entering Styria, you reach Schladming, a resort internationally renowned for the World Cup skiing competitions held on the Planai slopes

(1,894m/6,214 feet). Four peaks in the Hohe Tauern can be reached via lifts in this area. Rising majestically on the other side, to the north, is the Dachstein; the mountain road that passes through Ramsau leads in 15km (9 miles, last stretch toll) to the Türlwandhütte (1,707m/5,600 feet), the station of the cableway that climbs to the Hunerkogel. At a height of 2,836m (9,304 feet) there's a sweeping view over the dramatic landscape of the Hoher Dachstein (2,995m/9,826 feet), beyond which lie the Hallstätter Gletcher glaciers.

ℹ️ *Erzherzog-Johann-Strasse 213*

▶ *Continue along the E651 to Pruggern, where, after following a stretch of the 712 to Stein an der Enns, you take road 704 (Erzherzog-Johann-Strasse) southwards to Gross-sölk and St Nikolai im Sölktal. The final section of road 96 leads to Murau.*

7 Murau, Styria

Stein an der Enns, 3km (2 miles) southeast of Gröbming, marks the start of the stretch of scenic road known as Erzherzog-Johann-Strasse (closed in winter between St Nikolai and the Sölk pass, 1,788m/5,866 feet). This

Schladming, one of the ski slopes used by competing champions

passes through the magnificent Sölktal nature reserve, wedged between the Schladminger and Rottenmanner Tauern (west and east, respectively).

At Schöder, the southernmost tip of the scenic road, you're close to Murau, the first large Styrian town in the lush Mur valley. Murau's grand old centre recalls its golden age, when the Liechtenstein and Schwarzenberg families ruled the roost. One founded the first, 13th-century castle; the other built the still surviving Schloss Obermurau on its ruins in the 17th century. Visit the Heimatmuseum, a folk museum in the former Capuchin convent, and the Brauereimuseum, if possible during September's Oktoberfest, which commemorates 500 years of local beer production.

ℹ️ *Bundesstrasse 13a*

▶ *Drive to St Lambrecht on road 502.*

8 St Lambrecht, Styria

Set on the slopes of the Metnitzer Berge, an ideal spot for country hikes, St Lambrecht grew up around the famous Benedictine Stift (abbey)

To the north, local road 502, between St Lambrecht and Neumarkt, skirts the Naturpark Grebenzen, a nature area around the mountain of the same name (1,892m/6,207 feet). The abundance of woods in this part of Styria inspired the creation of the 'Styrian forest way', a clearly signposted theme route that visits Murau, St Lambrecht and Neumarkt plus another 22 locations, venturing westwards as far as Tamsweg. Attractions include the amazing Styrian larch-wood bridge (45m/148 feet) that crosses the Mur river at St Georgen (8km/5 miles west of Murau) and the St Ruprecht museum of wood (another 4km/2 miles).

founded in 1076 and rebuilt in Renaissance style by Domenico Sciassia (1645). Although it suffered under the anti-monastic policy of Emperor Joseph II (1765–90), the Stift has managed to preserve some fine baroque rooms (particularly the Kaisersaal, now a concert hall), the 15th-century Stiftkirche (church), with a precious drape of the Passion (c1460), and works of art dating from the 15th and 16th centuries, kept in the Kunsthistorische Sammlung (art collection). Also here is a collection of baroque crib statues and a display of stuffed birds.

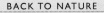 *Hauptstrasse 1*

▶ *At Neumarkt in Steiermark, road **502** intersects road **83** to the east; follow this south to Friesach.*

9 Friesach, Carinthia
The oldest town in Carinthia and once one of the most important centres in the southeast alpine area is also known as the home of the 'medieval euro' (the Friesacher Pfennig). Its rich medieval district was once the possession of the archbishop-princes of Salzburg; among surviving features are the moat and the walls, with 12th-century bastions and watchtowers. Once past the fortifications, enjoy the atmosphere of days past in Hauptplatz, adorned with old mansions and, in the centre, a pretty, octagonal fountain in Italian Renaissance style (1563).

Follow the road up to the east to reach the top of the Petersberg. From a rise above it, the bishops' old castle dominates the town. Its remains now house a restaurant, the Petersberg Museum of local history and culture and an open-air theatre, and still convey the splendour of the original 13th-century fortified residence, likened at the time to an imperial palace.

Back in town, there are several lovely churches, as well as that of the castle on the Petersberg (1130). There's the elongated Dominikanerkirche St Nikolaus, a Gothic convent church with a famous sandstone statue of the Madonna of Friesach (14th century); the Deutchordenskirche, a mixture of Romanesque, Gothic and

Castle towers and abbey bell-towers at St Lambrecht, in Styria

baroque styles with a wealth of Gothic sculpture (39 statues and two altar frontals); and the Stadtpfarrkirche St Barthlmä, a basilica with Romanesque touches and fine stained-glass windows in the choir (13th and 14th century). For something a little different, try the Virtuelle Mythenwelt, a multi-media museum dedicated to the great myths and legends of the past.

i *Hauptplatz 1*

▶ *The 62B westbound and then 63 southbound lead to*

later, lost her only son. She found herself having to manage the great family wealth by herself – no easy task for a woman in those days. Eventually, Hemma used it to found two sanctuaries: a monastery at Admonta and a convent at Gurk, where she herself was subsequently forced to retreat.

Gurk's Dom (cathedral) is one of the most beautiful and famous Romanesque churches in Austria (1140–1200), with overlapping and blending styles both inside and out. Two square

cycles (13th century); on the other side is the entrance to the crypt, a forest of marble columns (at least 100), which conceal the baroque chapel containing the tomb of St Hemma (1174).

i *Dr Schnerichstrasse 12*

▶ *Continue on the same road to Strassburg.*

⑪ Strassburg, Carinthia
The lush and unspoiled wooded slopes and wide, grassy clearings of the Gurktal have borne witness to over a thousand years

Gurk, a detail of the gilded main altar in the cathedral

Kleinglödnitz, where you take road 93 eastbound to Gurk.

⑩ Gurk, Carinthia
Anyone visiting Gurk will soon come across the story of St Hemma, a significant female figure in the medieval world. The wife of Count Friesach, the richest noble of the duchy of Styria and Carinthia, she was widowed in 1016 and, 20 years

towers dominate the exterior, crowned with onion domes – a baroque touch added to a very Gothic façade. Inside, the simplicity of the original layout, with nave and two aisles, is in striking contrast to the rich baroque furnishings, seen to dazzling effect on the main gilded altar by Michael Hönel (1629). From the right aisle you climb to the Bischofskapelle, the Episcopal chapel where you can admire one of the most valuable German Romanesque fresco

of turbulence. Their legacy is a pair of mighty castles that dominate the valley: Schloss Strassburg and the castle of Pöckstein at Zwischenwässern (10km/6 miles east), the principal seat and summer residence of the bishop-princes of Gurk. Both buildings, undermined by the passing of time and a violent earthquake, were extensively rebuilt from the late 18th century on, and Pöckstein today stabds as a perfect example of neo-classical architecture (1782). Schloss Strassburg, high above the village of the same name, still has two 12th-century towers, a fine, arcaded courtyard, portals and a baroque chapel (14th- to 17th-century). As well as the folk and history museum and the Jagdmuseum (history of Carinthian hunting), it's a venue for regular temporary exhibitions and events.

ℹ️ *Hauptplatz 1*

▶ *After returning to Gurk on road 93, turn left on to road*

very seriously: from spring to autumn the old centre and the medieval moat are a sea of colours.

In the middle of the historic central square, Hauptplatz, stands the Pestsäule (1715), a marble column commemorating a plague. Flanking this are a 17th-century fountain dedicated to the famous Minnesänger (medieval entertainer) Walther von der Vogelweide and the Schlussebrunner fountain, with a Roman basin excavated from Virunum, in nearby Zollfeld. No 1 on the square features the

the seat of the Stadtmuseum of local history.

ℹ️ *Hauptplatz 1*

▶ *Turn left off road 82 for Fiming and St Georgen.*

🔟 St Georgen am Längsee, Carinthia

A relaxing pause on the shore of Längsee, a small lake with excellent facilities and swimming, can be combined with a visit to the nearby Burg Hochosterwitz (5km/3 miles south of St Georgen), an

striking baroque façade of the Rathaus (the building actually dates from 1468) and at No 29 you can visit the original Verkehrsmuseum, which traces the evolution of transport from carriages to the present day. Sections of wall (5–7m/16–23 feet high) survive of the 14th-century fortifications.

Dating from the first half of the 16th century, the Herzogsburg was converted from ducal mansion to arsenal with a defence tower and is now

Burg Hochosterwitz, a formidable fortress not far from Sankt Georgen am Längsee

impressive fortress that seems to grow from the rock on its solitary hill.

First built in 860, it was strengthened against the Turks between 1570 and 1586 by Georg Khevenhüller, who erected the complex system of fortifications that still glowers over the winding path to the top of the hill (20 minutes' walk, but

67 for Pisweg and Kraig; at the junction with road 94, take it southwest to St Veit.

🔟 St Veit an der Glan, Carinthia

The former capital of Carinthia (until 1518) proudly maintains the exclusive atmosphere of a 'ducal town'. This is the setting for one of the first 'art hotels' – the Ernst Fuchs Palast – with its splendid Tiffany-glass windows. The town's annual floral decoration competition is taken

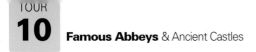

there is also a lift). Even if the enemy had managed to enter one of the 14 gate-towers along the walls, they would have been exposed to attacks by defenders on the upper levels. True to the prediction engraved by the 16th-century owner on a slab in the castle courtyard, Burg Hochosterwitz still belongs to the Khevenhuller family. Visitors can see a collection of weapons and medieval armour, the Gothic church and the chapel.

☐ *Längseestrasse 6*

▶ *Return to road **82** and follow it towards St Veit before turning left on to road **83** for St Donat and Maria Saal.*

14 **Maria Saal,** Carinthia
'Heart of Carinthia', Maria Saal's soubriquet, refers to its position and to its important historic role. The village stands on an area of intense Roman colonisation, which started with the settlement of *Virunum*, founded in AD 45 slightly further north, on the fertile Zollfeld plain. Little remains of the flourishing capital of the district of *Noricum*, though a large arena is currently being excavated, but many blocks of stone and several sculptures were reused in subsequent eras as building material and ornamental motifs for local churches.

FOR HISTORY BUFFS

The Magdalensberg, 9km (5 miles) west of Maria Saal, is a vast archaeological excavation site, first explored in 1948 and still turning up parts of an important 1st-century BC Roman settlement. The open-air museum arranged on the site allows visitors to stroll along ancient roads, through the forum and in the 22 buildings brought to light thus far.

Maria Saal, the Gothic parish church of Mariä Himmelfahrt

Stone from *Virunum* is believed to have been used in the Herzogstuhl (1301), the ducal seat beside road 83, just before you enter Maria Saal. Roman bas-reliefs (3rd- to 4th-century) can be seen in the wall on the right side of the parish church of Mariä Himmelfahrt, a Gothic architectural gem and place of pilgrimage. Inside are particularly lovely frescoes found in the late 19th century in the choir and

attributed to an anonymous artist from Friuli (1435). On the main altar is a statue of the Virgin Mary dating from 1425. There's a wonderful view from outside this simple and austere church, which dominates the village from its high perch, surrounded by a lovely cemetery and protected by medieval fortifications.

☐ *Am Platz 7*

▶ *Road **83** leads to the **A2/E66** between Klagenfurt and Villach.*

The Green
Lands of Styria

4 DAYS • 400KM • 248 MILES As the European capital of culture in 2003, Graz has buffed up its splendid old buildings and provides the perfect introduction to a journey through the green lands of Styria, with its white horses and fragrant lavender.

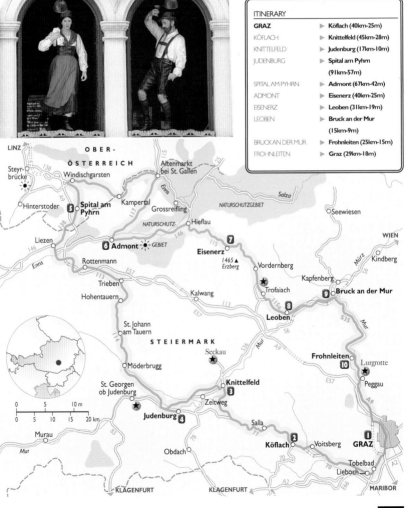

ITINERARY	
GRAZ	▶ **Köflach (40km-25m)**
KÖFLACH	▶ **Knittelfeld (45km-28m)**
KNITTELFELD	▶ **Judenburg (17km-10m)**
JUDENBURG	▶ **Spital am Pyhrn (91km-57m)**
SPITAL AM PYHRN	▶ **Admont (67km-42m)**
ADMONT	▶ **Eisenerz (40km-25m)**
EISENERZ	▶ **Leoben (31km-19m)**
LEOBEN	▶ **Bruck an der Mur (15km-9m)**
BRUCK AN DER MUR	▶ **Frohnleiten (25km-15m)**
FROHNLEITEN	▶ **Graz (29km-18m)**

1 **Graz,** Styria

'The historic centre of the city of Graz reflects artistic and architectural movements originating from the Germanic region, the Balkans and the Mediterranean, for which it served as a crossroads for centuries. [...It] is an exceptional example of a harmonious integration of architectural styles from successive periods. Every age is represented by typical buildings, which are often masterpieces'. The UNESCO declaration in support of Graz centre's status as a Cultural Heritage Site (1999) conveys the Styrian capital's unique spirit and charm.

The second most densely populated city in Austria sits in the shadow of the Schlossberg (473m/1,552 feet, climbed via a steep flight of steps or by cableway), where the famous 1569 hillside clock-tower (Uhrturm) is visible among the trees. Start your exploration of Graz at Hauptplatz, setting of the 19th-century city hall, and Herrengasse, the city's main thoroughfare. No 16 is the Landeszeughaus, an arsenal designed in 1644 by Andrea Solari, now housing the world's largest collection of historical weapons – more than 30,000 pieces, including armour and helmets, mainly from the 16th and 17th centuries. On the other side of the street you will see the Italian face of Graz when you cross the threshold of the Landhaus, a 16th-century building by Domenico D'Allio.

SPECIAL TO...

The baroque castle of Eggenberg, in the western suburbs of Graz, was completed in 1655. Besides its sumptuous reception halls and vast English garden, it owes its fame to extensive prehistoric and coin collections. Here you can admire the original Strettweger Kultwagen found at Strettweg (see Judenburg).

Graz, the city lying on the two banks of the Mur

Its elegant Renaissance inner courtyard (1581–85), by Antonio and Francesco Marmoro, has an arcaded structure with tiered loggias and is used as a space for theatrical performances.

Pass through the so-called 'Bermuda triangle' (after spending time in the busy nightspots of this pedestrian precinct you may not be able to emerge), near Glockenspielplatz – where a carillon plays Styrian music three times a day (at 11, 3 and 6) – to reach the cathedral, a late-Gothic building next to the baroque mausoleum of the Emperor Ferdinand II. The cathedral interior reveals the baroque influence of the Jesuits summoned by the Habsburgs in the 16th century to stem the tide of Protestantism. Two particularly precious reliquaries flank the choir, adorned with ivory bas-reliefs (Triumphs of Petrarch) attributed to Andrea Mantegna (1477), originally from the marriage chests of Paola Gonzaga. The vaulted ceiling of the choir bears the letters AEIOU, presumably standing for *Austria erit in orbe ultima* (Austria will live forever).

To round off your visit, ask for directions to the double Gothic stairway (1499) in the courtyard of the Burg, behind the cathedral. The climb is traditionally a favourite of young lovers, as it separates and reunites them at every turn.

ℹ️ *Herrengasse 16*

▶ *Drive to Köflach by travelling southwest on road 70 to Tobelbad and Lieboch, then northwest.*

2 Köflach, Styria

Set among rolling hills west of Graz, sheltered by the Stubalpe and Gleinalpe ridges, Piber (2km/1 mile northeast of Köflach) is the home of the famous Lipizzaner, the stallions that demonstrate their elegance and skill in the Spanish Riding School of the Hofburg in Vienna. Around 1850, the Archduke Charles of Styria decided to crossbreed Italian, Spanish and Arab horses at the Lipizza stud-farm, near Trieste (now Lipica, in Slovenia). At the end of World War I the Lipizzaner were transferred to Piber, where they are still bred today. As foals they have brown coats, which turn pure white after three years. The most promising stallions are sent to the Viennese riding school where, for seven to ten years, they perfect the art of 'dancing' to music. Every summer and on their retirement, the Lipizzaner are sent back from Vienna to Piber to enjoy some well-earned freedom.

ℹ️ *Peter Rosegger Gasse 1*

▶ *Follow road 77 northwest to the junction with road 504 on the right heading for Grossming and Knittelfeld.*

3 Knittelfeld, Styria

Almost entirely reconstructed after World War II, Knittelfeld is today a modern town, home to major industries and a neighbour of the famous Zwelteg circuit used for Formula 1 Grand Prix racing. Its past is still evident in the Renaissance Schloss Hautzenbichl, which dominates the town from the northeast, and the castle of Spielberg (1560), on the way to the racetrack (not open to visitors).

About 10km (6 miles) north of Knittelfeld is the Seckau Benediktinerabtei (Benedictine abbey), founded in 1140 but rebuilt in its present guise in the 16th and 17th centuries.

ℹ️ *Hauptplatz 15a*

Shops and buildings in a street in the old centre of Graz

▶ *The main **S36** road leads to Judenburg.*

4 Judenburg, Styria

It's easy to lose yourself in meandering Judenburg, a delightful little town with a thousand-year history and an ideal Mur valley base for hikes into the Seetaler Alpen, which rise to the southwest. Evidence of its prehistoric origins comes in the form of the Strettweger Kultwagen, a miniature votive wagon found in the Strettweg suburb and attributed to the Hallstatt culture (600 BC; a copy is displayed in the local Stadtmuseum).

The town of Mercatus Judenpurch began to develop in the 11th century, helped by the arrival of a colony of Jewish merchants. From then on its commercial fortune grew, reaching a peak in the 14th and 15th centuries thanks to booming trade with the powerful Venetians, who minted the only gold currency on Habsburg territory, the Judenburger Gulden. A legacy of that period can be seen in the

---

FOR CHILDREN

At the Märchenwald Steiermark theme park in St Georgen ob Judenburg (8km/5 miles west of Judenburg) children can encounter fairy-tale characters in the enchanted wood and enjoy a host of games and activities.

---

monolithic Stadtturm (late 15th century), a tower 75m (246 feet) tall with a flight of steps to the gallery, which gives a grand view of the town and the surrounding Aichfeld.

ℹ️ *Hauptplatz 1*

▶ *Follow road **77** westbound until you come to the turning*

The splendid library – the Stiftbibliothek – of the Benedictine abbey of Admont

on the right to the *114*; at
Trieben, turn left on to the
113 for Rottenmann and
Liezen, and continue north-
east from there to Spital am
Phyrn on road *138*.

5 Spital am Pyhrn,
Upper Austria
From Judenburg, head due
north across the Styrian ridge
of the Niedere Tauern, the
Rottenmanner Tauern, along

A little way after the pass,
just after entering Upper
Austria, you'll see on the left the
terminus of the Wurzeralm rack-
railway, linked to the Frauenkar
chairl-ift (1870).

These slopes offer
wonderful hiking opportunities
and skiing in winter, using Spital
am Phyrn, just 4km (2.5 miles)
to the north, as a base. Tourism
has always been part of the local
economy here; during the

▶ Take the *138* northbound to
Windischgarsten, where you
turn right on to the *550* for
Rosenau, Kampertal and
Altenmarkt bei St Gallen.
Here head southwest on
road *117* to Admont.

6 Admont, Styria
Stop at Admont for a relaxing or
sporting break in the lush Enns
valley and, above all, to visit the
famous Benediktinerstift

one of the ancient communication routes between southern
Europe and the Danube valley
– the road to the Phyrn Pass
(954m/3,130 feet), used since
the times of the Celts and
Illyrians.

RECOMMENDED TRIP

You can walk or drive from
Spital to the Gasthaus Grünau
and make the easy ascent
through the Dr Vogelgesang
Klamm gorge (open May to
October). At the exit from the
romantic gorge, stop for
refreshments at one of the huts
before returning to the
Gasthaus Grünau.

SCENIC ROUTES

A beautifully scenic road winds
through the mountains west of
Windischgarsten, past meadows
and woods, to Hinterstoder
(18km/11 miles). Here, take
the cableway to the Hutterer
Höss peak (1,853m/6,079 feet)
for a better view of the
barren Totes Gebirge
('mountains of the dead')
from above.

Crusades passing knights found
hospitality at the pass in the
Spital inn, hence the name of
today's resort.

ℹ️ No 350, Spital am Pyhrn

Admont's Stiftbibliothek – a detail
of one of the sculpted groups by
J T Stammel

(Benedictine abbey) founded in
1074 by St Hemma of Gurk.

In the Middle Ages, the Stift
housed an important school of
scribes, and now boasts 1,405
manuscripts and incunabula
(pre-1501 books) and 150,000
other volumes – the richest
monastic collection of its kind.
The abbey complex (repeatedly
altered over the centuries) was
almost entirely destroyed by fire
in 1865 but, fortunately, one of
the few parts to escape the
flames was the Stiftbibliothek
(library).

The other areas were
reconstructed in neo-Gothic

i Hauptstrasse 36

▶ Drive along road **146** to the east till you come to Hieflau; here take the **115** southeast to Eisenerz.

SCENIC ROUTES

The 25km (15 miles) that separate Admont from Hieflau run almost entirely through the amazing Gesäuse canyon, wedged between rocks that rise sheer above the Enns river. At this point the river is particularly turbulent and perfect for kayaking. The area is environmentally protected (Naturschutzgebiet).

SPECIAL TO...

The Eisenstrasse, or 'iron route', runs between Hieflau and Leoben and is signposted along the way. Its focus is the Erzberg at Eisenerz, but there are many stops along the way, such as the Vordernberg blast furnaces and mines, and the Heimatmuseum of Trofaiach, dedicated to the history of the mining industry.

style by Wilhelm Bucher. The 72m (236-foot) long oval hall housing the library is a masterpiece of rococo style and contains splendid frescoes painted by Bernardo Altomonte in 1776, as well as baroque sculpted groups by Josef Thaddeäus Stammel (1760). The force of expression in his *Death, The Last Judgement, Heaven and Hell* almost detracts from the room's real treasure, the precious books and incunabula displayed in glass cases. The abbey museum has an interesting natural history collection, comprising 250,000 insects.

7 Eisenerz, Styria

For over 2,000 years the slopes of the Erzberg have been mined for the iron ore that constitutes almost a third of its rock mass. As a result this pyramid-shaped mountain is just 1,465m (4,806 feet) high today, compared with its original estimated height of 1,534m (5,033 feet). The Schichturm watchtower over the Erzbach valley (1580) gives a beautiful view of the terraced slopes of the open-air mine, still operational and open to visitors travelling by special bus or reinforced truck. The train that once carried miners to work now carries visitors into the heart of the mountain.

To the west, the valley folds of the Eisenerzen Alps offer superb hiking opportunities. On the opposite side, a lovely 5km (3-mile) detour northwest of Eisenerz explores the protected nature area around Lake Leopoldstein. In Eisenerz itself

the Gothic parish church of St Oswald, which towers high on a relief, is perhaps the only one in Austria to have retained its ring of fortifications intact, erected as protection against the Turks in 1532.

i Freiheitsplatz 7

▶ Take the **115**, then the **115a** to Leoben.

8 Leoben, Styria

At Eisenerz you may well ask where all that iron goes. The

The open-air iron mine on Mount Erzberg, near Eisenerz

flourishing metal industries of Leoben, the second most densely populated town in Styria, provide the answer. Most visitors will be more interested in *Gösser*, a locally made beer of international renown.

The now lively economy of this pretty little town, first settled in the 13th century on a bend in the Mur river, hasn't spoiled the charm of its well-preserved old centre, still partially enclosed by walls and reached via the Mautturm, a medieval toll station.

Cycling enthusiasts will be pleased to know that Leoben is on the Murradweg, a cycle route that runs 359km (223 miles) along the Mur river between Salzburg and Styria.

i *Peter-Tunner-Strasse 2*

▶ *Drive to Bruck an der Mur on the E7/S6.*

9 Bruck an der Mur, Styria
Bruck an der Mur's two emblems can be found on the spacious main square, Koloman-Wallisch-Platz. The Eiserner Brunnen, named after an old fountain, is actually a well-head, a delicate wrought-iron work by the local artist Hans Prasser (1626). On the corner with Herzog-Ernst-Gasse stands the Kornmesserhaus, once the home

of wealthy merchant Pankraz Kornmess, and considered the finest late-Gothic secular building in Austria (1485). Its elegant ground-floor arcades are echoed by the first-floor loggia in a Venetian-inspired design. Close to the Kalvarienkirche, in the southeast of the town, you can explore the Weitental, Bruck's 'green lung'.

The Naturfreunde Rundwanderweg, a well-signposted 7.5km (5-mile) circular nature trail, and a mountain-bike track lead to the Arten-und Naturschutzzentrum, a centre for the study and conservation of the valley's ecosystem, set in lovely wooded surroundings.

i *Koloman-Wallisch-Platz 1*

▶ *Follow the S35 to Frohnleiten.*

10 Frohnleiten, Styria
This pretty resort overlooking the river is surrounded by mountains and filled with flowers in summer. In medieval times, and again in the 18th century, trade brought privilege and wealth to the town (the Leobner and Tabor gates are all that remain of the fortifications), but it suffered devastation in 1809 at the hands of Napoleon's troops. The parish church of Mariä Himmelfahrt escaped a

Iron forged into precious armour in the Landeszeughaus, Graz

fire in 1701 and still stands on the westernmost edge of Hauptplaz, in the Augustinian convent, which houses frescoes and paintings by J A Mölk (1764).

In nearby Murhof (some 4km/2.5 miles south), golfers can play on an 18-hole course set among splendid natural surroundings.

i *Brückenkopf 1*

▶ *To return to Graz, continue on the S35 then take the A9 at Friesach.*

BACK TO NATURE

On the return journey to Graz, 5km (3 miles) past Frohnleiten, you can access one of Austria's most spectacular natural underground networks, the Lurgrotte. Within the hills between Peggau and Semriach (entrances in both locations) there's a labyrinth of corridors and caverns featuring impressive stalactites and stalagmites, white or veined red and grey. Only 1km (0.6 mile) of the total 6km (4 miles) can be reached from Peggau.

HOT WATER SPAS

Austria's spa culture has a long history. Celtic rituals centred around natural springs, and archaeological excavations have suggested that the Roman conquerors, well aware of the benefits of hydrotherapy, made ample use of many water sources around their settlements.

Some spas in Salzburg, Upper and Lower Austria enjoyed a glorious revival in the 19th century, as the aristocracy and members of the imperial family began 'taking the waters'. A fashion emerged for healthy holidays, based on spa baths, walks through the countryside and relaxation in the form of light opera and waltzing.

Nowadays the perceived link between spas and physical well-being is, if anything, even stronger. There's a widely shared faith in treatments and cures that focus on prevention, relaxation and a return to a more conscious and balanced relationship with the body. These are likely to combine oriental medicine with bathing in hay and milk, beauty treatments, fitness and diets.

Along Austria's roads, and particularly in the areas around the historic spa towns, there are over a hundred resorts with facilities and hotels offering a range of treatments, some of which are listed below. Even on a short stay, they can at least help release the tensions of a long day in the car.

is known mainly – and somewhat superficially – for the cold bath therapy applied to cure certain ailments. At least 20 Austrian spas have adopted this method, but if you can't follow a complete course of treatment, enjoy a walk along the pleasant 'Kneipp paths' found everywhere.

The great Austrian *Bads*
Vorarlberg Vorarlberg has no traditional spas, but there are modern family baths such as the Alpen-Erlebnisbad Val Blu of Bludenz (see Tour 1), and treatment centres such as Bad Reuthe (see Tour 1), which exploit the therapeutic properties of the mineral and peat springs.

The spa elegance of days past in the Kurpark of Baden bei Wien

The Kneipp method
Since 1886, when a little book called *My Water Cure* was published, the method proposed by Bavarian priest Sebastian Kneipp (1821–97)

has been widely adopted in Austria as well as Germany. The treatment is based on five principles: hydrotherapy, phytotherapy, movement, diet and lifestyle. Kneipp's method

Tirol The only spa in Tirol is Bad Häring, near Wörgl (see Tour 6), where sulphurous waters, mudpacks and massage are used to treat cirulatory and locomotive complaints.

The winter spa at Bad
Kleinkirchheim, in Carinthia

Carinthia Warmbad Villach
(see Tour 8) is the only spa
centre in Europe where the
water flows into the pool
directly from a spa spring below.
Don't miss the revamped
Erlebnisbad, offering aquatic
fun for all the family.

At Bad Kleinkirchheim (see
Tour 10) the Römerbad and St
Kathrein spas use water rich in
radon. In the Roman-style
tepidarium these reach a
temperature of 30–50°C
(86–122°F) and are particularly
good for the blood pressure.
There are also mud treatments
and packs using lavender, algae
and rosemary.

In Bad Bleiberg (west of
Villach) a doctor is always
available to help at the
Kristallbad. The subterranean
tunnel, with a temperature of
9°C (48°F) and humidity at 99
per cent, is recommended for
those suffering from allergies.

Styria At Steirische
Thermenland (eastern Styria)
an entire region has become a
'spa realm', with centres in Bad
Waltersdorf (see Tour 25;
treatments for skin complaints
and circulatory, respiratory and

Spas offer beauty and health
treatments – here one of the
many popular establishments
in Carinthia

motor problems), Loipersdorf,
Bad Gleichenberg (see Tour
12), Bad Radkersburg (see Tour
12) and Blumau (see Tour 25).
In this last resort, three springs
supply the hydro-massage baths
and swimming pools of the
Hotel Rogner-Bad Blumau, a
resort conceived by the artist
Fritz Hundertwasser.

Salzburg The Gasteinertal (see
Tour 9) starts with Felsenbad at
Dorfgastein, where you plunge
into an open-air rock pool,
continue in the 35°C (95°F)
swimming pools of the
Kurzentrum at Bad Hofgastein
and finish off in the Kurhaus in
Badgastein, which now as in
Roman times uses the curative
waters of 18 hot springs.

Upper Austria The saline
water of Bad Ischl (see Tour 14)
has for 175 years been used as a
remedy for complaints of the
respiratory and locomotive
systems (chronic rheumatism,
osteoporosis, etc) and for the
circulation.

Bad Hall (see Tour 16) is
surrounded by a vast park and
the spa uses one of the richest
sodium chloride and sodium
iodide springs in central
Europe.

Lower Austria Baden bei
Wien (see Tour 24) is a
sulphurous spa offering a
Caribbean atmosphere in the
modern Römertherme and fun
for all in the spa bathing
establishment with beach.

At Bad-Deutch-Altenburg
(see Tour 23), a short distance
from the ancient Roman spa in
Carnuntum archaeological park,
you can recharge your batteries
in the Kurzentrum
Ludwigstorff.

Burgenland Bad
Tatzmannsdorf (see Tour 25) is
an emerging tourist resort with
a golf-drome and a famous
tennis school, which has always
been known for the alkaline
and ferrous waters of its spas.

Vienna Oberlaa (south of the
centre) has a spa park and
swimming pool supplied with
sulphurous waters that flow out
at 54°C (129°F). Completing
the experience are a Finnish
sauna, relaxation areas and anti-
stress massage.

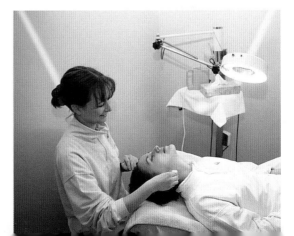

Medieval Towns
& Fortresses

After sampling the delights of Styrian pumpkins, grapes and wine
in Graz, set off on a wonderful journey to discover their origins –
and raise a toast to Carinthia with a delicious glass of cider.

3/4 DAYS • 355KM • 220 MILES

ITINERARY	
GRAZ	▶ **Wolfsberg (80km-50m)**
WOLFSBERG	▶ **Griffen (23km-14m)**
GRIFFEN	▶ **St Paul im Lavanttal**
	(15km-9m)
ST PAUL	▶ **Deutschlandsberg**
IM LAVANTTAL	**(69km-43m)**
DEUTSCHLANDSBERG	▶ **Leibnitz (34km-21m)**
LEIBNITZ	▶ **Bad Radkersburg**
	(44km-27.5m)
BAD RADKERSBURG	▶ **Feldbach (36km-22m)**
FELDBACH	▶ **Graz (54km-33.5m)**

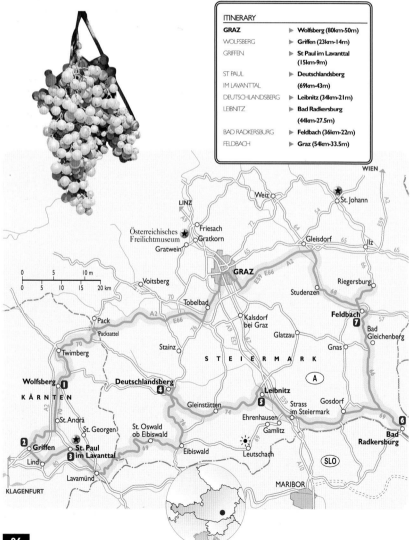

FOR CHILDREN

Take a journey through rural
Austria from Vorarlberg to
Burgenland at the
Österreichisches
Freilichtmuseum of Stübing
(15km/9 miles north of Graz),
including visits to old
farmhouses and craft
demonstrations. Children can
learn about schools in the past
and try their hands at
craftwork.

[i] *Herrengasse 16, Graz*

▶ *Continue south on road **70** to
Lieboch, where you take the
A2 towards Klagenfurt. Exit
this at Packsattel and
continue on the **70** southwest
to Twimberg and Wolfsberg.*

❶ Wolfsberg, Carinthia
Lying between Saualpe and
Koralpe, whose peaks reach
2,000m (6,562 feet), Lavanttal is
an ideal holiday location if you
enjoy fine walks through
blossoming apple orchards or
summer meadows filled with
rhododendrons.

The main valley town is
Wolfsberg, a pretty and ancient
little place on the banks of the
river. Until 811 the local
settlements in this area
belonged to the diocese of
Aquileia. The parish church,
built in 1242 and named after St
Mark, has a late baroque altar
with a remarkable altarpiece of
St Mark and the Lion, painted
in 1777 by Martin Johann
Schmidt, better known as
Kremser Schmidt (Schmidt from
Krems). The lovely castle
towering high on a rise to the
northeast stands on the site of
the original 13th-century
fortress, altered in Renaissance
style in the 16th century and
given a mock-Tudor appearance
in 1854 (open to visitors during
special events).

[i] *Minoritenplatz 1*

▶ *Road **70** continues to Griffen.*

❷ Griffen, Carinthia
The ruins of a 12th-century
castle stand on Schlossberg
mountain, which dominates the
village of Griffen. Traces of
prehistoric human life have
been discovered in a cave deep
inside the mountain, which
features coloured calcareous
forms and can be entered from
the centre of the village,
opposite the parish church. The
Tropfsteinhöhle also contains
an exhibition of rudimentary
utensils and animal bones (cave
bear, giant deer, mammoths).

[i] *Rathaus, No 5*

▶ *Drive to Lind on the **127** and
turn left on to road **126**,*

**The hilly region between Styria
and Carinthia, a land of vineyards
and fine wines**

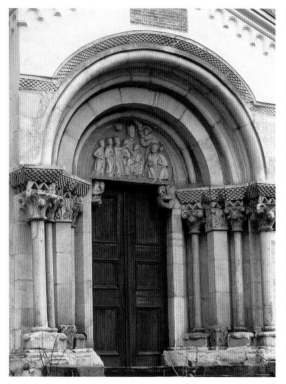

Entrance to the church of the
Benedictine abbey in St Paul

*for Deutschlandsberg on
the **76**.*

4 Deutschlandsberg, Styria
Deutschlandsberg was
developed in the shadow of the
castle of Landsberg, now
partially restored to house a
hotel-restaurant and an
archaeological museum. This is
the perfect place for a wine and
culinary break.

Thanks to a particularly mild
climate and its setting amid
rolling hills cloaked with
chestnut trees and vineyards,
Deutschlandsberg has earned a
reputation as one of the most
renowned producers of *Schilcher*,
a prized rosé wine, and of
Kernöl, Styrian pumpkin seed
oil, typically thick in consistency
and with a slight walnut smell.

i Hauptplatz 37

▶ *Return briefly south on road
76 before turning left (east)
on to road **74** for Leibnitz.*

5 Leibnitz, Styria
The area near the present
border with Slovenia was for
centuries a defensive outpost
against repeated Turk and
Hungarian invasions – as is
evident from the numerous
castles and fortresses scattered
over the hills of lower Styria.

One of the most impressive
is the Schloss Seggau, which
from the west dominates the
farming town of Leibnitz,
founded in the Lassnitz valley in
860. Its reception rooms
(Fürstenzimmer), decorated by
Carlo Formentini in 1747, house
archaeological finds from the
Roman site of *Flavia Solva* (AD
70), excavated at Wagna, 2km
(1 mile) south.

i Sparkassenplatz 40

▶ *Travel southeast on the **67** to
Strass in Steiermark. When
you reach road **69**, follow
this eastbound to Bad
Radkersburg.*

*which leads to St Paul im
Lavanttal.*

3 St Paul im Lavanttal,
Carinthia
The Benedictine abbey (Stift) of
St Paul im Lavanttal is known as
the 'treasure chest of Carinthia',
for the valuable works of art
kept in its Kaiserzimmer and
Kunstsammlung rooms,
including paintings by Rubens
and ancient reliquaries, and for
its rich library, which contains a
store of 5th- to 9th-century
manuscripts second only to the
Nationalbibliothek in Vienna.
Founded in 1091 as a Christian
outpost on the edge of the Slav
world, the great abbey complex
was last rebuilt in the 17th
century, though the church has
maintained its original
Romanesque design. The 14th-
century vaulted ceilings are
painted with frescoes by
Michael and Friedrich Pacher
(1468) of a heavenly vision; a
series of saints in the left

transept (1493) is attributed to
Thomas von Villach.

i Hauptstrasse 10

▶ *Continue along the **135**
southeast to Lavamünd,
where a short stretch of
road **80** leads to the turning
on the left for road **69** to
Eibiswald. Here turn north*

RECOMMENDED WALK

A fine circular 8km (5-mile)
route starts from St Georgen
im Lavanttal (5km/3 miles
northeast of St Paul) to visit
several sites of historical and
cultural interest: the
Dörrkeusche, which reveals the
secrets of the craft of linen-
making; the Burg Stein, former
stronghold of the bishops of
Lavant; the Spitzelofen marble
quarry, and, lastly, the Duller-
Mühle mill, still in operation.

SCENIC ROUTES

The Südsteirische Weinstrasse (wine route) winds from Ehrenhausen, south of Leibnitz, over vineyard-covered slopes to the Slovenian border. One of the idyllic villages visited along this 25km (15-mile) circular way is Gamlitz (15km/9 miles south of Leibnitz), renowned for its wines (Weissburgunder, Muskateller, Traminer and Schilcher). There is an interesting Weinmuseum dedicated to the history of wine-making in Styria.

6 Bad Radkersburg, Styria

For seven centuries, Bad Radkersburg was a flourishing trading centre on the Mur river. Over the past 30 years or so it has also become an elegant spa resort. Nearly all the baroque façades in the old town, refortified in the 16th century, conceal splendid Renaissance arched courtyards, such as that of Palais Herberstorff at No 27

Bad Radkersburg, a pretty spa town in the Styrian hills

Langgasse (1583), linked to a medieval defence tower. The great spa establishment, set in parkland, has seven pools and a beauty and treatment centre. Vines are cultivated all around, taking advantage of the temperate Pannonian climate and fertile volcanic hills.

ℹ️ *Hauptplatz 14*

▶ *Return northwest on road 69 to the junction with road 66, and follow this northbound to Feldbach.*

7 Feldbach, Styria

The road that crosses the Oststeirisches Hügelland, the hilly region of eastern Styria, is ringed with castles and fortresses. At Feldbach, an old town (1188) in the Raab valley, you can visit the Tabor, a traditional square stronghold built in the 17th and 18th centuries to defend against the Turks. Part of the fortified complex now houses the Heimatmuseum, with exhibits about local history and culture.

Continue the journey northwards for about 4km (2.5 miles) to reach the 15th-century

Schloss Kornberg, rebuilt in the 17th century and now used for temporary exhibitions.

Another 6km (4 miles) leads to Riegersburg, a small village dominated by the fortress of the same name, which has loomed high on a spur of volcanic rock since the 12th century. There's an excellent view from this high point of the woods and vineyards of the Styrian spa region. You can bathe in the small lake near by in summer.

ℹ️ *Hauptplatz 1*

▶ *Follow road 68 northwest to Gleisdorf then take the A2 southwest to return to Graz.*

BACK TO NATURE

The Tierpark Herberstein, near the Renaissance Schloss Herberstein at St Johann (about 40km/25 miles north of Feldbach), is a wildlife park containing exotic and alpine animals. Here you can also visit a Florentine-style courtyard, knights' hall and the castle's weapon collection.

NORTHERN SALZBURG & UPPER AUSTRIA

The city of Salzburg is one of Austria's greatest centres of art and culture, but the 'Rome of the Alps' owes much of its popularity to the beauty of the surrounding region, also called 'Salzburg'. This modern-day *Land* (province) has a proud and distinctive history, having maintained its independence from central Habsburg government until 1816. Before then, it was under the strong rule of the powerful archbishop-princes.

Just outside Salzburg city, you can drive through the idyllic wooded scenery of the Salzburg Pre-Alps to reach the popular Salzkammergut, a lake district shared with neighbouring Upper Austria. Further south are the beautiful and at times grandiose mountain landscapes of the Tennengebirge massif and the Dachstein range, bordering with Styria and Upper Austria.

Lake waters and mountain backdrops form the picturesque landscape of the Salzkammergut

Besides countless abbeys scattered among Upper Austria's hills, the region's main attractions are the historic towns of Linz (the dynamic capital), Wels and Steyr, forming the points of a triangle in the heart of the *Land*. Many other places of interest are dotted around the region. To the northeast is the granite Mühlviertel plateau, where traditional crafts have survived despite the encroaching industrialisation; to the northwest, lush woods and the great farming estates of the Innviertel-Hausruckwald are enclosed within the lower Danube and the upper reaches of the Inn river; and to the south are the Salzkammergut, and the Nationalpark Kalkalpen, a protected natural area, which offers a selection of trekking tours.

Themed routes running through this northwest part of Austria include the Salt Trail, celebrating the 'white gold' that brought prosperity to Salzburg over the centuries, and the Iron Trail, recalling the manufacture of goods using iron transported from Styrian mines to southern Upper Austria and nearby Eisenwurz (Lower Austria).

Tour 13

Salzburg is a jewel among Austrian towns and it is no coincidence that it attracts so many visitors from all over the world. Music-lovers come for its association with its most famous son, the composer Wolfgang Amadeus Mozart and to attend the prestigious Salzburger Festspiele, a world-famous music festival. The standard of the performances complements the superb setting and atmosphere of the town. Lovers of art and historic architecture will enjoy the Altstadt (upper town), declared a World Heritage Site by UNESCO, and fans of

Hollywood musicals and classics can see the locations made famous by the musical *The Sound of Music*.

Tour 14

This tour sets off from Salzburg to explore one of the most fascinating regions in Austria, which straddles Salzburg, Styria and Upper Austria. It starts by travelling south through the Salzach valley, in Tennengau, a land of salt mines and dense woods. The route then unfolds around the Tennengebirge calcareous massif, venturing as far as St Johann im Pongau, a popular skiing centre, and climbing the Lammer valley with its spectacular views of the Dachstein glacier. Lastly, it visits Salzkammergut, where tranquil lakes lie among the gentle slopes of the Salzburg Pre-Alps; all are navigable and some offer water sports.

Tour 15

Circumscribed by the Danube to the south and the slopes of the Böhmer Wald (Bohemian Forest) to the north, the granite Mühlviertel extends north of Linz, acting as a link between Austria, Germany and the Czech Republic. This is one of the lesser-known regions, yet is one of the easiest to explore on foot, horseback or bicycle thanks to its gentle, rolling hills interspersed with valleys and settlements.

The Cistercian abbey of Wilhering, on the banks of the River Danube

Within sight of Salzburg, on the bank of the Salzach river

Starting from (and returning to) the left bank of the Danube, the tour climbs to the northwest extremes of Austria in search of old craft traditions and the scenery described by author Adalbert Stifter (1805–68) in *Rock Crystal*: a Christmas tale.

Tour 16

From Linz, this tour enters the heart of Upper and Lower Austria, passing the great mountain abbeys of St Florian Kremsmünster and Seitenstetten. Travelling via Phyrn-Eisenwurzel and the Kalkalpen national park, you follow the 'iron trail' (Steyr and Waidhofen an der Ybbs), continuing through Mostviertel, a land of apple orchards and cider. Before returning to Linz there's a final visit to the Enns river, which flows into the Danube near the resort of the same name.

Tour 17

This tour follows two of Austria's greatest rivers, the Inn and the Danube, for a short stretch of their long journey. It sets out from Linz on the trail of ancient legends along Nibelungen Strasse, which follows the Danube to Passau, at the confluence with the Inn and the northernmost point of the tour. It then returns south, exploring the Innviertel-Hausruckwald region amid the thick woodland and endless wheat fields of the 'granary of Upper Austria'.

Salzburg

From high on the Kapuzinerberg and Mönchsberg hills, or from one of the bridges spanning the Salzach river, which divides its old centre into the left bank and right bank, Salzburg is a captivating vision of domes and bell towers, framed against a backdrop of green hills.

MOZART

2/3 DAYS

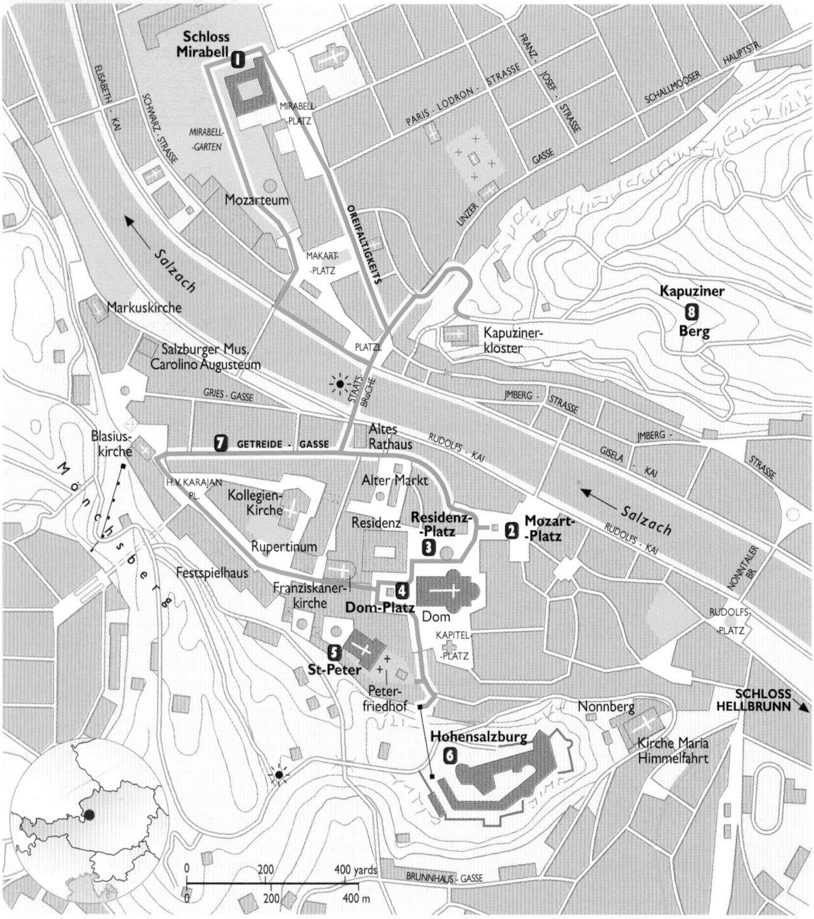

▶ *Cars have access to part of the city centre before 11 am, though this is inadvisable because of the shortage of car parks; the multistoreys on the city's hills don't always have spaces. It's better to leave the car in one of the car parks outside the centre, such as the Auersperg-Garage, near Schloss Mirabell. Buying a Salzburg Card gives free use of public transport.*

❶ Schloss Mirabell

Start your visit to Salzburg from Schloss Mirabell (entrance on the Kurgarten side), on the right bank of the Salzach river. There's a marvellous view of the Altstadt, across the river from the gardens, and of the Hohensalzburg fortress on the Mönchsberg hill, justifying the palace's name (Mirabell means 'beautiful view').

Restored to its baroque appearance after a fire in 1818, the building now serves as the city hall, but was originally a residence erected by

archbishop-prince Wolf Dietrich von Raitenag (1589–1612) for his mistress and their 15 children. This enterprising archbishop, a descendant of Pope Pius IV, studied in Italy and subsequently promoted the great works of architecture that gave Salzburg its reputation as the 'Rome of the Alps'. Highlights inside the palace include a monumental 18th-century staircase and the Marmorsaal (marble hall); outside, there's a splendid baroque garden, with a Zwerglgarten ('dwarves' garden') containing copies of its original gnomes, and a rose-garden with a hedge maze.

▶ *Pass the Landestheater (regional theatre) on the right to come to Makartplatz; here turn right into Schwarzstrasse, along the Salzach (No 9 is the birthplace of conductor Herbert von Karajan; No 5 is the Hotel Sacher, No 3 the Café Bazar). Cross the river over the Staatsbrücke (with a good view of the Altstadt), pass in front of the Altes*

The mass of domes and bell towers in Salzburg, dominated by the great Hohensalzburg fortress

FOR HISTORY BUFFS

St Rupert founded Salzburg, the 'citadel of salt' in 696, on the site of Roman *Juvavum*, which had been devastated by the barbarians. The mining of 'white gold' brought profits and power, and from 1200 the archbishops who succeeded St Rupert were granted the title 'princes of the Empire'. Salzburg thus maintained its independence from Habsburg Austria until 1816, and some of its citizens are still eager to point out that Wolfgang Amadeus Mozart was of Salzburg, rather than Austrian nationality.

Rathaus (old city hall) and follow Juden-Gasse to reach Mozartplatz.

❷ Mozartplatz

As part of his project to rebuild the city, in around 1598 Wolf

Dietrich had the cemetery around the old cathedral dismantled and demolished 55 dwellings to make room for five great new communicating squares, to a design by Vincenzo Scamozzi of Vicenza.

In the centre of Mozartplatz, the square nearest the Salzach river, is a statue dedicated to Salzburg's greatest citizen, the composer Wolfgang Theophilus (Amadeus) Mozart (1756–91). The monument was built in 1842, a year before the first

Festspiele, in the presence of Mozart's children, in an attempt to make amends for the city's neglect of the great composer in the last 10 years of his life.

3 Residenzplatz
The south corner of Mozartplatz leads into the great Residenzplatz, bustling with visitors and the setting for some of the city's most interesting buildings.

Extending along the west side is the façade of the

Wolf Dietrich for royal guests (not open to visitors).

Salzburg citizens are particularly fond of the Glockenspiel, a 17th-century carillon on the tower that plays its melodies three times a day (at 7, 11 and 6). The south side of the square is closed, between the two residences, by the left side of the cathedral.

One of the sumptuous gala rooms in the Residenz, furnished to suit baroque tastes

SPECIAL TO...

A few steps from the Schloss Mirabell garden exit, at No 8 Makartplatz, is the Mozart-Wohnhaus, the eight-room home of the Mozart family from 1773 to 1780, the year before the composer left Salzburg permanently for Vienna. Faithfully restored in period style, it houses the Mozart Ton-und Film-Sammlung, an audio-visual collection about Mozart's life and times. Just pick up a headset and wander around the rooms. Exhibits include the pianoforte the composer used for his concerts.

Residenz, the medieval palace of the archbishop, founded in the 12th century and sumptuously redecorated in baroque style between 1596 and 1619. On the second floor, you can see the magnificent gala rooms (Prunkräume), with a wealth of stuccowork, statues, frescoes and original furnishings. The Residenzgalerie, on the third floor, houses the art collection and has important paintings from the 16th to the 19th century.

Opposite, beyond the monumental Residenzbrunnen, the loveliest baroque fountain north of the Alps, is the Residenz-Neugebäude (new residence) commissioned by

4 Domplatz
The imposing, twin-towered façade and distinctive dome of the baroque Dom (cathedral) dominate this beautiful square, the perfect summer setting for performances of the mystery play *Jedermann* by the poet and dramatist Hugo von Hoffmannsthal (1874–1929). The church that originally stood here was founded in 774 by St Virgil, and the cathedral has been altered and enlarged several times since to reflect the power of the archbishop-princes, including extensive alterations by Wolf Dietrich, which were completed in 1628. Mozart was baptised in the 12th-century font (note the copper lions

guarding its base). In 1959 the cathedral was reconsecrated after restoration of the dome, which had been badly damaged by World War II bombing.

Inside, richly decorated with stuccowork, four side chapels open on to the nave; the first on the left contains a precious font resting on lions (1321). The cathedral organ (1703), at the back of the cathedral, is one of the most important in Austria, second only to that of St Stephen's in Vienna. It's played

secluded spot with a forest of wrought-iron crosses and doors leading to catacombs dug into the rock. This is where the people of Salzburg gather to listen to carols on Christmas Eve. You can visit the catacombs, a network of caves used as a cemetery by Christians in the 3rd century AD.

Just outside the inner square is the famous Stiftkeller restaurant, established in 803. To its right is the entrance to the convent church of St Peter

temporary refuge for the city's rulers in times of danger – including Archbishop Leonhard von Keutschach, who spent the longest time in hiding there (1495–1519), during the peasants' war.

It was then that the fortress took on its present appearance, with additions such as the arsenal and granary, and the embellishment of the interiors with Gothic furnishings and wood panelling. After it was used as a prison for Wolf

in conjunction with the other four, situated at the pillars of the transept, during the Salzburg Festival.

5 St Peter
A passage runs to the right of the cathedral façade to Kapitelplatz, closed at the back by the present-day archbishop's mansion. Keep to the right and you'll come to a gate leading into the complex of St Peter Erzabtei, an abbey founded in the 7th century near the Mönchsberg rock.

With no advance warning, you will find yourself passing through a cemetery, the Petersfriedhof, right in the city centre – a beautiful and

(Peterskirche), the only one in Salzburg to have maintained its Romanesque layout.

▶ *Beside the entrance to the Petersfriedhof, at the beginning of Festunggasse, is the terminus of the cableway that climbs to the Hohensalzburg on Mönchsberg hill.*

6 Festung Hohensalzburg
The nucleus of what is now central Europe's biggest complete fortress was built in 1077 by Archbishop Gebhard, who was alarmed by the enmity between Pope and Emperor. In subsequent centuries, the Hohensalzburg served as a

The porticoes and crosses in the lovely Petersfriedhof, the oldest cemetery in Salzburg

---

FOR CHILDREN

In the Spielzeugmuseum, at the end of Getreidegasse near the Gothic Blasiuskirche, 300 years of toys are traced through its beautiful displays of wooden, tin and earthenware toys. The collection includes a number of interesting musical instruments.

Dietrich when he fell out of favour, the Hohensalzburg was further enlarged and fortified in

The sweeping view from the bastions of the Hohensalzburg, the great fortress of Salzburg

1619 and again in 1810, when Napoleon seized the city.

Visits start at the Kuenburg-Bastei and go on to the royal apartments and the two museums – the Burgmuseum, with a collection of weapons and armour, and the Rainermuseum, established to commemorate the regiment based in the fortress from 1871 to 1918.

▶ *From the base station of the cableway, cross Kapitelplatz and Domplatz and turn into Franziscanergasse on the southeast corner. Pass Max-Reinhardt-Platz and continue along Hofstallgasse (festival offices on the left) to Herbert-von-Karajan-Platz. Turn northwards into Bürgerspitalgasse and continue until you come, on the right, to Getreidegasse.*

7 Getreidegasse

The heart of the Altstadt is the 'street of grain', a narrow street running between high façades adorned with wrought-iron signs (every business has its own traditional style, McDonald's included!). Getreidegasse's main claim to fame is the Mozart Geburtshaus, at No 9, the 17th-century house where the great composer was born on 27 January, 1756, now a museum.

At the end of Getreidegasse, just past Rathausplatz, is Alter Markt, an elegant square that is also home to the famous Café

BACK TO NATURE

Salzburg zoo is on the west side of Hellbrunner Berg, reached by car or on foot from the park. Animals from all over the world roam in large enclosures that blend in with the environment. Vultures, which fly free on the mountains around Salzburg, return to the zoo regularly for their meals.

Tomaselli, where in 1703 the inhabitants of Salzburg tasted their first cup of coffee, imported from Italy. A few steps away at No 13 Brodgasse you can buy *Mozartkugeln*, chocolates made by hand to Paul Fürst's original recipe.

▶ *Back in Rathaus-Platz, cross the Salzach river over Staatsbrücke and turn into Linzergasse.*

8 Kapuzinerberg

Salzburg's old centre extends to embrace the area on the right bank of the Salzach, between the Mirabell gardens and the Kapuzinerberg. From No 14 Linzergasse (a lovely ascending street lined with 13th-century buildings), climb to the Kapuzinerkloster (about 15 minutes) and the 17th-century church. Scattered below the monastery are the remains of towers and the medieval ring of walls; from Hettwer Bastei there is a sweeping view of the entire Altstadt.

▶ *Dreifaltigkeitsgasse leads off the south end of Linzergasse to Schloss Mirabell square.*

EXCURSION

▶ *Hellbrunner Strasse runs from the river's left bank, just outside the Altstadt, into Alpenstrasse (southbound). Turn right on to Fürstenweg to reach Schloss Hellbrunn (about 5km/3 miles in all).*

Schloss Hellbrunn

After ridding himself of his tedious predecessor (his uncle Wolf Dietrich), Archbishop Markus Sittikus von Hohenems rewarded himself by commissioning Santino Solari, in 1612, to build the Lustschloss ('palace of pleasure') at the foot of the Hellbrunner Berg (495m/1,624 feet).

The result was a sombre suburban villa, used then as now for parties and special events and surrounded by beautiful landscaped gardens. Its main attractions are the water features

(Wasserspiele) dotted around the gardens and supplied by the hill's many springs. They include trick fountains, grottoes, fish ponds and a mechanical theatre operated by water.

The zoo is an ideal place to take the children (see **Back to nature**).

RECOMMENDED WALKS

On Mönchsberg hill you can climb along Festungsgasse, passing the cableway terminus, or take the flight of steps from Toscanini-hof to the Dr-Herbert-Klein-Weg and the Kokoschkaweg. Both options offer a pleasant walk through green spaces (only the final stretch to the fortress is steep), and fine views of the old city.

A detail of Schloss Hellbrunn, the first example of a suburban villa north of the Alps

AUSTRIA'S TRADITION OF MUSIC

In a country where even the official anthems were written by great maestros (the Hapsburg anthem is by Haydn, the national anthem by Mozart), musical tradition is so deeply rooted in the cultural and social fabric that it's become a tourist attraction in itself. In homage to the great musicians and composers who were born and worked in Austria, every corner of the country organises events, concerts, and festivals.

Anton Bruckner
(1824–96). 'God's minstrel' was the organist in Linz cathedral and at the abbey of St Florian, where he is buried. As well as being an outstanding instrumentalist he composed several masses and nine monumental symphonies.

Joseph Haydn
(1732–1809). Haydn was in the service of the counts Esterházy at Eisenstadt for nearly 40 years, and transposed music from late baroque into Viennese classicism, providing a basis for the innovations of Beethoven and Mozart. He wrote symphonies and works for solo instruments and quartets.

Gustav Mahler
(1860–1911). This orchestra conductor and composer began his career as a pupil of Bruckner and worked chiefly in the symphonic field, introducing a distinctive impressionism of his own.

Wolfgang Amadeus Mozart
(1756–91). As a child prodigy, he composed and played for courts all over Europe from the age of six. After giving up the patronage of the archbishop-prince of Salzburg he moved to Vienna, where he died in poverty at just 35 years of age.

Arnold Schönberg
(1874–1951). After his first compositions, influenced by Wagner and Mahler, Schönberg turned away from the conventional tonal system. He founded the School of Vienna and introduced the 12-tone scale, based on a chromatic range of 12 semitones. With the advent of Nazism, he was forced to seek refuge in the United States.

Franz Schubert
(1797–1828). Mental fragility and adversities plagued Schubert's short life, and were expressed in his romantic and poignant compositions. As well as *Lieder* (songs with an instrumental accompaniment), he wrote choral and sacred music.

Johann Strauss the Younger
(1825–99). The Strauss family of composers, led by the elder Johann (1804–49), embodied the spirit of 19th-century Vienna in joyous and memorable waltzes. Johann Senior wrote the famous *Radetzky March*, his son the even better known *Blue Danube*.

Special events
Vorarlberg At Bregenz, the Bregenzer Festspiele (late Jul–late Aug) is held every two years, staging an open-air opera on the shores of the Bodensee. At the same time, the Festspielhaus hosts concerts of the Wiener Symphoniker and other famous international orchestras.

Tirol At Innsbruck, the Innsbrucker Festwochen der Alten Musik (Jul–Aug) has a repertoire of early music, from medieval to baroque, including

Mozart's birthplace, Salzburg

Monuments to great musicians in Vienna; above, Wolfgang Amadeus Mozart; below, Johann Strauss

rarely performed works. Venues include the Spanish hall in Ambras castle, the imperial palace, the cathedral of St Jakob and Wilten abbey.

Carinthia At Ossiach am See, Carinthischer Sommer (Jul–Aug) organises concerts for choir and orchestra and operas in the church of Ossiach abbey and in the Grosser Saal of the Villach conference centre. There are also special events for children. At Millstatt, the Internationalen Musikwochen (May–Oct) has concerts of chamber music for organ and other soloists in the abbey church.

Styria At Graz, Styriarte (Jun–Jul) provides classical and sacred music, opera, and concerts for choir and orchestra.

Steirischer Herbst (Oct–Nov) has a festival of avant-garde music; Graz University of Music also holds an international conference.

Salzburg In Salzburg, the Salzburger Festspiele (mid-Jul–late Aug) is one of the most prestigious festivals in the world with operas, concerts and drama in the Festspielhaus. The Osterfestspiele (Easter) was instituted by Herbert von Karajan in 1967 and is divided into two cycles, each comprising an opera and three concerts.

Lower Austria At Baden bei Wien, the Badener Operettensommer (late Jun–mid-Sep) is inspired by Baden's long musical tradition of light opera and held in the Sommerarena.

Upper Austria At Linz the Brucknerfest (Sept–Oct) traditionally opens with the

Linzer Klagenwolken (an audiovisual show) in the Donaupark, with a programme of orchestral and solo concerts featuring world-class musicians, in the Brucknerhaus and cathedral. At Bad Ischl, the Operettenfestspiel (Jul–early Sep) has two light operas a year, one by Franz Lehár. There are also concerts and recitals.

Burgenland At Eisenstadt, the Haydn Festspiele (Sep) has music by Haydn, played by his best-known interpreters.

Vienna At the Frühlingfestival (Apr–May) classical masterpieces are performed by the Wiener Philarmoniker and the Mahler Chamber Orchestra, and special showings of silent film classics are accompanied by an orchestra at the Konzerthaus.

The Musikfest der Wiener Festwochen (mid-May–mid-Jun) features concerts by the world's leading musicians in the Musikverein and Konzerthaus.

Resonanzen (Jan) is a festival of ancient music held in the Konzerthaus.

The Jazz-Fest (Jul–Aug) is one of the most important events of its kind, with performances at the Staatsoper and in the open air.

Salzburg &
the Salzkammergut

After a cultural break in Salzburg and an intriguing look at its sources of wealth along the salt routes, you can enjoy countryside pursuits and water sports at the shimmering lakes of Salzkammergut and the resorts that have made them famous.

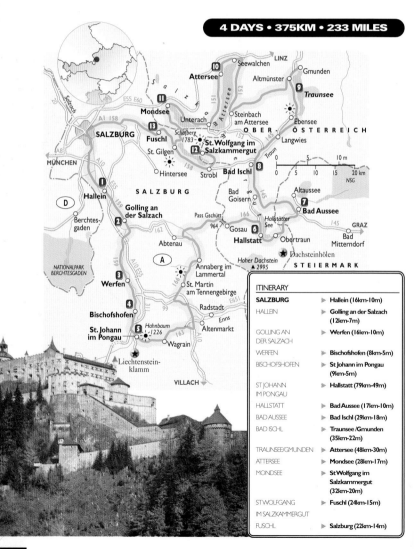

4 DAYS • 375KM • 233 MILES

ITINERARY		
SALZBURG	▷	**Hallein (16km-10m)**
HALLEIN	▷	**Golling an der Salzach (12km-7m)**
GOLLING AN DER SALZACH	▷	**Werfen (16km-10m)**
WERFEN	▷	**Bischofshofen (8km-5m)**
BISCHOFSHOFEN	▷	**St Johann im Pongau (9km-5m)**
ST JOHANN IM PONGAU	▷	**Hallstatt (79km-49m)**
HALLSTATT	▷	**Bad Aussee (17km-10m)**
BAD AUSSEE	▷	**Bad Ischl (29km-18m)**
BAD ISCHL	▷	**Traunsee /Gmunden (35km-22m)**
TRAUNSEE/GMUNDEN	▷	**Attersee (48km-30m)**
ATTERSEE	▷	**Mondsee (28km-17m)**
MONDSEE	▷	**St Wolfgang im Salzkammergut (32km-20m)**
ST WOLFGANG IM SALZKAMMERGUT	▷	**Fuschl (24km-15m)**
FUSCHL	▷	**Salzburg (22km-14m)**

ⓘ *Mozartplatz 5, Salzburg*

▶ *Proceed south on the 150 and then follow the 159, towards Bischofshofen.*

❶ Hallein, Salzburg

Dominated by the Barmsteine, high outcrops on the nearby Austrian-German border, Hallein has for thousands of years been the economic and cultural centre of the Tennengau region. The Celts settled here in the Dürrnberg area (3km/2 miles southwest) as early as 2,500 years ago, to mine rock-salt; workings still extend into the bowels of the mountain. Any tour of the town and Bad Dürrnberg above soon touches the history of salt-mining, which made the fortune of nearby Salzburg, and Celtic civilisation. One obligatory stop at Hallein is at the Keltenmuseum, constantly supplied with finds from excavations. In town, on

the Dürrnberg, not far from the entrance to the subterranean world of the Salzbergwerk mine-museum, you can stroll past the stelae and mounds of a Celtic settlement reconstructed in detail and called the Keltendorf.

ⓘ *Pernerinsel*

▶ *Continue south on road 159 to Golling an der Salzach.*

❷ Golling an der Salzach, Salzburg

Waterfalls and steep gorges characterise the wild countryside around Golling, a pretty holiday resort in the Salzach valley dominated to the south by a well-preserved medieval castle containing the Heimatmuseum (natural history and folk museum).

Romantic painters were particularly fond of the waterfall at St Nikolaus/Torren, reached after a lovely 3km (2-mile) walk

Hallein, an old Celtic town and millinery capital of the Tennengau region

west of the village. Flowing directly from the rock, it performs a double leap of 76m (249 feet). Continuing south, two beautiful gorges offer a spectacle worthy of Dante's *Inferno*. The Salzachöfen can be admired from a trail starting at the Lueg pass (2km/1 mile from Golling). To reach the Lammeröfen, a narrow gorge of the Lammer stream, take road 162 eastbound, shortly before the pass, and follow it for 8km (5 miles).

ⓘ *Markt 51*

▶ *Road 159 leads to Werfen.*

❸ Werfen, Salzburg

The old town of Werfen has two highlights – one natural, the other man-made. The former

The Eisriesenwelt, the largest ice cave in the world

alternating of hot and cold air currents in the subterranean spaces.

For a less energetic experience, venture to the northern outskirts of Werfen and visit the Burg Hohenwerfen, erected in the 11th century by Archbishop Gebhart and altered several times. Nowadays it houses a falconry museum with displays of birds in flight.

[i] *Markt 35*

▶ *Remain on road 159 to reach Bischofshofen*

4 Bischofshofen, Salzburg
The Salzburg capital of ski-jumping has three different 'culture trails', specially designed to take in all its many artistic and natural attractions. Of note are the parish church of St Maximilian, founded in 696 by St Rupert and re-decorated in late-Gothic style in the 14th and 15th centuries, and the 15th-century Frauenkirche, which houses a copy of the oldest work of Austrian sacred art, the cross of St Rupert (9th century; the original is kept in the local museum in the Kastenturm). Near by is the Romanesque Georgskirche, with frescoes dating from 1230.

The Georgskirche has frescoes dating from 1230. A lovely natural history trail (west of town) passes via the Gainfeldwasserfall, a 50m (164-foot) high waterfall protected as a national monument, arriving at the ruins of the Bachfall fortress above (12th century).

[i] *Salzburger Strasse 1*

▶ *Continue southwards on road 311 towards St Johann im Pongau and Schwarzach.*

5 St Johann im Pongau, Salzburg
The Amadé skiing area, which includes the well-known resort of St Johann, stretches eastwards

can be reached by driving up a mountain road (6km/4 miles north) to the Fallstein car park, then walking (15 minutes) to the base station of a cableway for a 4-minute ascent. It's all worth it when you get to the entrance of the world's largest ice cave, the Eisriesenwelt, containing unique forms sculpted by the

FOR CHILDREN

Children will have great fun at Abenteuerland adventure park, Kleinarl, 7km (4 miles) south of Wagrain, thanks to the many attractions, which include inflatable games, slides, a 'fun farm' and constantly changing entertainment programmes.

as far as Filmoos; a single ski pass gives access to 100 lifts. At St Johann itself, a cableway climbs to the top of the Hahnbaum (1,226m/4,022 feet) and a sweeping view in all seasons over the Hochkönig (2,941m/9,649 feet) to the northwest and the peaks of the Hohe Tauern to the south. The village and the entire valley are dominated by the majestic towers of the Dekanatskirche St Johannes, the 'cathedral of Pongau', rebuilt in neo-Gothic form after a devastating fire in 1855.

Running southwards from St Johann, parallel to the Gasteinertal, is the Grossarl valley, its river flowing through the impressive Liechtenstein-klamm; a tunnel and walkways allow visitors to pass through the gorge for nearly 1km (0.6 mile) to the Schleier waterfall.

> i *Am Hauptplatz, Ing-Ludwig-Pech-Strasse 1*

> ▶ *Follow road 163 eastbound to reach the A10 and take this for a short stretch northbound to the exit at Eben im Pongau. After 4km (2 miles) on road 99 heading west, take road 166 to the north at Niedernfritz St Martin and then east to Gozauzwang on the Halstätter See. You reach Hallstatt by following shore road 548 to the south.*

6 Hallstatt, Upper Austria
Due to its scenic beauty and historical importance, the area around the Hallstätter See,

SCENIC ROUTES

The stretch of Lammertal road between Niedernfritz St Martin to the south and Abtenau to the north – about 20km (12 miles) – is known as the Salzburger Dolomitenstrasse, and follows a narrow gorge between the Tennengebirge mountains to the west and the Dachstein mountains to the east. There are fine views of dense woodland and many waterfalls from here.

dominated by the Dachstein massif, has been declared a World Heritage site by UNESCO. Again, as in the Hallein zone (the Celtic prefix 'hall' means 'salt'), the region's historical and economic development has depended on rock salt.

St Johann im Pongau, the route around the Liechtensteinklamm

RECOMMENDED EXCURSION

Along road 166, between St Johann im Pongau and Hallstätter See, cross the Gschütt Pass and turn right at Gosau to come to Vorderer Gosausee (937m/3,074 feet). This lake set in the mountains has an extraordinary view of the Dachstein glacier. If you follow the lake eastwards on foot, you reach a second one, Hinterer Gosausee, and from here an ascent of about three hours leads to the Adameck refuge hut (2,196m/7,205 feet).

From Hallstatt, perched high on a mountain on the southern lakeshore, a cableway climbs to the Salzbergwerk, the oldest salt-works in the world. Visitors descend into the galleries on a long slide to explore the beautiful salt lake.

In town, a covered flight of steps leads to the high Pfarrkirche Mariä Himmelfahrt, the parish church of the Assumption, with a valuable 16th-century altarpiece in the choir.

A pedestrian route, the Ostuferwanderweg, takes in the east shore of the lake from Bad Goisern in the north to a pretty railway station in the south, and the landing-stage for the ferries that cross from Hallstatt opposite or sail to Steeg (Jul–mid-Sep), at the northern tip of the lake.

i Seestrasse 169

▶ *Continue along the road that follows the lake to Obertraun, where you continue northeast on the local road (closed in winter) to Bad Aussee.*

7 Bad Aussee, Styria
The therapeutic properties of its salt-rich waters have brought fame to Bad Aussee, a resort in

FOR HISTORY BUFFS

A vast necropolis was uncovered at Hallstatt, containing over 2,000 tombs, along with some fascinating finds. As a result, the Iron Age period from the 12th to the 5th century BC is universally known as the 'Hallstatt era'. Although most objects are now in Vienna and Salzburg, the local archaeological museum warrants a visit.

The town of Halstatt is linked to important prehistoric finds

Styrian Salzkammergut, set in particularly dramatic surroundings. On one side is the monumental ice-capped Dachstein, on the other the unsettling spires of Totes Gebirge, and in between are the Traun river and three lovely little lakes.

On the other side of the Grundlsee (5km/3 miles to the east), whose northern shore you follow, is the romantic Toplitzsee, a sheet of water enclosed between rocks and woodland. Slightly further north (6km/4 miles from Bad Aussee), on the lake of the same name, stands Altaussee. In a scenic spot above it you can visit a salt mine and the Barbarakapelle, the chapel of St Barbara.

i Kolloman Wallisch Platz

▶ *Drive to Bad Ischl on the 145 northwest.*

8 Bad Ischl, Upper Austria
'Salt children' was the name given to the offspring of Archduke Franz Karl (who died in 1878) and Sophie of Bavaria, referring to the salt water of Bad Ischl which the couple took to

cure their presumed sterility. Their son, who became Emperor Franz Joseph (1830–1916), visited this spa resort even more than his parents. Here he met his adored wife Elizabeth (Sissi) and the family spent summers here together from 1854 to 1914.

The town retains a refined and slightly old-fashioned atmosphere, and recalls its imperial connections in the solemn Kaiservilla, a

Biedermeier residence designed in the shape of an 'E', in homage to Elizabeth of Bavaria, who was assassinated in 1898. Another celebrated visitor to the resort was the great Franz Lehár (1870–1948), composer of light operas. Memoribilia of his stay here (1912–48) and his work are found in the museum which now occupies the house where he lived.

> *i* Bahnhofstrasse 6

> ▶ Road 145 leads northeast to Trunsee, via Ebensee, Traunkirche and Altmünster; here turn right on to road 120 for Gmunden

❾ Traunsee, Upper Austria
One of the loveliest lakes in Salzkammergut, and the deepest in Austria, can be seen in all its magnificence from the south by climbing to the Feuerkogel scenic viewpoint, reached by cable-car from Ebensee (mid-May–Oct).

Follow the west shore of the lake and pass through the picturesque resorts of Traunkirchen, famous for its delightful Corpus Christi boat procession, and Altmünster,

---

BACK TO NATURE

The famous Dachstein caves are found on the road between Hallstatt and Bad Aussee, near Obertraun. The first complex of caves and passages is reached via the Krippenstein cableway (intermediary stop) with access to the Rieseneishöle, with its ice 'cathedral', and the Mammuthöle, which has extended vertically over 1,180m (3,871 feet). Continue from Obertraun 5km (3 miles) east to reach the Koppenbrüllerhöhe (mid-Apr–late-Sep), where stalactites have formed around a subterranean spring.

FOR HISTORY BUFFS

A vast necropolis was uncovered at Hallstatt, containing over 2,000 tombs, along with some fascinating finds. As a result the Iron Age period from the 12th to the 5th century BC is universally known as the 'Hallstatt era'. Although most of the objects are now kept in the museums of Vienna and Salzburg, the local archaeological museum also deserves a visit.

---

which offers cycling enthusiasts the chance of excursions and a visit to the Radmuseum (bicycle museum).

After reaching the northernmost tip of Traunsee, stop at Gmunden, a pretty town arranged in a semicircle around the lake promenade, the famous Esplanade (2km/1 mile). Pottery production has a long history here, and at the town-hall porcelain bells ring at regular intervals during the day. A particularly beautiful sight is the

Spectacular ice formations in the Dachstein caves, near Obertraun

Seeschloss Ort (17th century), a castle built on an artificial islet, linked to the mainland by a wooden bridge 130m (426 feet) long. For a final view of the lake from the side opposite Ebensee, take the cableway to the Grünberg (984m/3,228 feet, late-Apr–Oct).

ⓘ *Graben 2, Gmunden*

▶ *Return to Altmünster by the same route and take local road **544** to Steinbach am Attersee. Here, follow the lake north on the **152** and, from Seewalchen, head south on the **151** to Attersee.*

⑩ Attersee, Upper Austria

Attersee is the name given to both the largest alpine lake in Salkammergut (20km/12 miles long, 3km/2 miles wide) and one of the prettiest villages on the western shore, which is more densely populated than the opposite shore and dominated by the Höllengebirge. If you don't fancy water sports, you could set off on one of the many lovely walks that explore the surrounding mountains and woods, such as the easy trail from Attersee to Palmsdorf and Buchberg.

ⓘ *Nussdorfer Strasse 15*

▶ *Road **151** follows the western shore of Attersee, then the east shore of Mondsee to the resort of the same name.*

⑪ Mondsee, Upper Austria

According to legend, while out on a shooting party in the Salzkammergut the Bavarian Duke Odilo was overtaken by darkness and only the sudden appearance of the full moon saved him from falling into a lake. In thanks for his narrow escape he founded a convent in the year 748 on the shores of that lake, and both convent and lake were named Mondsee, 'lake of the moon'.

The church of the oldest Benedictine house in Upper Austria is still the biggest draw at the holiday resort of Mondsee, on the northeast tip of the lake. The Stiftkirche's basic design is Gothic, but a concave baroque façade has been added. To the left of the main altar there's access to the Heimat-und Pfahlbaumuseum, in the abbey's lovely Gothic rooms, displaying finds associated with the prehistoric 'Mondsee culture' (2800–1800 BC) and masterpieces of illuminated work executed by the monks in Carolingian times.

ⓘ *Dr-Franz-Müller-Strasse 3*

▶ *Follow the west shore of Mondsee southbound on road **154** to the northern tip of Wolfgangsee at Pöllach. Turn left on to road **158** and, at the southern tip of the lake, turn left for Strobl-Schwarzenbach, then left again for Au and St Wolfgang.*

⑫ St Wolfgang im Salzkammergut, Upper Austria

The journey around the lake to reach the popular resort of St Wolfgang can be delightful,

The Attersee, the largest alpine lake in Salzkammergut

traffic permitting, but if you want to avoid it, you can take a boat between May and October from St Gilgen. From the top of the Schafberg (1,783m/5,850 feet), reached via a rack-railway driven by special steam locomotives (May–October), there's a wonderful view of the whole area.

In the town is the Hotel Im Weissen Rössl, a modernised version of the inn made famous by the operetta *The White Horse Inn*. Near by, the Wallfahrtkirche St Wolfgang overlooks the water and is visited mainly for its splendid Pacher-Altar in the choir in the right aisle. It took Michael Pacher 10 years to complete this Gothic altarpiece dedicated to the Coronation of the Virgin in his Brunico workshop (1471–81). Then, given its size (12m/39 feet tall), a terrific effort was required to transport it across the Brenner pass to Wolfgangsee. The Schwanthaler-Altar, a double baroque altar of 1676, is another gem.

i Au 140, St Wolfgang

▶ Return to Pöllach and continue to Fuschl on the same road.

B Fuschl, Salzburg
The romantic resort of Fuschl overlooks the eastern tip of the lake of the same name,

Above: St Wolfgang im Salzkammergut
Below: the famous Pacher-Altar in the church of St Wolfgang

particularly enchanting when approached from above, shrouded in the morning mist. Its a view that was exploited to the full in a number of films about the life of the Empress Sissi and shot in Fuschl castle (15th century; now a luxury

hotel, at the other end of the lake).

Fun excursions are offered on barges between May and October to the castle fishpond, where visitors can learn to identify and buy the fish found in Fuschlsee.

i Dorfstrasse 65

▶ Return to Salzburg along road 158.

Mühlviertel's
Forests & Meadows

The capital of Upper Austria is also the southern gateway to a part of the country untouched by mass tourism. With its undulating scenery, a patchwork of woods, meadows, cultivated fields and marshes, Mühlviertel is an unspoiled area of natural beauty and age-old traditions right on the edge of Bohemia.

2/3 DAYS • 238KM • 148 MILES

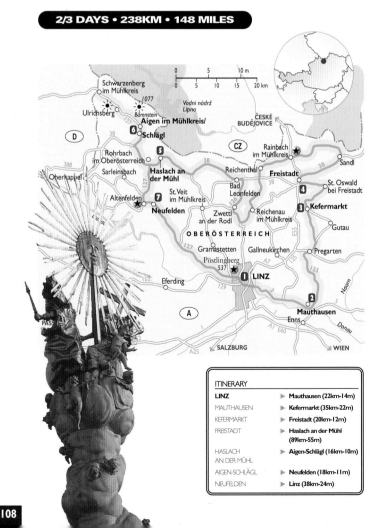

ITINERARY

LINZ	▶ Mauthausen (22km-14m)
MAUTHAUSEN	▶ Kefermarkt (35km-22m)
KEFERMARKT	▶ Freistadt (20km-12m)
FREISTADT	▶ Haslach an der Mühl (89km-55m)
HASLACH AN DER MÜHL	▶ Aigen-Schlägl (16km-10m)
AIGEN-SCHLÄGL	▶ Neufelden (18km-11m)
NEUFELDEN	▶ Linz (38km-24m)

❶ Linz, Upper Austria

Linz, the capital of Upper Austria, straddles the River Danube, its old centre on the right bank, the new town on the left, linked to each other by the modern Nibelungenbrücke. Its history is inextricably linked with the Danube, which is still navigated regularly, for both tourist and commercial purposes, towards Passau in Germany and eastwards as far as Vienna.

The centre of city life is Hauptplatz, one of Austria's largest squares, as it was in the 13th century. Dominated by its gleaming column, the Dreifaltigkeitssäule (1723), it is surrounded by 15th- to 18th-century mansions (No 1 is the Altes Rathaus, 1513), some with fine courtyards containing vaults and fountains.

Altstadt – the main city-centre street – is reached from Klosterstrasse, passing in front of the Renaissance Landhaus Palace (1564–74), seat of the regional parliament. Its porticoed courtyard with loggias makes a delightful setting for *Serenadenkonzerte* (musical evenings).

Tummelplatz is overlooked by the Hofberg castle, built in 1477 by Emperor Friedrich III, who lived here in voluntary exile during Matthias Corvinus' siege of Vienna. It was rebuilt by Rudolph II in the 17th century. Visit the Schlossmuseum with its art, ethnological, coin and

The 18th-century Dreifaltig-keitssäule towers high above the Linz trams

applied art collections, then walk through the park to Freidrichstor, the only surviving gate of the Renaissance castle. Carry on to Römerstrasse, site of Austria's oldest church, consecrated to St Martin (the support walls date from the 8th century). Circle the old centre to the south along the Promenade and, before returning to Hauptplatz, visit the baroque Alter Dom (cathedral) at No 3 Domgasse, designed in 1669–78 by Pietro Francesco Carlone. Composer Anton Bruckner was the organist here between 1856 and 1868. See also the Stadtpfarrkirche (in Pfarrplatz), originally Gothic but transformed to baroque style in the mid-17th century.

A quicker way of seeing the city is aboard the Linz City Express, a tourist train that, in half an hour, visits all the main sights (Mar–early Nov).

Young visitors will enjoy the Ars Electronica Center, a multimedia museum with electrifying virtual experiences.

🛈 *Hauptplatz 1*

▶ *Follow road 3 (Donau Bundesstrasse) eastbound. About 5km (3 miles) past Steining, turn left on to the local road for Langenstein-Mauthausen.*

FOR CHILDREN

Linz offers adventure on the steepest tramline in the world (as certified by the Guinness Book of Records), which climbs to the top of the Pöstlingberg (537m/1,762 feet), northwest of town. After enjoying the splendid view, you can accompany children on the Grottenbahn dragon-train – a magical journey into a world of elves and fairy-tales inside a fortified tower.

The Mauthausen concentration camp, a physical reminder of past atrocities

2 Mauthausen, Upper Austria

Thanks to its strategic position at the confluence of the Enns and Danube rivers, Mauthausen was a busy toll station as early as 1208, in the service of the Babenberg family (predecessors of the Habsburgs). Its importance was underlined in 1491 with the construction of Schloss Pragstein, a mansion overlooking the river and now home to the Heimatmuseum (history and folk museum).

Despite the town's present-day atmosphere of tranquillity, its recent past has been grim. Terrible crimes were perpetrated by the Nazis between 1938 and 1945 in nearby Gedenkstätte (3km/ 2 miles northwest), a granite quarry turned into a camp where more than 100,000 deportees died. The camp is open to visitors as a chilling reminder of the atrocities committed there.

i *Heindlkai 13*

▶ *A short stretch of local road leads east to road 123; follow this northbound to Pregarten and here continue on the local road to Kefermarkt.*

3 Kefermarkt, Upper Austria

In 1467 a country squire called Christoph von Zelking settled into Schloss Weinberg, the majestic castle that has dominated Kefermarkt's northern approach since 1305. He donated the monumental

---

SPECIAL TO...

The Mühlvierteler Museumstrasse is a themed route that visits about 30 museums and other places exploring the local economy, ecology and history. Many of the sites of interest in the Pregarten-Bad Leonfelden section of this tour have joined the initiative.

---

altar (13.5m/44 feet high by 6.3m/20.6 feet wide) that was to bring fame to the local Pfarrkirche St Wolfgang. Nobody knows who was responsible for its superb limewood carvings and life-sized figures.

i *Oberer Markt 15*

▶ *Continue northwards and turn right for Lasberg; here bear northeast on the local road to St Oswald bei Freistadt and take road 579 to Freistadt.*

4 Freistadt, Upper Austria

The cultural and economic capital of Mühlviertel is a romantic medieval town enclosed within 15th-century walls punctuated by two gates and five towers.

From Böhmertor, a flower-decked street leads to Hauptplatz, featuring old Gothic houses resting on granite arches, that conceal beautiful courtyards lined with loggias. A great 14th-century castle with a square tower rises to the northeast of the square. This contains the Mühlviertel Heimatmuseum, with its interesting collection of works made using Hinterglasmalerei (glass-painting technique). Sometimes incorrectly called *verre églomisé* (gilded glass), this craft was first developed in Bohemia and Upper Austria in the 17th century.

The procedure lent itself well to production-line methods and, in nearby Sandl (15km/9 miles northeast), just one family-run artisan workshop was able to produce 386,000 pieces between 1852 and 1864. The Sandl Hinterglasmuseum arranges special painting courses.

[i] *Hauptplatz 14*

▶ Road **38** leads northeast to Sandl. Turn northwest for Windhaag bei Freistadt. Here drive southwest and then

---

FOR HISTORY BUFFS

If the frenetic modern pace of travel is getting you down, pay a visit to Rainbach im Mühlkreis. Here you'll find the oldest horse-drawn tram in Europe (1832), complete with period station and restaurant.

---

west on the local road to Rainbach im Mühlkreis and Reichental. Where the houses end, turn left for Schenkenfelden and Reichenau im Mühlkreis, then climb northwest on the local road to Zwettl an der Rodl and Bad Leonfelden. Here proceed northwest on road **38** to Haslach.

5 Haslach an der Mühl, Upper Austria
The most obvious features of note in the medieval village of Haslach are the Gothic parish

---

church of St Nikolausa with its great bell tower, and the Torturm, an old fortified gate housing the history and folk museum. Harder to find but more characteristic and fascinating are the small theme museums and craft workshops, which offer an insight into the history, culture and customs of this region on the edge of the Bohemian Forest.

The Webereimuseum focuses on the history of weaving, a flourishing local industry thanks to an abundance of linen; the Kaufmann-museum and the Schulmuseum, are replicas of, respectively, a grocer's shop and a classroom of the past; the Museum für Mechanische Musik & Volkskunst has some exquisitely decorated mechanical musical instruments on display; and the Ölmühle illustrates phases in

Kefermarkt, the superb altarpiece in the church of St Wolfgang

the production of oil from linen seeds. There are many more, and half the fun is in the search.

ⓘ *Marktplatz 45*

▶ *Follow road 38 northeast to Oepping, then road 127 north to Aigen-Schlägl.*

❻ Aigen-Schlägl, Upper Austria

A stop in these two pretty adjoining villages, united under the same municipality, is an excellent opportunity to experience both culture and nature.

RECOMMENDED WALK

From Aigen, a scenic road climbs 1,077m (3,533 feet) up the Bärenstein, the starting point for excursions into the lush Böhmer Wald (Bohemian Forest).

The sumptuous Premonstratensian Stift (abbey) of Schlägl is the main attraction. Founded in 1218 and revamped in baroque style in the 17th century, it evaded secularisation by Emperor Franz Josef II and began to flourish under Abbot

The rich library in Schlägl abbey

SCENIC ROUTES

The scenic road from Aigen to Schwarzenberg (18km/ 11 miles), and on across the border, is called the Mühlviertel Weberstrasse. It runs over the wooded slopes of the Böhmer Wald and the final stretch has remarkable views of the Plöckstein (1,378m/4,521 feet), the high point of the border between Austria, Germany and Bohemia.

Fähtz, to whom we owe thanks for its rich Gemäldegalerie (more than 200 paintings by primitive masters) and a neo-baroque library (60,000 volumes, manuscripts and prints), arranged in a large room splendidly decorated with inlay. In the Stiftsbrauerei (abbey brewery) the monks will be happy to give visitors a taste of their home-brewed Austrian beer, made with rye.

Continuing along the road northeast, you reach Ulrichsberg and Schwarzenberg, both famous glass-production centres.

Just past the first of the two, Ulrichsberg, a road climbs on the right to Hochficht (1,338m/ 4,390 feet), the region's main skiing resort.

ⓘ *Hauptstrasse 2*

▶ *Return to Oepping and continue on road 127 to Arneit; after 2km (1.2 miles) turn left for Neufelden.*

❼ Neufelden, Upper Austria

First the salt trade, then linen-processing and finally beer-production brought profits to this old market town, where fine houses line the Markt (17th- to 18th-century). The valley is dominated by Burg Pürnstein (4km/2.5 miles north), a stronghold that originally belonged to the Birchenstainer family, who founded it at the end of the 10th century and subsequently passed it to the Starhembergers.

ⓘ *Markt 22*

▶ *After following a short stretch of local road southeast, take road 127 to Linz.*

BACK TO NATURE

The Altenfelden Wildpark (4km/2.5 miles west of Neufelden) is home to 950 species of animals, including wapiti, prairie dogs, kangaroos, and trained birds of prey, that fly in daily displays.

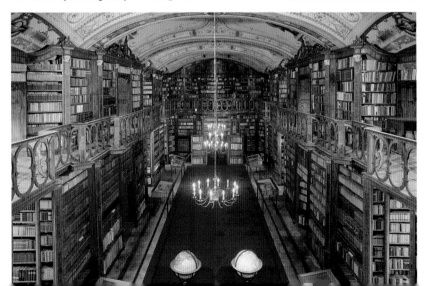

Famous
Abbeys

The green hills that extend to the south of Linz beyond the boundary of Upper and Lower Austria conceal old forges, blacksmiths' shops and tempting 'cider houses', all in a tranquil rural landscape guarded for centuries by great abbeys, the custodians of priceless works of art.

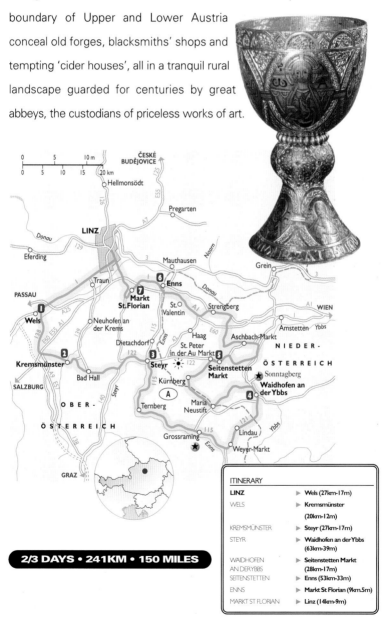

2/3 DAYS • 241KM • 150 MILES

ITINERARY		
LINZ	▶	**Wels** (27km-17m)
WELS	▶	**Kremsmünster** (20km-12m)
KREMSMÜNSTER	▶	**Steyr** (27km-17m)
STEYR	▶	**Waidhofen an der Ybbs** (63km-39m)
WAIDHOFEN AN DER YBBS	▶	**Seitenstetten Markt** (28km-17m)
SEITENSTETTEN	▶	**Enns** (53km-33m)
ENNS	▶	**Markt St Florian** (9km.5m)
MARKT ST FLORIAN	▶	**Linz** (14km-9m)

☐ *Hauptplatz 1, Linz*

▶ *From Linz take road 1 to Wels.*

❶ Wels, Upper Austria

This is a town with a strong rural tradition – a major agricultural fair is still held here every year – as well as an incomparable historic charm.

You enter beautiful Stadtplatz through the west entrance, which is guarded by the Ledererturm (the only surviving tower of the 13th-century fortifications). There are no fewer than 60 distinctive mansions here, but the eye is immediately drawn to the baroque façade of the Rathaus (1748) and the multicoloured Renaissance Haus der Salome Alt, with its picture of the famous mistress of Wolf Dietrich, Archbishop of Salzburg. An alley on the right leads to the idyllic open gardens of the Burg, the old fortress (776), now housing the local history museum; visit the room where Emperor Maximilian I died (1519).

Everyone cycles in Wels and there are lovely excursions into the surrounding countryside, such as the one to the Schmiding ornithological park (7km /4 miles northwest).

FOR CHILDREN

A plunge in the water-park swimming pool, a visit to the Puppenwelt museum of old toys and a visit to the zoo are just some of the activities available for children in Wels.

☐ *Kaiser-Josef-Platz 22*

▶ *Follow road 138 southwards to Sattledt, where you turn left on to the 122.*

❷ Kremsmünster, Upper Austria

The famous Benediktinerstift (Benedictine abbey) can be admired in all its majesty from beautiful, medieval Kremsmünster. The building has an unmistakable square profile with the twin towers of the collegiate church and the Mathematischer Turm, the astronomical observatory erected between 1748 and 1759. The present abbey, founded in 777 by the Bavarian Count Tassilo III, is a late 17th-century baroque work by Jakob Prandauer and Carlo Antonio Carlone, the latter also responsible for transforming the abbey church. The Schatz-kammer (treasure chamber)

The attractive façades of the houses in Steyr

contains the Tassilokelch, a gilded copper chalice considered to be a masterpiece of its age (c770).

☐ *Rathausplatz 1*

▶ *Drive along road 122 eastbound to Steyr, passing via Bad Hall.*

❸ Steyr, Upper Austria

Capital of the Enns valley mining area and an important industrial, metallurgical and mechanical centre (two thirds of all BMW engines are manufactured here), Steyr still

---

BACK TO NATURE

Grossraming (34km/21 miles southeast of Steyr) is home to one of the information centres of the Nationalpark Kalkalpen, a protected natural area that extends over 75,000sq km (28,950 square miles) in Upper Austria. It has high-mountain scenery (Sengsengebirge and Reichramiminger Hintergebirge ranges) and three different types of forest. Trekking tours are available, lasting six days.

From on high, there are beautiful views of the confluence of the town's two rivers, the Steyr and the Enns.

☐ *Stadtplatz 27*

▶ *Take road 115 southbound, then southeast, passing via Ternberg and Grossraming; turn right at Weyer-Markt, then left on to the 121, northwest to Waidhofen.*

▣ Waidhofen an der Ybbs, Lower Austria

Waidhofen, on the left bank of the Ybbs, maintains its medieval appearance and celebrates its centuries-old association with iron in the Eiserne ('iron') display of armour at the Heimatmuseum. The metal was essential to the economy of this region of Eisenwurzen, which straddles Styria and Lower Austria. It was transported from Eisenerz (see Tour 11) to be worked in the forges along the 'iron route' of Lower Austria, between Steyr and Waidhofen.

☐ *Freisingerberg 2*

▶ *Drive northwest for about 4km (2.5 miles) on road 121, then turn left on to the local road 88 for Seitenstetten; at the Seitenstetten turning, continue straight on, then turn right at Maria Neustift for Ertl, Tiefenbach and St Peter in der Au. Here, turn right on to the 122 for Seitenstetten.*

SPECIAL TO...

The sanctuary of Christkindl (1708) stands on the western outskirts of Steyr and is regarded as the 'home' of the infant Jesus. Children asking for Christmas gifts address their letters to the post office here. The Christkindlmarkte (traditional markets selling decorations and sweetmeats) and the special crib exhibitions make Steyr a favourite destination during Christmas festivities.

has the charm of a well-preserved medieval town.

Elegant Stadtplatz is surrounded by the almost imperceptibly concave façades of the old houses, in a mix of styles: Gothic, Renaissance, baroque and rococo. Of particular interest is the Gothic Bummerlhaus of 1497 (No 32). The pretty, narrow streets and romantic courtyards are dominated by Schloss Lamberg, rebuilt in the 18th century on the site of the legendary fortress of the dukes of Styria (Styriaburg, 985–91).

A picturesque view of Waidhofen an der Ybbs

5 Seitenstetten Markt, Lower Austria

Bucolic Seitenstetten, set among apple orchards, owes its fame to an important Benedictine abbey, founded in 1112 and rebuilt in 1719. Its interesting painting and sculpture gallery includes works by Brueghel. A lovely wrought-iron gate opposite the abbey leads to the Historischer Hofgarten, baroque public gardens filled with the scent of roses and herbs.

Take a refreshing walk along Mostobstwanderweg, a circular route that starts from the abbey,

SCENIC ROUTES

The stretch of road that cuts across the tour between Steyr and Seitenstetten passes through a wonderfully fertile region of rolling hills reminscent of Tuscany, in Italy, or parts of Kent, in England – except that the hills are blanketed with conifers.

northwest. A short stretch of the 42 leads southwest to the A1, which you take to Enns.

☐ *Mauthausner Strasse 7*

▶ *Follow road 1 westwards and turn left, passing over the A1, to continue southwest on local road 566 to Markt St Florian.*

7 Markt St Florian, Upper Austria

On the spot where St Florian was martyred in 304 stands the famous Chorherrenstift St Florian, an abbey founded in 1071 by Augustinian canons and, in its present form, one of Austria's baroque masterpieces,

A view of the Stift in Markt St Florian, a masterpiece of Austrian baroque style

one of many stops on the 'Mostviertel cider route', which visits every centre between Waidhofen and Strengberg.

☐ *Steyrer Strasse 1*

▶ *Follow road 122 for about 4km (2.5 miles) to the turning on the right for Biberbach, where you proceed northeast to Gimpersdorf. Here take the local road to the north to link up with the 122; follow this westbound through Aschbach-Markt. Turn right on to the road for Wolfsbach, and from here drive to Strengberg first on the local road northwards, and then on road 1*

6 Enns, Upper Austria

From the terrace of the 16th-century Stadtturm (60m/197 feet) there's a fine view of the old buildings of Enns, founded in the 2nd century AD on the site of the major Roman settlement of *Lauriacum*. Alternatively, visit the 25 stages of history recommended on the town tour.

Your journey back in time starts from the Gothic basilica of St Laurentius, on the northwest edge of the town; inside the remarkable 14th-century building are the remains of a church at least a thousand years older.

Fascinating items excavated here are kept in the Stadtmuseum Lauriacum and Schloss Ennsegg, built in the 16th century, with a panoramic view of the Danube.

designed by Carlone and built between 1686 and 1750 by Prandtauer. Visit the library on the first floor, with its splendid inlaid cupboards and 140,000 books, and the Altdorfer Altar room; this features 16 panels depicting the martyrdom of St Sebastian, created by the great 'master of the Danube' Albrecht Altdorfer (1518). The Imperial apartments on the second floor have mementos of composer Anton Bruckner (1824–96), who was a treble in the Florianer Sängerknaben (boys' choir) and later the official organist; he now lies in the abbey crypt.

☐ *Marktplatz 2*

▶ *Follow the local road northwest and turn right after Olkam for Ebelsberg and road 1 to Linz.*

South of the
Danube

3 DAYS • 355KM • 220 MILES

ITINERARY

LINZ
WILHERING
EFERDING

ENGELHARTSZELL
SCHÄRDING

BRAUNAU AM INN

RIED IM INNKREIS

LAMBACH

▶ **Wilhering (10km-6m)**
▶ **Eferding (17km-10m)**
▶ **Engelhartszell (33km-20m)**
▶ **Schärding (42km-26m)**
▶ **Braunau am Inn (49km-30m)**
▶ **Ried im Innkreis (122km-76m)**
▶ **Lambach (40km-25m)**
▶ **Linz (42km-26m)**

Driving is only one of many ways to follow the Inn and Danube rivers to their confluence. Whether you go by car, bicycle, boat or on horseback, every historic location lining the banks offers new delights.

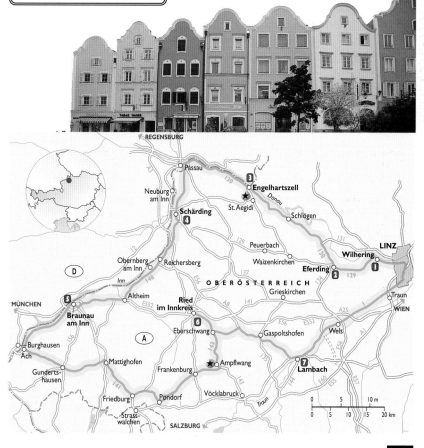

ⓘ Hauptplatz 1, Linz

▶ *Take road 129 westbound from Linz to Wilhering.*

❶ Wilhering, Upper Austria
From 1146, the spiritual and cultural life of the region of Wilhering was dominated by the famous Cistercian abbey, the Zisterzienserabtei, entirely rebuilt after a fire in 1733. The sumptuous decorations of the new abbey church were the work of Andrea and Martino Altomonte, from Italy, champions of the baroque and rococo styles in Austria.

Wilhering is renowned for its pretty surroundings; the Wald-schule, in the former brewery, organises group excursions into the nearby Kürnberger Wald (woods), to the southeast.

ⓘ Linzer Strasse 14

▶ *Continue on road 129 to Eferding.*

❷ Eferding, Upper Austria
Eferding has had a lively past – from its beginnings as a Celtic settlement to its development as a Roman cavalry encampment, culminating in its role in the the 1524 peasant revolt. Ancient tombs are housed in the

---

FOR HISTORY BUFFS

The ruins of Schaunburg, built in 1161 and extended in the 15th century, hint at a glorious past. This imposing fortified complex in Upper Austria lies 5km (3 miles) northwest of Eferding and can be visited on request with a guide.

Spitalskirche and Schloss Starhemberg (15th- to 17th-century), which also contains historic exhibits and a folk museum.

ⓘ Stadtplatz 31

▶ *Take the 130 northwest to Engelhartszell.*

RECOMMENDED WALKS

Strolling through the woods, near Schlögen, northwest of Eferding, you can enjoy one of the most spectacular and most frequently photographed views of the Danube, which at this point forms a narrow bend (Sclögener Schlinge) dreaded by navigators.

A detail of the rich rococo decorations in Wilhering abbey

❸ Engelhartszell, Upper Austria
Engelhartzell grew up on the bank of the Danube around an old abbey called Cella Angelica (Engelszell), founded by the Cistercians in 1293 and rebuilt in baroque style. This has been

FOR CHILDREN

It's not only dolphins that perform. Take a look at the trained trout that leap, pirouette and play ball games in the Forellenzirkus, near St Aegidi, 5km (3 miles) south of Engelhartszell.

the only Trappist monastery on Austrian territory since 1925. Fine rococo furnishings can be seen in the Stiftkirche (church).

ⓘ Marktplatz 61

▶ *Continue on road 130 northwest to Innstadt (entering Germany); then head south towards Schärding on local road 2625, which becomes the 506 back in Austria.*

4 Schärding, Upper Austria

The baroque façades of the houses overlooking the Silberzeile ('silver side') of Obere Stadtplatz are the most obvious – but not the only – evidence of Schärding's past affluence. Until 1779 this border town on the Inn river belonged to Bavaria, and the elegant rounded gables of the brightly coloured houses echo the styles on the German side of the river. Around the square are the remains of the old fortifications, extended between 1428 and 1436; the Burgtor, the gate of the old castle adorned with frescoes, houses the Heimatmuseum, dedicated to folk culture and local handicrafts. A traditional wooden barge shuttles between the main natural and cultural sights along the Inn to Passau.

ℹ️ *Unterer Stadtplatz 19*

▶ *Proceed south on road 149 via Reichersberg, where you take the 148 southwest to Altheim and Braunau.*

5 Braunau am Inn, Upper Austria

The old town of Braunau, birthplace of Adolf Hitler, has a more innocuous claim to fame in the Gothic parish church of St Stephen. It dates from the 15th century and houses a fine pulpit

---

BACK TO NATURE

Birdwatchers shouldn't miss a stop at the Europareservat Unterer Inn, a nature reserve shared with Germany and stretching along the Inn river east of Braunau.

---

and organ loft of the same period. Once across the bridge over the Inn, which for centuries carried a flourishing salt trade, you're on German territory.

ℹ️ *Stadtplatz 2*

▶ *Follow local road 501 southwest to Ach. Take the 503 southeast for Hochburg, Gundertshausen and Mattighofen; turn south on to road 147 for Friedburg, then continue east on the local road to Höcken, where you turn right for Pöndorf. A turning left leads to Fornach; continue east to the turning on the left for Frankenburg. A local road travels east to Rödleiten and the turning on the left for Ampflwang, where you continue north on road 143 to Ried.*

6 Ried im Innkreis, Upper Austria

The old centre of Ried, capital and soul of Innviertel, is

arranged around four elegant squares in a chequerboard pattern. Handsome sculptures by the Schwanthaler family (17th to 18th century) and the Zürn brothers (17th century), natives of the town, can be admired in the baroque Pfarrkirche St Peter und Paul (1721–32) and in the nearby Innviertler Volkskundehaus museum.

ℹ️ *Kapuzinerberg 8*

▶ *Head southeast on the 143 to Eberschwang, where you turn left on to a stretch of local road that leads to the 520 for Lambach.*

SPECIAL TO...

The wooded Innerviertel-Hausruckwald region, east of the Inn, is a horse-trekking paradise. Even novice riders, adults and children, can enjoy a comfortable ride on the docile Icelandic horses of the large Ampflwang stud farm, 19km (12 miles) south of Ried.

---

7 Lambach, Upper Austria

An artificial islet on the Traun river, with a picnic area, is the best place from which to admire the two landmarks of Lambach and Stadl-Paura, opposite. The Benedictine abbey, founded in 1056 and rebuilt in the 17th and 18th centuries, houses precious Byzantine-style frescoes in its church, and the 18th-century sanctuary, dedicated to the Holy Trinity and designed to a triangular plan, with three portals, three towers, three altars, three organs, three sacristies and mosaics in three colours.

ℹ️ *Marktplatz 8*

▶ *Follow road 1 to Traun, where you turn left on to road 139 for Linz.*

A ferry on the Danube at Engelhartszell

VIENNA, LOWER AUSTRIA & THE BURGENLAND

The eastern part of Austria extends from north to south, taking in the *Länder* (provinces) of Lower Austria (Niederösterreich) and the Burgenland, as well as borders with four other countries: Germany, the Czech Republic, Slovakia and Hungary. As a result, it has strong social and cultural ties with the Slavs, especially in the regions near the borders; Burgenland, for example, has substantial Hungarian and Croatian minorities.

The former Imperial city of Vienna, now a *Land* in its own right, was the capital of Lower Austria until 1920, and continues to exert an influence over the beautiful surroundings. To the north lie the vast wooded Waldviertel plateau which reaches up to the Czech border, and the vine-clad hills of the Weinviertel where the connoisseur can drop in on one of the many wine cellars dotted about the landscape. To the east you will find the fertile Marchfeld plain and the Danube region of Wachau, declared a World Heritage site by UNESCO. To the south is the agricultural Mostviertel, a land of orchards bordering with Styria, and the Wienerwald (Vienna Woods), a region of woods and spas leading to the easternmost Alpine spurs, the Scheenberg, Ötcher and Roxalpe mountains, with peaks rising above 2,000m (6,562 feet).

A long strip of territory south of the capital, near Hungary, constitutes the Burgenland, the 'land of castles', occupying a strategic position as the last bastion to the east. Nature-lovers will be keen to explore the area around the Neusiedler See, the great lake that determines the landscape and climate of this area on the edge of the Magyar steppe (*puszta*). The brackish pools and canebrakes that surround it (designated the Neusiedler See–Seewinkel National Park) support a diversity of bird species, including rare herons.

The following tours prove that Vienna is not only a star in its own right but a superb base for fascinating excursions into the surrounding countryside.

The church of St Nikola an der Donau overlooks the Danube

Tour 18

This tour takes the road south from St Pölten, renamed Niederösterreichische Barock-Strasse, the Lower Austria Baroque Route, because of the gems of art and architecture found along the way. It skirts the Eisenwurzen region along the 'iron route' as far as the unspoiled Ötscherland nature zone and the ancient Styrian sanctuary of Mariazell, one of Austria's best-known pilgrim centres and a summer and winter resort.

Tour 19

From the wine area of Krems, this tour ventures north to the westernmost edge of Lower Austria, and explores the wooded Waldviertel, a region known for its strong craft traditions and mystical legends. Then you descend to Ybbs and begin the drive across the Wachau, a stretch of the Danube of such scenic value that it's been declared a World Heritage site by UNESCO, visiting Melk, one of the country's most important baroque abbeys en route.

Tour 20

Vienna is a wonderful city, crowned by the green Wienerwald hills, with vineyards almost reaching its suburbs and traditional inns (*Heuriger*) selling new wine on its outskirts. Despite a reputation for stiff formality, it's more likely these days to attract visitors who want to have fun as well as to appreciate the city's majestic architecture. You can do both in Vienna, still the proud Imperial city, the world capital of music and the venue for a thousand exhibitions. It's impossible, looking at the large number of city theme tours, not to find one that suits you. Schloss Schönbrunn, southwest of the city, is a popular excursion.

Tour 21

The highlights of this tour northwest of Vienna are two river valleys, both with cultural and natural highlights. The Kamptal,

Inside the museum of baroque art in Vienna's Belvedere

surrounded by far-reaching forests and vineyards, reveals intriguing examples of its past along a scenic road that follows the course of the Kamp river. Further north is the Thaya river – or, rather, the two Thaya rivers that meet at Raab – which marks the profile of this region on the border with Moravia, where, over the millennia, it has carved out contrasting landscapes of extraordinary beauty.

Tour 22

The Weinviertel region extends north of Vienna into gentle hills cultivated with vines and boundless expanses of wheat fields. This is a place for relaxed exploration and frequent food-and-wine stops. Not far from the border with Moravia, you turn south towards the Danube across the fertile Marchfeld plain and the lush Donauland river woods.

Tour 23

A totally different landscape and climate confronts you on this tour. After seeing how the ancient Romans lived at Carnuntum, you travel from the Danube plain to northern Burgenland and the Neusiedler See, a great marshy lake that dominates the landscape around its expanse of nearly 40km (25 miles). From the southern tip of the lake, you quickly come to the capital of Burgenland, Eisenstadt, former base of the powerful Hungarian Esterházy family and of the composer Joseph Haydn (1732–1809).

Tour 24

The centres of the southern Wienerwald reveal the strong influence of the Habsburgs and of Vienna's aristocracy. Mansions and castles along the way are interrupted by a journey through the mountains of Lower Austria, a summer and winter holiday destination, and you can visit the spas of Bad Vöslau and Baden bei Wien on the way back.

Tour 25

This final tour is a themed route that explores the castles that formed the Burgenland defence line against invaders from the east – Turks in particular. Along the way you take a detour to visit the splendid Wechsel mountain region, between Styria and Lower Austria, enjoyable all year round.

History &
Nature

From St Pölten, the youngest *Länder* capital (1968) with the oldest code of civic law (1159), you follow the Traisen river across eastern Mostviertel towards Styria and the sanctuary of Mariazell, along the baroque, iron and pilgrimage routes.

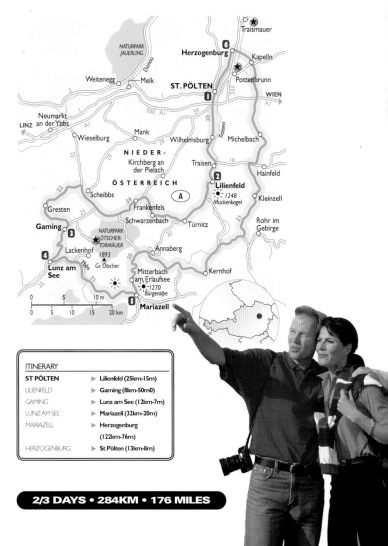

ITINERARY

ST PÖLTEN	►	**Lilienfeld (25km-15m)**
LILIENFELD	►	**Gaming (8km-50m0)**
GAMING	►	**Lunz am See (12km-7m)**
LUNZ AM SEE	►	**Mariazell (32km-20m)**
MARIAZELL	►	**Herzogenburg**
		(122km-76m)
HERZOGENBURG	►	**St Pölten (13km-8m)**

2/3 DAYS • 284KM • 176 MILES

❶ St Pölten, Lower Austria

The old centre of the city of St Pölten – which began life as the Roman settlement of *Aelium Cetium* – bears the stamp of two great baroque architects, Jakob Prandtauer (1660–1726) and his nephew Josef Munggenast (1680–1741), who revamped many of its religious and secular buildings in the early 18th century.

The four squares that form the centre's nucleus are spread over just a few hundred metres. The westernmost is Rathausplatz, on which stand the solemn 16th-century city hall, with a façade by Munggenast (1727), and the Franziskanerkirche, completed in rococo style in 1779 (the altarpieces of the side altars are the work of Kremser Schmidt, who is buried in St Pölten). Walking along Rathausgasse and then Wiener Strasse (in the middle of the pedestrian zone), you come to Riemerplatz, surrounded by fine mansions with wrought-iron balconies and delightful inner courtyards, and Herrenplatz, where the fountain of the 'chattering women' commemorates the daily rendezvous at the market. Near by is Domplatz, with a Romanesque cathedral dedicated to Our Lady of the Assumption, Mariä Himmelfahrt, its sumptuous

St Pölten's modern district on the Traisen river (above); Herrenplatz in the old town (right)

FOR HISTORY BUFFS

Schloss Pottenbrunn, 6km (4 miles) northeast of St Pölten, is home to the Österreichisches Zinnfigurenmuseum, a tin soldier museum. More than 10,000 figurines re-create major events in Austrian history, from the siege of Vienna by the Turks in 1693 to the Battle of the Nations against Napoleon at Leipzig (1813).

A sweeping view of Lilienfeld, an old village in Lower Austria

baroque interior bearing the imprint of Prandtauer (1722). Back in Rathausplatz, follow Linzer Strasse a short way south and admire another 18th-century façade: that of the Institut der Englischen Fräulein, featuring tabernacle-style portals and statues of saints.

When Vienna was made an independent *Land*, St Pölten became the capital of Lower Austria, in 1968. The transfer of government machinery and cultural assets such as the Niederösterreichisches Landesmuseum prompted the construction of a new, ultra-modern district close to the Traisen, the river on which the city stands. One particularly notable structure is the Festspielhaus (festival theatre), designed by Klaus Kada.

ⓘ *Rathausplatz 1*

▶ *Drive south to Lilienfeld on road 20.*

2 Lilienfeld, Lower Austria
The village and Cistercian abbey of Lilienfeld, founded by Duke Leopold VI of Babenberg in 1202, sit on the Traisen river among the green foothills of the Ötscher. Although altered structurally in baroque times, the abbey still has its exemplary 14th-century cloister, its chapter-

BACK TO NATURE

A little way north of Gaming (about 3km/2 miles) is a road leading into the Naturpark Ötscher-Tormäuer, a protected natural area on the north side of the Grosser Ötscher (1,893m/6,211 feet), which is full of waterfalls and an ideal setting for hiking and mountain-bike excursions. After about 8km (5 miles) the road reaches the Schindlhütte refuge hut; from here you can proceed on foot to an interesting subterranean cave (Ötscher-Tropfsteinhöhle).

house, the Dormitorium and the Cellarium of 1250, among the few surviving examples of pure medieval architecture in Austria (with a permanent exhibition on the Babenberg dynasty).

For a spectacular view of Lilienfeld and the valley, take the chair-lift to the Muckenkogel (1,248m/4,094 feet), the starting point for walks and excursions.

ⓘ *Dörflstrasse 4*

▶ *Road 20 leads southwest to Türnitz. Then turn right on to local road 102. Drive via Schwarzenbach to the 30, which you take left for Frankenfels and Winterbach. Continue northwest on the 28 and the 25 to the turning for Scheibbs, where you turn left on to road 22 for Gresten.*

Take local road 92 southbound to Gaming.

3 Gaming, Lower Austria
A pretty holiday resort surrounded by greenery, Gaming owes much of its fame to the Kartause, the charterhouse founded here in 1330 by Duke Albrecht II of Habsburg (buried here with his wife), which was one of the largest in the Germanic area until 1782. Partially converted to a hotel and venue for cultural events, it still has an elegant, soaring Gothic convent church (1332–42); the lovely balconied courtyard leads to rooms inside, including the Prälatensaal and the domed Bibliotheksaal, adorned with 18th-century stuccowork and frescoes.

From the village there are lovely walks (some circular) in the mountainous region around the Ötscher.

ⓘ *Im Markt 1*

▶ *Drive southwest to Lunz am See on road 25.*

SCENIC ROUTES

The road from Lunz am See to Mariazell follows the Ois river valley past glorious views of mountain slopes cloaked with vegetation. Rounding off the journey is the lovely Lake Erlauf, near Mariazell.

4 Lunz am See,
Lower Austria

Between Scheibbs and Lunz you are once more on the Niederösterreichische Eisenstrasse, the 'iron route' that winds around Eisenwurzen (see Tour 16). The Heimat-

> #### RECOMMENDED TRIP
>
> Take the cableway from Mariazell to the Bürgeralpe (1,270m/4,167 feet), a skiing destination and an exceptionally scenic spot. In summer months, you can return to the valley along a pleasant path that passes via the Höhlenstein cave (about two hours).

museum, with a large section on the local mines, is in the pretty Amonhaus (1551), with a façade adorned with sgraffiti. In late May thousands of narcissi flower in the meadows around the nearby Lunzersee, a lake frozen over in winter; you can also swim here in summer.

ℹ️ *Amonstrasse 16*

▶ *Take the scenic road 71 southeast and, at the eastern tip of Erlaufsee, turn right for Mariazell.*

5 Mariazell, Styria

For centuries, pilgrims have set off from all over Europe to a green hollow in northern Styria, on the edge of the eastern Alps. Their destination is Mariazell, the 'Austrian Lourdes', the sanctuary of Maria Geburt. It was founded in 1157 by the Benedictines, where the venerated Magna Mater Austriae ('great mother of Austria'), a Madonna sculpted in the 12th century, is kept.

The 14th-century church was extensively altered between 1644 and 1683 by Domenico Sciassia (as is evident in the façade, with the baroque twin towers flanking the original Gothic tower); the interiors were then embellished by the Fischer von Erlach family, father and son. Modern pilgrims and mountain-lovers can also travel

to Mariazell from St Pölten in the carriages of the Mariazellerbahn, a historic narrow-gauge railway.

ℹ️ *Hauptplatz 13*

▶ *Follow the 20 northbound and, shortly before Annaberg, turn right on to local road 101 for Gscheid. Turn left on to road 21 and pass Kernhof and St Aegyd to reach the turning on the left for local road 133 to Kleinzell. Here, drive north again to the local road that goes via Furth, Reith and Maria Jeutendorf. Turn right on to road 1 and, after 1km (0.6 mile), turn left for Herzogenburg.*

6 Herzogenburg,
Lower Austria

Some of the most eminent and prolific artists of 18th-century Austria are associated with the construction and decoration of the baroque Augustinian abbey of Herzogenburg, the Augustiner Chorherrenstift, originally founded in 1112. The architects were Jakob Prandtauer, Josef Munggenast and Fischer von Erlach the Elder, the painters Daniel Gran, Bartolomeo and Martino Altomonte. There are notable collections of Gothic and baroque art in the Stiftsmuseum.

ℹ️ *Rathausplatz 22*

▶ *Return to Sankt Pölten on the S33 dual carriageway southbound.*

> #### FOR CHILDREN
>
> The mysterious world of dinosaurs can be explored in the Saurierpark at Traismauer (north of Herzogenburg). The park is inhabited by huge and frightening giant lizards (fortunately only life-size sculptures).

The great abbey of Herzogenburg

North of the
Danube

3 DAYS • 304KM • 189 MILES

This journey past woods and vineyards, abbeys and castles starts on the banks of the Danube – and the Krems – in a town with a medieval heritage and a fine old centre.

ITINERARY

KREMS AN DER DONAU	▶ Zwettl (50km-31m)
ZWETTL	▶ Gmünd (41km-25m)
GMÜND	▶ Weitra (11km-7m)
WEITRA	▶ Rappottenstein (41km-25m)
RAPPOTTENSTEIN	▶ Grein (59km-37m)
GREIN	▶ Ybbs an der Donau (22km-14m)
YBBS AN DER DONAU	▶ Melk (28km-17m)
MELK	▶ Spitz an der Donau (19km-12m)
SPITZ AN DER DONAU	▶ Weissenkirchen in der Wachau (5km-3m)
WEISSENKIRCHEN IN DER WACHAU	▶ Dürnstein (6)km-4m)
DÜRNSTEIN	▶ Göttweig (13km-8m)
GÖTTWEIG	▶ Krems an der Donau (9km-5m)

Travelling on the Danube in the Wachau region

ⓘ *Undstrasse 6, Krems an der Donau*

▶ *Take local road **73** northwest and, after about 6km (4.5 miles), turn right for Gföhl; here follow the **37** to Rastenfeld, then go northwest on road **38** to Zwettl.*

❶ Zwettl, Lower Austria
Three artificial lakes stretch to the east of the medieval town of Zwettl; you can stop for a swim on the shores of the western-most, the Ottenstein Stausee, which, with its elongated form and high, wooded shoreline, evokes the scenery of the Scandinavian fiords.

The famous Cistercian abbey of Zwettl, the Zisterzienserstift, stands in the woods to the east of town, at the tip of the lake, and is notable for its mixture of three architectural styles. Founded in 1137, it was altered in Gothic (14th century) and then baroque (1722–27) style. Of particular note are the late-Romanesque cloisters, with their elegant pavilion and hexagonal fountain (Brunnenhaus), and the Gothic choir with 14 radial chapels (1360–83).

ⓘ *Gartenstrasse 3*

▶ *After travelling about 3km (2 miles) north on the **36**,*

*bear right for Gerotten-Schwarzenau. Turn left on to the **E49/303** and follow this to Schrems. Here, drive to Gmünd on road **41**, to the southwest.*

❷ Gmünd, Lower Austria
The Waldviertel's characteristic calcareous rocks took on magical significance in Celtic imagery, and still make a profound impression. At the Naturpark Blockhaide, on the northern outskirts of Gmünd, you can walk from monolith to monolith and learn about their geology, mythology and history.

Gmünd itself is an historic border town, across the Laisnitz river from Czech territory. You can see the work of Lower Austrian glass-workers and local stonecutters in displays

---

SPECIAL TO...

There are several treats for all the family along the Märchenschlossstrasse, the 'fairytale castle way', which on this tour visits Rosenau, Gmünd, Schwarzenau, Krumau, Gfhöl and Weissenkirchen. They include exhibitions of puppets and costumed dolls from all over the world. Good examples can be seen at the Märchenhaus & Puppenmuseum in Schloss Rosenau, between Weitra and Rappottenstein.

---

at the Glassmuseum and Steinmuseum.

ⓘ *Schremser Strasse 6*

▶ *Continue along road **41** to Weitra.*

❸ Weitra, Lower Austria
The historic stronghold of Weitra, partly surrounded by its old medieval walls and dominated by a mighty Renaissance castle (1590–1606), has an interesting Museum Alte Textilfabrik (textile art museum), an obligatory stop on the Waldviertler Textilstrasse (see also Tour 21).

The trains of the Wald-viertler Schmalspurbahn, a narrow-gauge local railway stop at the picturesque local station on their 43km (27-mile) journey between Gmünd and Gross Gerungs. In summer there are special tourist outings in period carriages.

ⓘ *Rathausplatz 1*

▶ *Take the **119** and then local road **71**, which continues southeast towards Zwettl. Once past Jagenbach, turn right for Schloss Rosenau, and here turn right again on to the local road for Gross-gerungs. At the crossroads with the **38**, continue left for Gross Meinharts, after which you turn right on to local road **7309** for Rappottenstein.*

4 Rappottenstein, Lower Austria

Burg Rappottenstein is a mighty fortress guarding the nearby village of the same name and the spot where the Kamp river forms from its subsidiaries, the Kleiner Kamp and the Grosser Kamp.

The castle's size and strength hint at the strategic importance of this area, the Waldviertel. Its polygonal keep was part of the original Kuenring castle (12th century); the five outer courtyards and seven gates are 16th-century additions.

Nowadays the castle is a setting for musical concerts.

i No 39

▶ *Follow road 124 southwest across Arbesbach to Königswiesen; here turn left on road 119a/119 for Grein.*

5 Grein, Upper Austria

Before the construction of the great dam and the Ybbs-Persenbeug hydroelectric station, sailors dreaded the treacherous stretch of the Danube between Grein and Ybbs, in the Strudengau valley. Various methods of negotiating the river feature in the Oberösterreichisches Schiffahrtsmuseum (Museum of Navigation) in Schloss Greinburg, the Renaissance castle that dominates the delightful surroundings of the attractive little town of Grein on the Danube.

i Stadtplatz 7

The compact Burg Rappottenstein, whose original nucleus dates from the 12th century

▶ *Follow the left bank of the Danube along road 3 to the viaduct that crosses the river. Ybbs is about 2km (1 mile) along the 25.*

6 Ybbs an der Donau, Lower Austria

The former Roman and medieval stronghold of Ybbs marks the beginning of the lovely Wachau region on the Danube, known as the 'smile of Austria'. At its westernmost section it takes the name of Nibelungengau (the anonymous author of the 13th-century *Nibelungen* epic came from this area).

There are unparalleled views of the river, the valley and the pre-Alps to the south from the terrace of the baroque sanctuary of Maria Taferl, reached from the other side of the Danube (13km/8 miles northeast).

Continuing for 6km (4.5 miles) in the same direction, you will reach Schloss Artstetten, where Archduke Franz Ferdinand and his wife, killed in Sarajevo in 1914, were buried.

The castle houses the permanent Für Herz und Krone ('for heart and crown') exhibition, illustrating the fatal

SCENIC ROUTES

The two parallel roads that wind along either side of the Danube in the Wachau, between Ybbs and Krems (about 40km/25 miles), have terrific views of one of the most beautiful river landscapes in Europe. Along the green banks are vineyards and apricot orchards (blossoming in April), as well as churches, castles and abbeys. In 2000 UNESCO designated the Wachau a World Heritage Site.

events of the final days of the Habsburg monarchy.

ℹ️ *Hauptplatz 1*

▶ *Cross the river again and follow road 3 to Emmersdorf, where a bridge crosses to the opposite bank of the Danube and Melk.*

7 Melk, Lower Austria
Melk abbey will be familiar to anyone who enjoyed *The Name of the Rose*, Umberto Eco's medieval whodunnit, later made into a film. Adso, the novel's narrator, comes from this Benedictine complex overlooking the Danube, a spiritual and cultural centre since 1089, and given a baroque overhaul by Jakob Prandtauer and Josef Munggenast (1702–36). A guided tour gives you a glimpse of the historic

documents and artworks in the gallery and imperial apartments (including the golden Melk Cross of 1365), the frescoes in the Marmorsaal (marvellous Danube valley views from the adjacent terrace) and the library's 90,000-plus books. The striking façade of the abbey church (clearly visible from outside the complex) is one of Prandtauer's most balanced and harmonious designs. Inside are statues and gilded altarwork by Antonio Beduzzi (1727–35).

End your visit to Melk with a boat trip on the Danube, or take a relaxing stop in Hauptplatz, where you can enjoy a coffee while admiring the baroque façades of the surrounding houses. Alternatively, you can explore the nearby Dunkerstainerwald woods.

ℹ️ *Babenbergerstrasse 1*

▶ *Cross the Danube again and follow road 3 to Spitz.*

8 Spitz an der Donau, Lower Austria
Spitz stands on a rise known as Tausendeimerberg (the 'mountain of a thousand vats'). Vine-growing and wine production are essential to the

---

RECOMMENDED WALK

From Melk, you can take a two-hour walk through natural surroundings along Leopold Böck-Weg to reach Schloss Shallaburg, one of the most beautiful Renaissance castles in Austria (1572–1600).

SCENIC ROUTES

A lovely scenic route starts from Wachau Strasse (left bank of the Danube) and climbs to the Jauerling vantage point (959m/3,146 feet), where the view sweeps over the surrounding Naturpark Jauerling-Wachau (hiking paths), the Waldviertel and the Wachau.
Halfway there, you can stop at the Gothic sanctuary of Maria Laach (14th century) and admire the venerated painting known as the Six-fingered Madonna; look at the hand holding the rosary.

---

local economy, here and all over the Wachau. In the shade of the vineyards, between one tasting and another, you can stroll past old houses adorned with frescoes (such as the Rathaus) and visit the ruins of Hinterhaus castle (13th century), the 14th-century Pfarrkirche St Mauritius, with an altarpiece by Kremser Schmidt (1718–1801), and the Schiffahrtsmuseum,

Vineyards on the banks of the Danube at Weissenkirchen in der Wachau

FOR HISTORY BUFFS

In the village opposite the ruins of Aggstein, visit the site where the famous Palaeolithic (25,000 BC) statuette Willendorf Venus was found. This 11cm (4in) figurine, with rounded forms evoking female fertility, is kept in the Naturhistorisches Museum, in Vienna.

dedicated to the history of navigation on the Danube.

i *Mittergasse 3a*

▶ *Road 3 continues to Weissenkirchen.*

🈹 **Weissenkirchen in der Wachau,** Lower Austria

Together with nearby Joching, Wösendorf and St Michael, this delightful village overlooking the left bank of the Danube is the most important wine-producing area in the Wachau. The wonderful Renaissance Teisenhoferhof mansion (1542), overlooking the market square and housing the Wachau-

museum, hosts conferences and seminars for the Weinakademie (the wine academy).

Take a stroll along the Danube promenade, or climb the steps to the 15th-century fortified church of Mariä Himmelfahrt, before refuelling at one of the many *Heurigen*, traditional inns run by local wine-producers.

i *No 32*

▶ *Continue along road 3 to Dürnstein.*

🈸 **Dürnstein,** Lower Austria

The first view of Dürnstein is the towering blue and white bell tower of the abbey church and the 12th-century ruins of Kuenring castle, high over the town. The abbey was given a baroque facelift by Jakob Prandtauer between 1720 and 1733, with M Steinl and Josef Munggenast adding their contribution to the Stiftskirche Maria Himmelfahrt.

Dürnstein's town centre is still surrounded by old walls and centres on Hauptstrasse, a pretty, romantic street lined with

fine 16th- to 17th-century houses with overhanging storeys.

i *No 25*

▶ *Follow road 3 to the bridge over the Danube to Mautern, where you turn southeast on to the local road for St Pölten to Furth-Göttweig.*

🈴 **Göttweig,** Lower Austria

This tour into the Wachau ends on a high note, with a climb to the Benedictine abbey of Göttweig, known as the 'Montecassino of Austria' for its wonderful position on a green hillside. The splendid baroque complex was designed by Lucas von Hildebrandt and was rebuilt by several craftsmen between 1720 and 1740, after the original 11th-century abbey was almost totally destroyed by fire. Around 60 monks still live in the abbey, and to find out about their daily routine you can visit the permanent Klostergang exhibition, attend prayers and even stay in a special reception area. Amazing views of the Danube and the Wachau open out from the terrace of the famous restaurant annexed to the abbey.

i *Untere Landstrasse 1*

▶ *Take the local road northwards to link up with the S33 dual carriageway to Krems.*

FOR HISTORY BUFFS

Richard the Lionheart was imprisoned in Dürnstein castle on his return from the third crusade. According to legend, he was saved by his minstrel, who heard a response from the castle dungeons while strumming the king's favourite song. In fact, he was freed after paying a huge ransom.

The tower of Dürnstein's Stiftskirche, on the bank of the Danube

Vienna

2/3 DAYS

Superb architecture and stunning museum collections are just two reasons to visit the Danube capital. No wonder UNESCO has seen fit to make Vienna's Innere Stadt (old centre) and Schloss Schönbrunn World Heritage Sites.

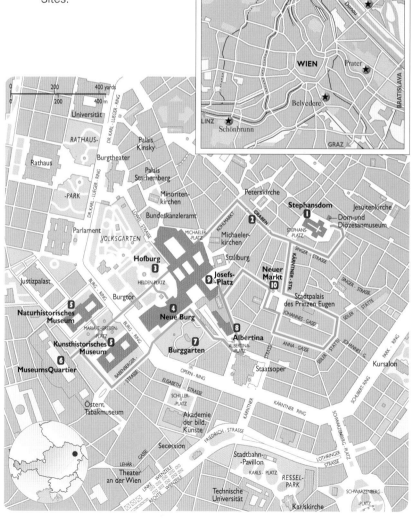

ℹ️ *Albertinaplatz*

▶ *Cars are banned in the Kärtner Strasse-Graben-Kohlmarkt ring, but you can park in the Kurparkzonen (short-stay pay car parks) found in Bezirke (city districts) numbers 1 (Innere Stadt) to 9, and in the 20th. A special card for hotel residents allows one day's free parking. The Vienna Card gives free access to public transport. Alternatively, it's easy to cycle around Vienna (hire available); cycle lanes are marked throughout the city.*

❶ Stephansdom

The cathedral of St Stephen dominates central Stephansplatz, a busy gathering-place on fine evenings. The Viennese have a particularly soft spot for the cathedral's south tower, Steffl, 136m (446 feet) tall, and the monumental Pummerin, the bell housed in the unfinished north tower. The great portal and the 'heathen towers' on the façade (12th century) are all that remains of the original Romanesque church. The internal structure of a nave and two wide aisles, and the rich pinnacle decorations on the exterior, are the results of a programme of alterations begun in 1359 and not completed until the 16th century. The ubiquitous baroque style is limited here to the aisle altars. Note in particular the details of the splendid pulpit by Anton Pilgram (1514–15) and the red

The glittering tiles on the roof of the Stephansdom and the silhouette of the famous Steffl

FOR HISTORY BUFFS

In accordance with Spanish ritual, until the 19th century the viscera, heart and remains of deceased Habsburgs were buried separately. In Vienna urns containing the viscera are kept in the cathedral catacombs, the hearts are in the Augustinerkirche and the actual tombs can be visited in the crypt of the Kapuzinerkirche.

marble mausoleum of Emperor Friedrich III, built between 1467 and 1513. In the Katakomben (catacombs, entrance in left transept) are the tombs of many nobles and prelates.

▶ *Follow Domgasse to the junction on the right with Grünangergasse. Turn right again into Singerstrasse and cross Stock-im-Eisen-Platz (note the ultra-modern Haas-Haus on the corner).*

❷ Graben

The baroque column that dominates Graben square is the greatest of the Pestsäulen – 'plague columns' – found in towns all over Austria, consecrated to the Holy Trinity in 1693 to commemorate a devastating outbreak of the plague. It was proposed by Emperor Leopold I and he is depicted at the base, kneeling in thanksgiving. Today it's a landmark in an area renowned for its quality shopping and elegant Viennese cafés.

▶ *The Graben leads on the left into Kohlmarkt. Further along you will find the Hofburg.*

3 Hofburg

The Kohlmarkt, once the coal market, is now a prestigious business address. If you're sweet-toothed don't miss the Demel cake shop, at No 14, a rival since 1786 of the famous shop at the Hotel Sacher in Philarmonikerstrasse.

In Michaelerplatz you come to the monumental 19th-century entrance of the Hofburg, the imperial Habsburg residence until 1918 and a city within the city. Its rotunda, crowned with a distinctive dome, opens on the right at the entrance to the Kaiserappartaments, where you can visit rooms once occupied by Franz Joseph and his beloved 'Sissi' (see page 139) and the Silberkammer, with its collection of court silver and tableware.

Continuing beyond the rotunda you come to the spacious courtyard of the In der Burg, where tournaments were held in the 16th century. It's now enclosed by reception buildings dating from four different phases of construction between the 16th and the 18th century.

The oldest wing, on the left, features a garish Renaissance gateway leading to the Schweizerhof, the courtyard of the original 13th-century castle (Alte Burg). Here are the entrances to the old Burgkapelle, the imperial chapel that resounds on Sundays with the sweet voices of the Vienna Boys' Choir, and to the Schatzkammer, depositary of the Habsburgs' treasure.

Back in the In der Burg, go left across a passage in the Leopoldinischer Trakt to emerge in the vast Heldenplatz, overlooked from the opposite side by the Burgtor, the isolated neo-classical monumental 'castle gate' that separates the Hofburg square and complex from the busy Ringstrasse. With a little

FOR CHILDREN

No more than half an hour's walk east of the centre (a couple of underground stops) is Vienna's great green space, the Prater park, extending between the Danube and its canal over 1,712 hectares (4,230 acres). It's an ideal place for families to enjoy a few hours of relaxation and amusement. Attractions include the giant fairground wheel (the famous Riesenrad featured in *The Third Man*, Carol Reed's 1949 movie); cycling along the Hauptallee, a 5km (3-mile) straight road through woods and meadows, or riding the charming miniature train.

imagination, you can hear horses pawing the ground and squeaking carriages entering the palace through the vast forecourt on gala occasions.

The interior of the Stephansdom, with its bundle pillars that support the nave and aisles

RECOMMENDED EXCURSION

After walking through the city along the Donaukanal see the real Danube on one of the mini-cruises (Apr–Oct) from Schwedenbrücke (5 minutes on foot from the cathedral). Beyond the Nussdorfer Schleusenanlage, a lock designed by Otto Wagner, you can see the modern buildings of the UNO-City business centre, on the east bank of the river. Follow the coast of Donauinsel, an artificial island, almost all the way, and return to the Donaukanal and the Schwedenbrücke.

4 Neue Burg

The Neue Burg, the new castle wing commissioned by Franz Joseph, stands back from Heldenplatz on the left. The entrance at the centre of the façade leads to the Ephesos-

The great Maria-Theresien-Platz

Museum, displaying a collection of artefacts found at Ephesos (1st to 4th century BC); the Waffernsammlung, exhibiting old weapons and armour, and the Sammlung alter Musik-instrumente, a collection of around 300 historical musical instruments. The gateway of the outermost Corps de Logis provides access to the Museum für Völkerkunde, an ethnographic museum.

▶ *Cross the Burgring and enter Maria-Theresien-Platz.*

5 Kunsthistorisches Museum and Naturhistorisches Museum

Between 1872 and 1891 Gottfried Semper and Karl von Hasenauer constructed twin buildings on the opposite sides of Maria-Theresien-Platz to house the royal collections of fine arts and natural history.

The former are in the Kunsthistorisches Museum, one of the most prestigious collections of its kind in the world, with exhibitions arranged in 91 rooms ranging from ancient Egyptian and Oriental art to tapestries (900 Flemish and French pieces of the 16th to 18th centuries), coins (500,000 in all) and fine arts and artefacts (including the famous salt cellar in embossed gold by Benvenuto Cellini, c1540). On the first floor is the Gemäldegalerie, a spectacular picture gallery with the largest collection of works by Pieter Bruehgel the Elder.

Empress Maria Theresa's consort, Francis of Lorraine, was fascinated by natural history and science, and founded the Naturhistorisches Museum, which contains an astounding 1,000 meteorites, 3 million fossils and 6 million insects.

▶ *Maria-Theresien-Platz is adjacent to Museumsplatz, which leads to the MuseumsQuartier.*

6 MuseumsQuartier

As demonstrated by the Hofburg's museums, Vienna likes to keep its collections in buildings that are works of art in

Relaxing in the Burggarten, the 'castle garden' created between 1819 and 1823

themselves. The Museums-Quartier, inaugurated in 2001 on the site of the old imperial stables, continues this tradition with three ultra-modern buildings of great visual impact. The Kunsthalle is the venue for contemporary art exhibitions; the Leopold Museum of modern Austrian art has the world's most important collection of works by Egon Schiele; and the Museum Moderner Kunst Stiftung Ludwig (MUMOK) exhibits major works of modern and contemporary art. Also within the museum district are open-air bars and restaurants, fountains and benches, where culture vultures can take a break.

▶ From Museumsplatz follow the back of the Kunsthistorisches Museum along Babenbergerstrasse, cross the Burgring again and enter the Burggarten.

BACK TO NATURE

Nature enthusiast Francis of Lorraine set up the Schönbrunn Tiergarten, the world's oldest zoo, in 1752. Its 750 residents, including domestic and exotic species, now live among the futuristic structures that lie within this baroque environment.

---

7 Burggarten
The imperial gardens, an elegant and tranquil oasis in the city, were created between 1819 and 1823 in place of fortifications demolished by Napoleon. The Palmenhaus is a Jugendstil (Austrian art-deco) conservatory on the northeast side of the garden. Hundreds of butterflies fly free in the Schmetterlinghaus and you can enjoy a good cup of Viennese coffee in the annexed café.

▶ In the garden, behind the Palmenhaus, follow Augustinerbastei and emerge in Albertinaplatz (on the corner is the booking office for Vienna's four state theatres).

8 Albertina
The recently restored Albertina building occupies the eastern section of the Augustinian convent, in turn incorporated into the southeast portion of the Hofburg.

The famous graphic art collection housed here is named after its initiator, architect Albert von Sachsen-Teschen, who lived in the palace from 1795 with his wife, Archduchess Marie Christine (favourite daughter of Empress Maria Theresa, who granted her the rare privilege of marrying by free choice).

Over a million drawings, engravings, prints and lithographs dating from the 14th century to the present day make the Graphische Sammlung the world's most prestigious collection of its kind.

▶ Follow Augustinerstrasse to Josefsplatz.

The Donnerbrunnen in Neuer Markt, a masterpiece by the sculptor Georg Raphael Donner

9 Josefsplatz

Returning towards the starting point of the Hofburg visit, you end up in Josefsplatz, named after Emperor Josef II, at the outermost section of the palace, the Stallburg (old court stables of 1558). Behind the equestrian monument to the emperor stands the Nationalbibliothek building, erected between 1723 and 1737 by Joseph Emanuel Fischer von Erlach the Younger to his father's design. Of interest besides the rich library, which contains 2 million books (including a Gutenberg Bible), are the huge Prunksaal, the former study, lavishly decorated and frescoed, and the Globenmuseum, with a collection of globes and maps.

On the left side of the square (looking towards the Nationalbibliothek) you enter the Augustinerkirche, a Gothic convent church closely associated with the Habsburgs in life and in death, having witnessed many elaborate wedding ceremonies and housing the Herzgruft der Habsurger (crypt), where the hearts of Habsburgs who died between 1637 and 1878 are kept in silver urns.

The wing of the riding school on the opposite side of the square, is where the famous Lipizzaner horses of the Spanische Hofreitschule (Spanish Riding School) perform. The story of these white stallions of Iberian origin, now bred at Piber in Styria, is told at the Lipizzaner Museum, in the Stallburg (entrance on Reitschulgasse).

▶ Go back along Augustinerstrasse and turn left into Dorotheergasse (note the Dorotheum at No 17 and the Jüdisches Museum der Stadt Wien at No 11). Turn right into Plankeng and right again into Neuer Markt.

10 Neuer Markt

The 12th-century 'new market square' contains the so-called Donnerbrunnen, the Providentia fountain sculpted by G R Donner (1739). The real attraction of the Neuer Markt, however, is the Kapuzinerkirche, a deceptively unassuming church beneath which are the rooms of the imperial crypt (Kaisergruft), where 140 members of the Habsburg family lie in brass and zinc sarcophagi.

▶ At the southern tip of the square, turn into Marco d'Aviano-Gasse, then turn right into Kärntnerstrasse and left into Annagasse. Emerging in Seilerstätte (at the junction is the Haus der Musik), follow this to the left before turning left into Himmelpfortgasse, which leads to Kärntnerstrasse. Follow this to the right and return to the Stephansdom.

EXCURSION

▶ You can drive to Schloss Schönbrunn from the centre

(Opernring, on the south side of the Burggarten) on Operngasse-Friedrichstrasse-Linke Wienzeile (car parks inside the castle). A much better and easier option, though, is to use public

SPECIAL TO...

Around 1720, the hero of the victory over the Turks, Eugene of Savoy (1663–1736), had a splendid summer residence built in baroque style on the outskirts of Vienna (now part of the city). Separated by the park, the Oberes and Unteres Belvedere house, respectively, a gallery of 19th- and 20th-century Austrian art and a museum of baroque art. At the southernmost tip of the park, visit the Alpengarten, a botanical garden of alpine flora.

transport (U4 underground line from Schwedenplatz, on Donaukanal).

Schloss Schönbrunn

The Habsburgs' summer residence was built in the early 18th century on the site of Emperor Maximilian II's 16th-century hunting lodge. The new palace was a particular favourite of Maria Theresa's, who had it embellished between 1744 and 1749. During a visit you can admire the imperial apartments on the first floor, the austere bedchamber where Franz Joseph died on 21 November, 1916, and the rooms where his wife Sissi (Elisabeth of Bavaria) retreated to write.

Across the park, with its splendid flower parterre, is the Neptune fountain (1780) and, on its right, the Irrgarten, a new maze of hedges laid out according to the original design (and particularly popular with children).

From here, climb to the top of the Gloriette mound, a neo-classical portico which has a beautiful view of the castle and Vienna behind it. In the wing that runs to the left (as you enter) around the Ehrenhof (the vast driveway) is the Hofbackstube, where a modern 'court baker' imparts the secrets of traditional Viennese apple strudel.

Schloss Schönbrunn below, and, above, inside the Belvedere

THE HABSBURGS

The history of Austria is inextricably bound to that of the Habsburgs, until 1918 the ruling dynasty of an empire that, during the reign of Charles V (1519–56), at the peak of its power, extended beyond Europe. By using strategic alliance and marriage, rather than wars of conquest, the family enjoyed a remarkable rise to power, graduating from dukes to archdukes and, from 1438, emperors of the Holy Roman Empire, and finally (from 1804) emperors of Austria.

Vienna is the main focus of any tour of locations connected with the Habsburgs. The imperial capital has a wealth of associations, including the Hofburg and its treasures, the crypt in the Augustinerkirche containing the emperors' hearts, the Kaisergruft (imperial crypt) in the Kapuzinerkirche and Schloss Schönbrunn (see Tour 20). Franz Josef's favourite dish of boiled beef (*Tafelspitz*) can be found on the menu of any typical Viennese restaurant, and *Kaiserkitch* – postcards and figurines of the aged emperor – fill the souvenir shops.

All over Austria there are monuments, monasteries and castles steeped in Austrian imperial history. It's not hard to imagine Maximilian I looking out from the Goldenes Dachl in Innsbruck (see Tour 4), or his father, Friedrich III, in his golden exile in the Linz Schloss (see Tour 15); Maria Theresa in mourning, after the wedding of her son in the Hofburg in Innsbruck (see Tour 4); or even Franz Joseph and Sissi in their Kaiservilla retreat at Bad Ischl (see Tour 14).

throne by default, in the absence of an heir to the Swabian dynasty. So the giddy ascent of the Habsburgs was based on the chance extinction of two dynasties and the enterprise of Rudolf himself.

Albert II, the first emperor

In the 14th century Carinthia, Tirol, Istria and Trieste were added to the territories inherited by Rudolf's heirs. In 1438 Duke Albert V (1404–39) played his ace card by marrying the daughter of Sigismund, the German Emperor of the Holy Roman Empire. In one fell swoop he had gained the kingdoms of Bohemia and Hungary and became Albert II, inheriting his father-in-law's imperial title. This was the first of a long series of dynastic marriages that inspired the famous motto: 'Let others war; thou, happy Austria, wed.'

Maximilian I, gathering power

Continuing this successful policy, Maximilian I, who became emperor in 1493, judiciously married Maria, heir to the throne of Burgundy, thus ensuring the annexation of much of the Low Countries. The marriage of his son Philip brought Aragon and Castile into the fold, and his grandson Charles V inherited Spain and its overseas colonies, parts of Italy and the Netherlands, as well as the dynasty's German and Austrian possessions.

In 1556 Charles retired from power, leaving Spain, the Netherlands, the Italian territories and the overseas possessions to his son Philip II, while Austria was inherited by Charles's brother, Emperor Ferdinand I, who would subsequently also govern Bohemia and Hungary. By the time of Charles V's death the Habsburg legacy had been split, but the Austrian branch kept its imperial title.

Rudolf I, father of a ducal family

The Babenberg family died out in 1246, after 270 years ruling the Eastern March, or Ostmark (origin of the name Österreich – Austria). In 1278 Rudolf I, the German sovereign, took possession of Austria, which then corresponded more or less to today's Upper Austria, Lower Austria and Burgenland,

Portrait of Emperor Franz Joseph and Elisabeth of Bavaria (Sissi), dated 1851

Carniola (part of Slovenia) and Styria. Rudolf had begun his career as the mere Count of Habsburg, a name taken from the 11th-century family seat, Habichtsburg ('Hawk's Castle') in Switzerland. He had succeeded to the German

Maria Theresa, an enlightened sovereign

There followed a troubled period of Turkish invasions (1529 and 1683), outbreaks of the plague, a war of succession following the extinction of the Spanish Habsburg line and the eventual transfer of Spain to the French Bourbons in 1706.

Charles VI died in 1740 without a male heir, but had taken the precaution of establishing his daughter, Maria Theresa's right to succession. Her marriage to Francis of Lorraine, the future Holy Roman Emperor, created the new house of Habsburg-Lorraine, though some territory was lost to Prussia during the War of Austrian Succession (1740–48). During her 40-year reign Maria Theresa had 18 children, including the unfortunate Marie Antoinette, and instituted many reforms, earning the real affection of her subjects.

Franz Joseph and Sissi

Napoleon abolished the Holy Roman Empire in 1801 and the Habsburgs' personal domains became the Austrian Empire, presently to be divided into two administrations and known as Austria-Hungary – the Dual Monarchy. During the 19th century the Habsburgs annexed part of Poland (Galicia), and in 1908 Bosnia and Herzegovina were annexed under Hungarian government.

The last great period of the Habsburg empire came with the long reign of Franz Joseph (1848–1916), who met and fell for his future wife, 15-year-old Elisabeth of Bavaria ('Sissi') at Bad Ischl. The marriage was not a happy experience for Elisabeth, who refused to eat during her obligatory visits to Schönbrunn and the Hofburg, and was increasingly isolated from the Emperor, who was distracted by affairs of state.

A number of violent deaths afflicted those years – the shooting in Mexico of the Emperor's brother, Maximilian (1867); the violent deaths of the heir to the throne, Rudolf, and his young lover (1889); the assassination of Elisabeth at the hand of an Italian anarchist in Geneva in 1898; and finally the murder of Archduke Franz Ferdinand (1914) in Sarajevo, which sparked off the events culminating in World War I.

Franz Joseph's own death in 1916 marked the end of an era that had endured almost 700 years. After Karl I's brief reign, at the end of World War I the Habsburgs were forced into exile. Karl's wife Zita lived for over 70 years after her husband's death and died in 1989 in her late 90s.

Above: Maria Theresa with her children in a painting by V L Maurice
Below: Emperor Franz Joseph

The Forests
North of Vienna

The Waldviertel and Wienerwald northeast of Vienna have many cultural, natural and gastronomic delights. Medieval towns sit among the vineyards and the forests of the dramatic Waldviertel frame mighty fortresses on the Bohemian and Moravian borders.

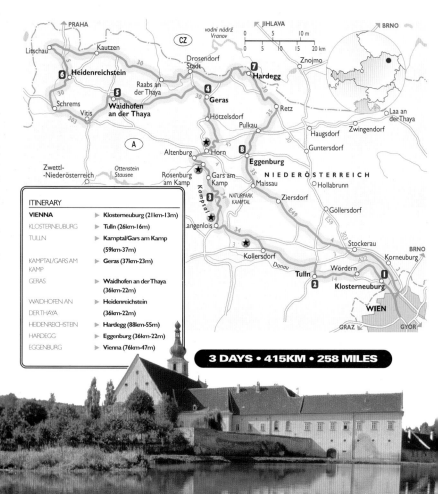

ITINERARY

VIENNA	▶	Klosterneuburg (21km–13m)
KLOSTERNEUBURG	▶	Tulln (26km–16m)
TULLN	▶	Kamptal/Gars am Kamp (59km–37m)
KAMPTAL/GARS AM KAMP	▶	Geras (37km–23m)
GERAS	▶	Waidhofen an der Thaya (36km–22m)
WAIDHOFEN AN DER THAYA	▶	Heidenreichstein (36km–22m)
HEIDENREICHSTEIN	▶	Hardegg (88km–55m)
HARDEGG	▶	Eggenburg (36km–22m)
EGGENBURG	▶	Vienna (76km–47m)

3 DAYS • 415KM • 258 MILES

i Albertinaplatz, Vienna

▷ From the centre of Vienna,
stay on the western bank of
the Danaukanal and follow
Höhenstrasse northwards to
Klosterneuburg

❶ Klosterneuburg,
Lower Austria

As you arrive from Vienna along
the winding and scenic
Höhenstrasse, the historic town
of Klosterneuburg appears in all
its splendour below the
Kahlenberg (484m/1,588 feet),
crouching between the Danube
and the vineyard-covered hills of
the Wienerwald. Your eye is
immediately drawn to the mass
of the austere Augustinian
abbey, founded in 1106 by the
Margrave Leopold III and the
greatest cultural and artistic
centre in the Austrian March
during the Middle Ages. Its
most precious possession dates
from that time: the Verduner
Altar, a superb altarpiece of 51
enamelled panels by Nicolas of
Verdun (1181). Most of the
abbey complex architecture
dates from the 18th century,
when Emperor Charles VI made
it his Austrian retreat. The new
design by D F D'Allio was
extremely ambitious, and the
existing structure represents
only a quarter of his original
plans.

i Niedermarkt 4

▷ Follow local road 118
northwest and then
southwest across Greifenstein;
at Wördern, take the 14
eastwards to Tulln.

❷ Tulln, Lower Austria

In *The Nibelungen* saga, Tulln, the
seat of the Babenberg dynasty, is
where Attila awaits his
Burgundian bride Kriemhild.
There's more to this pretty little
town than legend, however.
Formerly a major Roman
stronghold on the Danube, it
was fortified again in the 13th
century, when the Romanesque
portal of St Stephen's church
was built, along with the 11-
sided ossuary. More recent work
can be seen in the Egon Schiele
Museum, dedicated to the

The Augustinian abbey of
Klosterneuburg, its towers
enclosing the façade

famous and troubled Austrian
painter who was born at Tulln in
1890.

On the way to Langenlois,
on road 3 from Kollersdorf and
about 2km (1 mile) northwest of
Grafenwörth, is Schloss
Grafenegg, restored between
1840 and 1873 in Tudor style
and considered one of the most
beautiful and romantic castles in
Austria. You can stroll through
the immense English gardens
and, between April and
September, listen to fine music
at one of the Schlosskonzerte
(castle concerts).

i Minoritenplatz 2

RECOMMENDED
WALKS

The area surrounding Tulln
features wetland woods and
marshy meadows, thanks to the
many canals and old
watercourses that interweave
around the Danube. To
appreciate the beauty of this
river environment, walk along
the paths and small roads in the
footsteps of the great
ethnologist Konrad Lorenz,
who studied the geese of the
Danube in Altenberg, between
Klosterneuburg and Tulln.

▶ *A stretch of road 19 to the north leads to road 3; follow this westwards to Kollersdorf; here, turn left on to the 34 in the Kamptal for Langenlois and beyond.*

3 Kamptal, Lower Austria

Between Langenlois and Horn you drive along the Kamp river valley, passing wonderful scenery and several places of historical and cultural interest. After the first gentle slopes covered with vineyards comes the narrowest section of the valley, where river and rock move closer together along the scenic road.

There are so many attractions along the way – castles (Gars am Kamp), fortresses (Rosenburg) and abbeys (Altenburg) – that this area has been designated the Kulturpark Kamptal, a cultural

Demonstrations with birds of prey in the Rosenburg fortress, which rises sheer above the bank of the Kamp river

---

FOR CHILDREN

Children will love the picturesque 16th-century Rosenburg fortress, which rises sheer above the right bank of the Kamptal river, not so much for its rich interiors of period furniture and archaeological artefacts but for the free-flying displays of eagles, hawks, vultures and owls (at 11 and 3). They can also visit the Märchenwelt, a fairy-tale world created within the castle.

---

park that combines 45 sights and institutions demonstrating the valley's natural, geological and cultural diversity.

Two good examples are the Langenlois Heimatmuseum, in the 16th-century Ursin-Haus, with exhibitions on local history and viticulture, and the Höbarth und Madermuseum at Horn, with archaeological and farming exhibitions. The Kulturpark cycle route (450km/280 miles)

---

takes in some interesting excursions, with opportunities to taste local dishes and wines (Grüner Veltliner and Riesling) at the indicated stops.

ⓘ *Hauptplatz 83, Gars am Kamp*

▶ *Continue along road 34 to Rosenburg, and from here northeast to Altenburg on the local road. Road 38 northeast leads to Horn, where you head north on road 4 to Geras.*

4 Geras, Lower Austria

The baroque renovation of the Prämonstratenser-Chorherrenstift (Premonstratensian abbey) of Geras (1736–40) was mainly the work of architect Josef Munggenast and painter Paul Troger. They were responsible for the lovely Marienhof (Yard of our Lady), a courtyard enclosed on three sides, and the frescoes of the Sommerspeisesaal, the summer dining room. A visit to the complex, which also houses

an art academy and a hotel in the 17th-century Schüttkasten, ends with a walk in the fragrant Kräutergarten.

i *Hauptstrasse 16*

▶ *Follow road **30** northwest for about 3km (2 miles), then turn left for Pingerdorf and left again for Japons. Continue west towards Schweinburg and Aigen, where you follow the local road southwest for Gross-Siegharts. Finally, local road **60** leads northwest to Waidhofen.*

5 Waidhofen an der Thaya,
Lower Austria
Waidhofen is an old farming town whose fate has always been linked to its proximity to Bohemia – as demonstrated by the remains of the medieval fortifications. This is one of the 40 stops on the Waldviertler Textilstrasse (Waldviertel Textile Trail), which also visits nearby Gross-Siegharts, 10km (6 miles) southeast.

Textile production played a crucial role in this Lower Austrian region, and in the mid-19th century every family

owned at least one loom. In 1869 over two-thirds of the local population earned a living from textiles. The Erstes Waldviertler Webereimuseum in Waidhofen has some old craft looms and traces the history of weaving up until the present day, with a section dedicated to the latest technology.

i *Hauptplatz 1*

▶ *Road **36** leads southwest to Vitis, where you continue along road **49/303** to Schrems and then take road **30** to Heidenreichstein.*

6 Heidenreichstein,
Lower Austria
The pretty Waldviertel resort of Heidenreichstein grew up around the largest Austrian castle still surrounded by a moat, the 13th-century Wasserburg. In fact, the whole region has more than its fair share of water, in the form of lakes and marshes.

To learn more about the marsh environment visit the Haus des Moores, a natural history museum. Then, to test your knowledge, you can take a wonderful walk in the local

Wasserburg, a castle still surrounded by water-filled moats at Heidenreichstein

Naturpark Hochmoor-Gemeindeau.

i *Litschauer Strasse 18*

▶ *Follow road **5** north to Eisgarn, then turn northwest on local road **63** to Litschau. The local road to the east passes via Leopoldsdorf and*

SPECIAL TO...

An unusual adventure is provided at the Abenteuerpark Anderswelt in Heidenreichstein (no admission for under 8s). This remarkable amusement park sets the scene with the disappearance of two fictional scientists in the mysterious Waldviertel lands, some time in the recent past. With the help of their abandoned diary, visitors follow clues to retrace their steps through thrilling (and frightening) episodes with realistic settings and first-class special effects.

Hardegg's medieval fortress guards the border with Bohemia and Moravia

*Kautzen, where it reaches the **30** for Dobersberg, Raabs, Drosendorf and Riegersburg. Here, turn left on to the main road that leads to Hardegg.*

7 Hardegg, Lower Austria

A whole chain of fortresses once defended the border with Bohemia and Moravia along the banks of the Thaya river. En route, you pass one at Raabs and another at Hardegg, guarding the smallest town in Austria from the height of its rocky peak.

Burg Hardegg, originally dating from 1140 but partially rebuilt in the late 19th century, contains a collection of memorabilia associated with Emperor Maximilian of Habsburg, Emperor of Mexico (1832–67).

i *Pleissing 2*

▶ *Follow the local road southeast to Niederfladnitz, and from here take road **30** to Retz. Turn right on to road **35** for Pulkau, Gross-Reipersdorf and Eggenburg.*

8 Eggenburg, Lower Austria

A scenic walk climbs from the Kanzlerturm, a mighty watchtower, along the medieval walls that still surround Eggenburg, an old stronghold and wine-producing centre (on the Weinviertel wine route).

A good way to explore the town is to follow the Kulturrundgang, a waymarked tour that visits, among other places, the irregular Kornplatz, where the Renaissance sgraffiti-decorated façade of the Gemaltes Haus (Painted House) stands out among other baroque buildings, with its attractive sgraffito paintings.

After stopping to see the Gothic parish church of St Stephan, which echoes Vienna's cathedral in name and internal design, spend some time in the Krahuletz-Museum. This is one of the richest Austrian museums of local history and culture, with collections of minerals, archaeological finds, clocks, costumes and local crafts.

i *Krahuletzplatz 1*

▶ *Continue on road **35** south for Maissau; turn left on to road **4** for Stockerau. The A22 motorway leads back to Vienna.*

The watery and wooded landscape of the Thayatal national park, entered at Hardegg

BACK TO NATURE

Hardegg is the gateway to the Thayatal National Park, extending 25km (15 miles) along the southern bank of the Thaya river and adjacent to the Podyji park, on Czech territory. This protected area was created to try and safeguard the unique Thaya valley, where river erosion of the compact Bohemian plateau has, over thousands of years, fashioned rugged banks in stark contrast with the rolling hills around them.

The Wine District

Travelling from *Heuriger* (wine tavern) to *Keller* (cellar), you reach the stately aristocratic residences of the Marchfeld and woods so dense that you could be in a tropical rain forest.

2 DAYS • 236KM • 147 MILES

ITINERARY

VIENNA	► Korneuburg (20km-12m)
KORNEUBURG	► Mistelbach (49km-30m)
MISTELBACH	► **Asparn an der Zaya** (7km-4m)
ASPARN AN DER ZAYA	► **Gänserndorf (76km-47m)**
GÄNSERNDORF	► **Marchegg (26km-16m)**
MARCHEGG	► Orth an der Donau (26km-16m)
ORTH AN DER DONAU	► Vienna (32km-20m)

RECOMMENDED WALKS

Kellergasse are a major feature of the northern Wienerwald wine-producing region. These are traditional roads running past vineyards and flanked by cellars with whitewashed walls, most of which are open to the public. You can take your pick of places on a stroll along the wine routes such as Poysdorf or Staatz, between Asparn and Zisterdorf.

ⅰ *Albertinaplatz, Vienna*

▷ *Head northeast from the centre of Vienna, cross the Danube and take road **3** at Florisdorf for Korneuburg.*

❶ Korneuburg, Lower Austria

Korneuburg lies in the foothills of the Bisamberg, a mountain which forms the eastern end of the Alps. It is dominated by a Stadtturm (tower) of 1477 (now incorporated in the 19th-century neo-Gothic Rathaus), which makes a handy base for the 4km (2.5-mile) excursion north to Leobendorf and its spectacular castle, Burg Kreuzenstein. It was created in medieval style in the late 19th century by Count Hans Graf Wilczek, who wanted a worthy home for his collection of Gothic art. The museum here has old weapons, furnishings and examples of folk culture.

ⅰ *Hauptplatz 39*

▷ *Drive along the local road northwest to Wiesen, and here turn left for Leitzersdorf. Local road **26** leads north-east to Ernstbrunn via Niederfellabrunn, then you continue to Mistelbach on the **40**.*

❷ Mistelbach, Lower Austria

After learning about the history and customs of Mistelbach on a visit to the Heimatmuseum in the pretty Barockschlössel

(1729), climb one of the two flights of steps leading from the 18th-century parish house to the 14th-century Pfarrkirche St Martin. Its two most treasured possessions are the Schöne Madonna – a 15th-century painting – and the 13th-century ossuary portal.

ⅰ *Hauptplatz 6*

▷ *Local road **35** leads northwest to Asparn.*

❸ Asparn an der Zaya, Lower Austria

Imposing Schloss Asparn, rebuilt in the 17th century on the foundation of a previous castle surrounded by a moat (1421), houses an interesting history museum and, in its parkland, reconstructions of various period dwellings.

Southwest of Asparn is the Naturpark Leiserberge, with 43km (27 miles) of marked paths and countless options for scenic hill walks.

ⅰ *No 169, Asparn an der Zaya*

▷ *Follow local road **3088** north and take the **46** to Staatz. From here drive eastwards on the **219** to Poysdorf. Continue south on the **7/E461** and turn left at Wilfersdorf on to road **40** for Zisterdorf and Dürnkrut. Take local road **11** southwest to Spannberg and Matzen-Reyersdorf, then turn left on to road **220** for Gänserndorf.*

FOR CHILDREN

Children can reflect on the differences between the education of the 18th and 19th centuries and the schools of today on a tour of period classrooms in the Schulmuseum at Michelstetten, 6km (4 miles) west of Asparn an der Zaya.

Burg Kreuzenstein (1874–1906), a beautiful imitation of a medieval mansion at Leobendorf

❹ Gänserndorf, Lower Austria

Gänserndorf Safari-Park, 3km (2 miles) south of town, has 500 species, including lions, zebras, elephants, camels and ostriches. You can visit by car or use the transport provided by the park.

ⅰ *Rathausplatz 1*

▷ *After reaching Obersiedenbrunn travelling south on road **9**, turn left for Schönfeld and Marchegg.*

❺ Marchegg, Lower Austria

The fertile Marchfeld plain is dotted with handsome castles

SPECIAL TO...

The eastern Wienerwald is not only a land of vineyards. Zistersdorf and Matzen lie in the oil-producing region of Lower Austria, where a million tonnes of crude oil are extracted each year – hence the unexpected sight of oil wells among the fields along the way.

built as summer residences for Viennese and Hungarian nobility, but Schloss Marchegg, built by King Ottakar II of Bohemia in 1260, has a longer and more involved history. During the 16th century it was given to Count Salm, heroic defender of Vienna during the first Turkish siege, and underwent major alterations. It now contains a Jagdmuseum (hunting museum) and Afrikanmuseum, with exhibitions about the African continent.

A little way south of Marchegg, and the same distance from Groissenbrunn, are two small baroque castles that once belonged to Prince Eugene of Savoy: Schloss Niederweiden (3km/2 miles south), an elegant hunting

FOR HISTORY BUFFS

Deutch Wagram, 12km (7 miles) southwest of Gänserndorf, was the scene of a memorable battle in July 1809 between the Austrians and Napoleon's army, who took revenge for the defeat suffered two months earlier at Asparn. The local museum has relics of this bloody event, during which more than 100,000 Austrians were killed.

lodge, and the 17th-century Schlosshof (3km/2 miles east), re-designed by Johann Lucas von Hildebrandt in 1725–29.

i Hauptplatz 30

▶ Take road **49** southbound to Engelhartstetten, and here drive west on road **3** to Orth an der Donau.

⑥ Orth an der Donau, Lower Austria

Mighty Orth castle, erected in a wooded area along the Danube in 1137 and rebuilt in the 16th and 17th centuries after its destruction by the Turks, houses no fewer than four museums, dedicated to local culture, the history of navigation on the Danube, fishing, and bee-keeping over the centuries.

i Am Markt 26

▶ Return to Vienna northwest on road **3** and then on the **A23** motorway southwest.

BACK TO NATURE

At Orth an der Donau you will find the information centre of the Nationalpark Donau Auen, a nature park extending along the Danube to the confluence with the Morava river. It comprises central Europe's largest river forest, which provides a habitat for over 5,000 animal species.

TOUR

23

The Danube
& Neusiedler See

This region straddling the Wienerwald and Burgenland has a special appeal for bird-watchers and lovers of fine wine, but there are plenty of other charms to discover in this unusual area on the edge of the boundless Hungarian

puzta (steppe).

2 DAYS • 204KM • 127 MILES

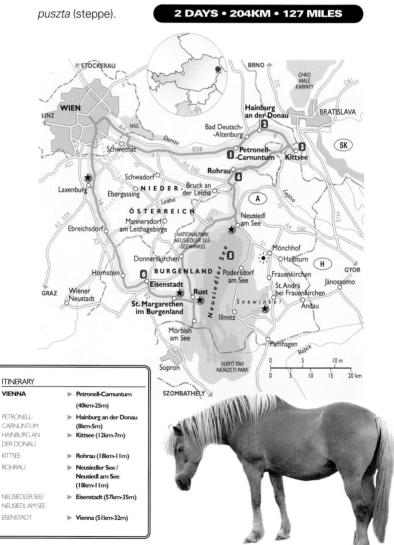

ITINERARY

VIENNA	▶ **Petronell-Carnuntum** (40km-25m)
PETRONELL-CARNUNTUM	▶ **Hainburg an der Donau** (8km-5m)
HAINBURG AN DER DONAU	▶ **Kittsee** (12km-7m)
KITTSEE	▶ **Rohrau** (18km-11m)
ROHRAU	▶ **Neusiedler See / Neusiedl am See** (18km-11m)
NEUSIEDLER SEE/ NEUSIEDL AM SEE	▶ **Eisenstadt** (57km-35m)
EISENSTADT	▶ **Vienna** (51km-32m)

Wienertor, the medieval Vienna gate in Hainburg an der Donau

ℹ️ *Albertinaplatz, Vienna*

▶ *Drive southeast from the centre of Vienna on the **A4** to the Schwechat exit, and here take road **9/E58** for Petronell-Carnuntum.*

❶ Petronell-Carnuntum, Lower Austria

The former capital of Upper Pannonia, visited by several Roman emperors, was founded in the 1st century AD as Carnuntum at the crossroads of the two major Danube and Amber border routes. Scattered all around the town of Petronell are remains of the ancient city; the extensive archaeological park is still being excavated and has an open-air museum. Already uncovered are two amphitheatres, baths, paved and channelled streets and the famous Heidentor, the heathens' gate. Art and artefacts found here are displayed at the Museum Carnuntinum, in the nearby spa resort of Bad-Deutsch-Altenburg.

ℹ️ *Kirchengasse 57*

▶ *Continue along the same road for Bad Deutch and Hainburg.*

❷ Hainburg an der Donau, Lower Austria

Like Bruck an der Leitha (22km/14 miles southwest), the town of Hainburg, well positioned in the Danube hills, has preserved much of its medieval fortifications, which surround the old centre interspersed with 12 towers and three gates. One gate, the mighty Wienertor, houses the Heimatmuseum, dedicated to local history and traditions.

Climb to the Schlossberg (291m/955 feet) to visit the lovely ruins of the Burg, a 12th-to 13th-century fortress in a scenic spot.

ℹ️ *Hauptplatz 23*

▶ *Continue along road **9** to the junction with road **50** and follow this southeast to Kittsee.*

RECOMMENDED WALK

Laxenburg (16km/10 miles south of Vienna) was a favourite residence of Empress Maria Theresa. Today, it's a popular country outing for the Viennese, who like to walk through the English gardens exploring streams, small lakes, romantic pavilions and 18th-century temples. Franzensburg, a castle built in 1793–1803 on an artificial islet named after Emperor Franz II, is particularly striking (guided tours Apr–Oct 11, 2 and 3).

---

❸ Kittsee, Burgenland

Most visitors to Kitsee are tempted to pay a quick visit to Bratislava, the capital of Slovakia, only 6km (4 miles) away, but it's well worth spending some time here to visit the baroque Schloss Kittsee (1730–40) and its ethnographic museum, dedicated to the popular art of eastern and southeastern Europe.

ℹ️ *Hauptplatz 11*

▶ *Go back for a short stretch to Berg, then turn left on to local road **165** for Prellenkirchen and Rohrau.*

❹ Rohrau, Lower Austria

The quiet village of Rohrau is a magnet for music-lovers and art-connoisseurs. On Hauptstrasse

A pleasant scene on the lakeshores at Rust, on the Neusiedler See

stands the unassuming birthplace (Geburtshaus) of the two composers Joseph (1732–1809) and Michael (1737–1806) Haydn. It is now a museum.

South of the village is Schloss Harrach, a fine 16th-century castle given a neo-classical overhaul in the 18th century. It now contains the art collection of the counts of Harrach, one of Austria's most impressive, with a substantial number of Spanish and Italian baroque paintings.

ℹ️ *Joseph Haydn-Platz 1*

▶ *Drive along road 211 southwest to the A4, which you follow to the Neusiedl am See exit, before taking road 51 for about 3km (2 miles).*

5 Neusiedler See,
Burgenland
The Neusiedler See, a vast lake shared by Austria and Hungary, is regarded by the Viennese as

their 'seaside', and has a highly unusual and fascinating environment.

The town of Neusiedl am See is set in low hills on the edge of the *puszta* (the great Hungarian steppe), covered with vineyards as far as the eye can see. As you leave it the vast lake appears in the distance like a mirage, apparently cut off from the western coast road by a surrounding strip of reeds, though in fact a road leads from Rust (reached via roads 50 and

---

BACK TO NATURE

The unusual nature of the Neusiedler See, which extends over 320sq km (123 square miles) and whose depth barely exceeds 2m (6 feet), has made it a paradise for wildlife, particularly migratory birds. Over 200 different species are said to breed here. The brackish pools and marshy meadows of the Seewinkel, on the eastern side, form the Nationalpark Neusiedler See, a biosphere reserve protected by UNESCO.

SPECIAL TO...

At St Margarethen im Burgenland (6km/4.5 miles west of Rust) visit the Römersteinbruch, a sandstone quarry mined in Roman times and later a source of supply for the churches and mansions of Vienna. Admire the works left by sculptors from all over the world, who meet here every year for a symposium.

---

52) to a lido with sailing boats, cabins, bars and restaurants. The seaside feel is enhanced by salty air produced by lashing east winds that evaporate the lake water.

A little way past Rust is the pretty resort of Mörbisch am See and the Hungarian border, marking the beginning of the Fertö-Tavi Nemzeti nature park, linked to the Austrian national park on the opposite lake shore.

Both Neusiedl am See and Rust offer opportunities to find out more about the region's natural and political history. At Neusiedl am See you can

FOR CHILDREN

On the approach to Rust, just outside St Margarethen, you'll see the Märchenpark Neusiedlersee, an amusement park set up in a green space with reconstructions of children's favourite fairy-tales and games for all ages.

recover from a few hours of watery fun at the Seepark with a visit to the Pannonische Heimatmuseum, which has about 7,000 items associated with the Pannonian area.

Rust, the 'stork town', offers an introduction to the other major feature of this region, vine-growing, favoured by the mild Pannonian climate. In honour of the renowned local product, Seehof has been made the seat of the Weinakademie Österreich, the national wine academy.

SCENIC ROUTES

Road 51 travels south of Neusiedl am See towards the Seewinkel National Park, crossing an area of great environmental importance. It also offers an opportunity to visit places of historic interest such as Mönchhof (Cistercian convent), Frauenkirchen (Franciscan convent) and St Andrä (traditional houses with reed roofs). To return to Neusiedl am See, follow the lake on the local road via Illmitz and Podersdorf.

i Hauptplatz 1, Neusiedl am See

▶ From Rust turn left on to road **52** for St Margarethen im Burgenland and Eisenstadt.

6 Eisenstadt, Burgenland
As a border town, Eisenstadt has been passed several times

Rust, the home of storks

between Hungarian and Austrian hands, before returning permanently to Austria in 1918 and becoming capital of Burgenland in 1925. During the last long period of Magyar rule, in the second half of the 17th century, the town enjoyed its golden age, and fine multistorey houses from that time still grace the old centre. This was also the period of the construction of Schloss Esterházy (1663–72), designed by C M Carlone in the style of Rome's baroque mansions. A century later, anxious to match the opulence of Vienna and Versailles, the Esterházy princes employed composer Joseph Haydn

(1732–1809), who stayed in their service for 40 years and performed nearly all his works in the auditorium now named after him. A museum and a music centre occupy the house where Haydn lived for 12 years.

Eisenstadt is above all a major wine-producing centre, and in the western suburb of Kleinhöflein new wine is served in the 17th- and 18th-century taverns.

i Schloss Esterházy 1

▶ Road **59** leads west to the turning on the right for road **16**, which you follow north to Vienna.

The Southern
Vienna Woods

This is a grand tour of the kind favoured by 19th-century Viennese aristocrats, starting with a trip to the Schneeberg and Rax mountains and the Semmering range, and taking a break on the return journey at Baden, for a refreshing visit to the spa.

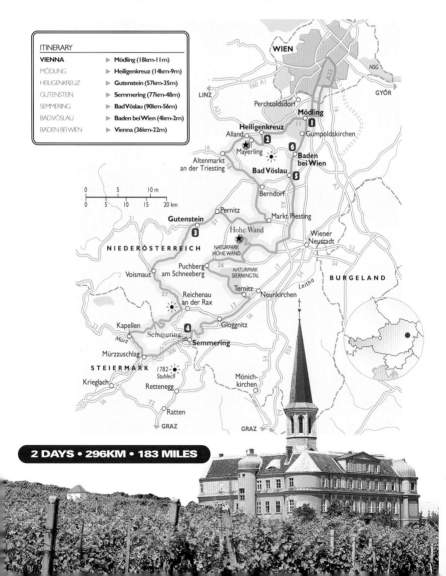

ITINERARY	
VIENNA	▶ Mödling (18km-11m)
MÖDLING	▶ Heiligenkreuz (14km-9m)
HEILIGENKREUZ	▶ Gutenstein (57km-35m)
GUTENSTEIN	▶ Semmering (77km-48m)
SEMMERING	▶ Bad Vöslau (90km-56m)
BAD VÖSLAU	▶ Baden bei Wien (4km-2m)
BADEN BEI WIEN	▶ Vienna (36km-22m)

2 DAYS • 296KM • 183 MILES

i Albertinaplatz, Vienna

▶ Leave Vienna southwards on the *17* for Wiener Neudorf; here, turn right on to road *11* for Mödling.

1 Mödling, Lower Austria

Mödling's romantic surroundings of woods and rocks at the mouth of a gorge appealed to such artists as Schubert and Beethoven, who spent long and productive periods here. Beethoven composed his *Missa Solemnis* in one of the old houses in the old centre, the 16th-century Hafnerhaus. At least two excursions are worth taking from Mödling. One visits Hinterbrühl bei Wien, 3km (2 miles) west, and the Seegrotte, where you cross the largest subterranean lake in Europe by motorboat. The other involves a 3km (2-mile) trip north to Maria Enzersdorf, where Burg Liechtenstein rises majestically against the sky, a fortress constructed in 1165 and almost entirely rebuilt in the 19th century in Romantic style.

i K Elisabethstrasse 2

▶ Continue along road *11* to Heiligenkreuz.

2 Heiligenkreuz, Lower Austria

Heiligenkreuz clusters around the austere Cistercian abbey founded in 1133, which was largely restored in the 17th and 18th century but retains some 13th-century Gothic elements. The abbey church has a beautiful interior, with sombre Romanesque aisles resting on mighty pillars, in contrast to the light Gothic choir, illuminated by 14th-century stained-glass windows. More than 300 red marble columns support the cloisters.

The abbey has a relic of the cross, donated by Leopold V on his return from the third crusade and the source of the name 'Heiligenkreuz', or Holy Cross.

i c/o Gemeindeamt (Municipio)

▶ Continue along road *11* to the junction with road *18*, which you follow southeast to Berndorf. Local road *4020* then leads south to Markt Piesting, where you proceed west on the *21* to Gutenstein.

3 Gutenstein, Lower Austria

Set at the point where the Piestingtal and Klostertal cross, Gutenstein is the gateway to the mountainous region of Lower Austria, already a high-society holiday destination by the late 19th century.

The Cistercian abbey of Heiligenkreuz

The scenic road that runs along the Klostertal and, subsequently, the Höllental to

---

SCENIC ROUTES

Just 12km (7 miles) separate Heiligenkreuz from Baden along the romantic Helenental road, in a valley cut by the Schwechat river. The beauty of the wooded heights scattered with old ruins inspired a popular song, *Kleines Wegerl im Helenental* ('The Path through the Helenental').

Kapellen and Mürzzuschlag in Styria overlooks the Schneeberg and Rax mountains (peaks above 2,000m/6,560 feet). There are well-equipped ski resorts here, and countless opportunities for summer excursions.

i Markt 21

▶ After another stretch of road *21*, turn left on to local road *134*, which leads, just past Vois, to road *27*. Continue southeast to Hirschwang and, shortly before entering Reichenau, turn right for Kapellen. Drive to Mürzzuschlag on the *23*

FOR HISTORY BUFFS

A Habsburg hunting lodge once stood in the Mayerling woods about 3km (2 miles) southwest of Heiligenkreuz. This is where the heir to the throne and his young lover, Baroness Maria Vetsera, died on 30 January, 1889. The event is still shrouded in mystery. The grief-stricken emperor, Franz Joseph, later had the building turned into a Carmelite monastery.

---

*southbound, then continue northeast on the **306** to the Semmering pass.*

RECOMMENDED WALKS

The Hirschwang district of Reichenau is the point of departure of the Rax cableway, which takes 10 minutes to climb to the ski slopes or, in summer, to hiking paths that link several refuge huts.

4 Semmering,
Lower Austria

The pretty summer and winter resort of Semmering lies at the pass of the same name, which marks the boundary between Styria and Lower Austria and has a long history as the communication route between the Danube basin and the Adriatic. The famous Semmering railway, a 41km (25-mile) mountain line, was built between 1848 and 1854 and declared a UNESCO World Heritage site in 1998 for its historical and technological value and for the spectacular surrounding scenery.

BACK TO NATURE

The Hohe Wand plateau (1,132m/3,714 feet) is reached by driving 6km (4 miles) along a toll road from Stollhof, halfway between Semmering and Bad Vöslau. This calcareous mass, a favourite with climbers for its sheer faces and precipices, is protected as a nature reserve because of its extensive forests of beech, fir and oak trees and varied Alpine wildlife.

🛈 *Passhöhe 248*

▶ *Road **306** leads to Gloggnitz, where you proceed along road **17** for Ternitz; here, take road **26** northwest to Purchberg and Grünbach am Schneeberg and turn left for Maiersdorf, Winzendorf and Weikersdorf. A brief stretch of road **26** leads eastwards to the **A2** for Bad Vöslau.*

5 Bad Vöslau, Lower Austria

Water and wine are a winning combination for Bad Vöslau. Its spa waters (24°C/75°F) are recommended for the circulation and nervous system, while the fine wine produced locally and served in the *Heurigen* lifts the spirits.

🛈 *Schlossplatz 1*

▶ *Follow road **212** northwards to Baden.*

6 Baden bei Wien,
Lower Austria

Baden is a resort famous for the curative powers of its sulphurous springs and for a long tradition of light opera. Its centre is a remarkably intact example of the Biedermeier style of buildings dating from the golden age of Franz I (1813–34). The famous Kurpark, an ideal place for walks, provides the setting for the Kurhaus (spa treatment centre, now a conference hall), Austria's largest casino and luxurious 19th-century hotels.

🛈 *Brusattiplatz 3*

▶ *Follow the signs northwards for Gumpoldskirchen and Mödling; from here, return to Vienna on the **A2/A23**.*

A viaduct belonging to the Semmering railway, built in the middle of the 19th century

Castles of
the Burgenland

Having reached the easternmost slopes of the Alpine range at Wiener Neustadt, you can visit the castle where Emperor Maximilian I was born and died. It's a fitting way to end an exploration of Austria which began on the other side of the country.

3 DAYS • 352KM • 219 MILES

ITINERARY

WIENER NEUSTADT	▶	Forchtenstein (24km-15m)
FORCHTENSTEIN	▶	Kobersdorf (24km-15m)
KOBERSDORF	▶	Lockenhaus (39km-24m)
LOCKENHAUS	▶	Bernstein (16km-10m)
BERNSTEIN	▶	Stadtschlaining (20km-12m)
STADTSCHLAINING	▶	Güssing (48km-30m)
GÜSSING	▶	Burgau (38km-24m)
BURGAU	▶	Kirchberg am Wechsel (103km-64m)
KIRCHBERG AM WECHSEL	▶	Wiener Neustadt (40km-25m)

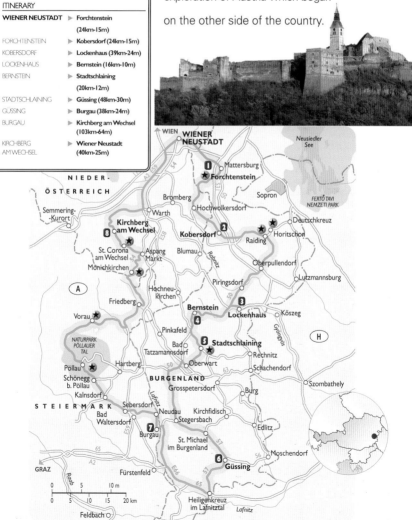

A reminder of times past around Kobersdorf castle

RECOMMENDED WALK

Horitschon, 17km (10 miles) southeast of Kobersdorf, is the main centre for the production of Blaufränkisch, one of southern Burgenland's famous red wines. The secrets of wine-making are revealed along the Weinlehrpfad, an educational trail 1.5km (1 mile) long.

this and after about 4km (2.5 miles) you'll see a turning on the left (road 55) for Lockenhaus.

3 Lockenhaus, Burgenland
You've now reached the slopes of the Geschriebenstein, near the Hungarian border, at 883m (2,897 feet) the highest mountain in Burgenland. The Burg dominating the town dates partly from the 13th century; adding to the charm of the old castle is a mysterious underground hall with two apses, possibly a secret gathering-place for the Knights Templar.

i *Hauptplatz 10*

▶ *Return to road 50 on road 55 and follow this to Bernstein.*

---

i *Hauptplatz 1–3, Wiener Neustadt,*

▶ *Follow road 53 to Neudörfl, then travel southeast on local road 219 to Mattersburg. Proceed to Forchtenstein on local road 223.*

1 Forchtenstein, Burgenland
Built in the 14th century and converted in 1635 into a Renaissance castle, Burg Forchtenstein houses important collections of art and weaponry. In July it hosts special family events.

i *Hauptstrasse 54*

▶ *Continue along the same road to the turning on the left for Hochwolkersdorf. Turn left again for Kobersdorf.*

2 Kobersdorf, Burgenland
Lying at the foot of the last active volcano in Austria, the Pauliberg (775m/2,543 feet), is Kobersdorf with its 13th-century Schloss (originally a Wasserschloss, or moated castle),

much altered in the 15th and the 16th century. The castle is private property but can be visited during the theatre events held in summer in its Renaissance porticoed courtyard.

i *Hauptstrasse 38*

▶ *Continue southeast past road S31 to Weppersdorf, where a brief stretch of the 50 leads southwards to the junction with road 62. Follow this eastwards to the turning on the right for Raiding. Continue southeast for Grosswarasdorf, where you turn right for road 50 towards Piringsdorf. Pass*

FOR HISTORY BUFFS

The great pianist and composer Franz Liszt (1811–86) came from Raiding, 13km (8 miles) southeast of Kobersdorf. The modest house where he was born has now been turned into a museum of his life and works.

4 Bernstein, Burgenland

Bernstein, which has a world monopoly on the extraction of green serpentine stone, is guarded by Burgenland's highest castle, one of the most important fortifications of the 13th century. Visit the Rittersaal, the knights' hall, and the outer courtyard. Much of the complex is now a hotel with restaurant and it commands a wide view of the southern Burgenland hills.

i *Alois Wesselyplatz 6*

▶ *Continue along road 50 and follow the signs for Bad Tatzmannsdorf to the turning on the left for Stadtschlaining.*

5 Stadtschlaining, Burgenland

Although extended and altered in the 15th century, Burg Schlaining (1230) retains much of its medieval character, clearly visible in the mighty ring of walls. It has an interesting

---

FOR CHILDREN

In the Wechsel region, at Mönichkirchen, there's a special track for skateboarders. Slightly further north, at St Corona, you can experience an exciting 8km (5-mile) sled descent during the summer months.

Gothic chapel with baroque decorations and a Rittersaal, knights' hall, with period furnishings.

i *Baumkircher Gasse 1*

▶ *Take local road 240 southwest to Oberwart; here take the 50 to the southwest for road 57 and follow this south–southeast, travelling via Stegersbach to Güssing.*

6 Güssing, Burgenland

Burg Güssing, which sits on an extinct volcano, is now a regional cultural centre hosting temporary exhibitions, and an ideal scenic point overlooking the great Pannonian plain. The original wooden fortification, built in 1157, was re-erected in stone in the 13th century. Fine art collections are on display in the Kunstkammer and in the Rittersaal.

i *Hauptplatz 7*

▶ *Continue along road 57 to Heiligenkreuz im Lafnitztal, where you follow road 65, then road 57a northbound to a turning on the left for Burgau.*

7 Burgau, Styria

Schloss Burgau stands right in the middle of the Styrian spa region and was once surrounded

---

SPECIAL TO...

Between Burgau and Kirchberg, about 20km (12 miles) apart on Styrian territory, are the two Augustinian abbeys of Pöllau (1504) and Vorau (1163). The former stands in the heart of Pöllauertal nature park; the latter possesses one of Austria's prime manuscript collections and, in the church, fine baroque wooden decorations.

---

by water (Burg an der Au). First recorded in 1367, it passed into the possession of the Hungarian house of Batthyány, as did nearly all the castles in Burgenland. A room on the second floor and the delightful porticoed courtyard host temporary exhibitions and concerts.

i *Schlossweg 296*

▶ *Take the local road north for Neudau where you bear west towards Bad Waltersdorf. Drive northeast to Kaindorf and Schönegg and turn left for Pöllau. Pass this and 9km (5 miles) later turn right for Vorau and Rohrbach, where you take road 54 north towards Aspang and Markt. Local road 137 leads northwest to Kirchberg via St Corona.*

8 Kirchberg am Wechsel, Lower Austria

Extending between the Schwarza and Pitten rivers, which meet to the east as the Leitha, is the mountainous region of Wechsel, a great place for trekking and skiing. About 4km (2.5 miles) from Kirchberg, one of the main resorts, is the Hermannshöhle, the largest cave labyrinth in Austria.

i *Markt 63*

▶ *Take road 134 first and then road 54 northeast to the A2 for Wiener Neustadt.*

The Gussing fortress

DRIVING IN AUSTRIA

AUTOMOBILE CLUBS
Austria has two national automobile clubs: ÖAMTC, based in Vienna, Schubertring 1-3, tel: 01 711990, www.oeamtc.at, and ARBÖ, based in Vienna, Mariahilfer Strasse 180, tel: 01 891217, www.arboe.or.at. Both are linked to local automobile clubs in numerous provincial towns.

BREAKDOWNS AND ACCIDENTS
In the event of a breakdown or accident, ÖAMTC (yellow vans and station wagons) and ARBÖ (white/orange vehicles) provide roadside recovery service. To call them, use the telephones along the motorways and on other roads. The vehicle must be removed from the carriageway as soon as possible. Activate hazard lights if the vehicle has them.

All vehicles must use a red emergency triangle, placed on the road at a safe distance and less than 1m (3 feet) from the kerb. Accidents with casualties or disputes must be reported to the police. All vehicles, including motorcycles, must carry a first aid box in a strong airtight container.

CAR HIRE
Vehicles can be booked through leading international car hire firms all over the country.

CHILDREN
Children under 12 and less than 1.5m (5 feet) tall can only travel in the front seat of vehicles in suitable safety seats; those taller must wear adult safety belts. Children older than 12 and less than 1.5m (5 feet) tall must wear a safety belt suited to their size.

Children's safety seats must not be used in the front seats of vehicles equipped with two airbags.

DOCUMENTS
Driving licences issued by all EU-member countries are valid in Austria. The vehicle's logbook (plus a letter of authorisation from the owner, unless present) and a third party liability insurance certificate must always be kept in the vehicle. Foreign cars must display a code identifying their country of origin (plate or sticker) on the back of the vehicle.

DRINKING AND DRIVING
Drink/driving rules are strictly enforced and breaches are severely punished. It's best not to drink alcohol at all if you are driving.

FUEL
There are fuel stations at frequent intervals on major roads and motorways, but they're harder to find in large towns. The following types of fuel are available: standard unleaded petrol (Bleifrei normal NO 91), Eurosuper (NO 95) and Super Plus (NO 98). If your car doesn't have a catalysing exhaust you can buy an additive for unleaded petrol from service stations.

HELMETS
Safety helmets are compulsory for all motorcyclists of all ages, passengers included.

INSURANCE
Third party liability insurance is compulsory in Austria.

LIGHTS
Motorcyclists must keep their headlights on all the time, day and night.

ROADS
Austria's main roads – *Bundenstrassen* (state roads) and *Schnellstrassen* (dual carriage-ways) – are in good condition, as are secondary roads. Some

mountain roads have steep gradients (up to 20 per cent) and are quite demanding; all have landslide protection. Some alpine passes above 2,000m (6,560 feet) are closed in winter; the most important include the Bielerhöhe, the Furkajoch, the Grossglockner road, the Hahtennjoch, the Sölk Pass, the Timmelsjoch/ Passo del Rombo, the Arlbergpass, the Gerlospass, the Lahnsattel, the Seefelder Sattel and the Wurzenpass.

Major road signs
Ausfahrt Exit (vehicles)
Ausgang Exit (pedestrians)
Autobahn Motorway
Bundesstrasse Main road
Einbahnstrasse One way
Einfahrt Entrance (vehicles)
Eingang Entrance (pedestrians)
Fahrräder Cyclists
Fussgänger Pedetrians
Gasse Street
Gefahr Pericolo
Gesperrt Closed
Glatteisgefahr Ice hazard
Maut Toll
Mautstrasse Toll road
Parkscheibe Time disc
Platz Square
Sackstrasse Cul de sac
Steinschlag Falling rocks
Strasse Street
Umleitung Detour
Verboten Forbidden

SAFETY BELTS
Safety belts are compulsory for drivers and front-seat passengers. Passengers in back seats must wear seat belts if the vehicle has them.

SPEED LIMITS
Speed limits are very strict. The maximum permitted speed is 50kph (31mph) in urban areas, 100kph (62mph) on non-urban roads and 120kph (75mph) on motorways. The speed limit for vehicles with caravans and trailers weighing in excess of 750kg (0.8 ton) on motorways is 100kph (62mph); for those with

studded tyres on non-urban roads it is 80kph (50mph) and 100kph (62mph) on motorways.

Speeding is severely dealt with and foreign motorists must pay on-the-spot fines. If immediate payment is not made, the Austrian police are entitled to confiscate personal belongings up to a value of €180 as surety.

TOLLS

In Austria the use of motorways and dual carriageways is subject to a toll (drivers with disabilities are exempt). A special sticker (*Vignette*) must be purchased from service stations, border posts or post offices before using the Austrian road network; this is displayed on the windscreen (centre top or left). Some bridges, tunnels and numerous Alpine roads are also subject to toll.

TRAFFIC RULES

In Vienna and in the large towns there is no parking in one-way streets used by trams, even if there are no signs, when only one lane is available beside the tramline. Many towns have a *Blaue Zone* (blue zone) where parking is allowed for a maximum of three hours; parking discs are on sale or free from tobacconists, fuel stations or banks. Those wishing to park for more than 2 or 3 hours should use one of the numerous underground pay car parks. If it snows, you must have snow or studded tyres (transit with studded tyres is permitted from 15 November to the first Monday after Easter). In winter, drivers should carry snow chains, which can be hired from Austrian automobile clubs.

ACCOMMODATION AND RESTAURANTS

Following is a selection of hotels (⌂), farm holiday centres (⌂≉) and camping sites (⛺) along the routes of each tour, along with suggestions for restaurants (〼〼) where you might like to take a break.

Accommodation prices

The prices indicated for hotels refer to the cost per night for a double room and are divided into the following three categories:

€	under €60
€€	€60–€100
€€€	more than €100

Restaurant prices

The prices indicated are for a three-course meal for one, excluding wine:

€	under €12
€€	€12–€22
€€€	more than €22

TOUR 1
BREGENZ
⌂ **Messmer €€**
Jürgen Haim, tel: 05574 42356.
⛺ **Lamm**
Mehrerauerstrasse 51,
tel: 05574 71701.
〼〼 **Goldener Hirschen €**
Kirschstrasse 8,
tel: 05574 42815.
Typical Austrian food. Closed Tue.

LECH AM ARLBERG
⌂ **Berghof €€–€€€**
tel: 05583 2635,
www.berghof-lech.com
⌂ **Theodul €–€€**
tel: 05583 2308,
www.theodul.at

ST ANTON AM ARLBERG
⌂ **Arlberg €–€€€**
Dorfstrasse 19,
tel: 05446 22100,
www.arlberg.com/hotel-arlberg
⌂ **Schwarzer Adler €€–€€€**
Dorfstrasse 42,
tel: 05446 2244,
www.schwarzeradler.com

BLUDENZ
⌂ **Schlosshotel Dörflinger €**
Schlosspl 5, tel: 05522 63016,
www.schlosshotel.cc

TOUR 2
SERFAUS
⌂ **Geiger €**
Untergasse 8,
tel: 05476 6266.
〼〼 **Noldi Stuben €**
Dorfbahnstrasse 42,
tel: 05476 6500.
Grills and Austrian fare.

MERANO
⌂ **Villa Tivoli €€€**
Via Verdi 72,
tel: 0473 446282,
www.villativoli.it
⌂ **Meisters Hotel Irma €€**
Via Belvedere 17,
tel: 0473 212000,
www.hotel-irma.it

SÖLDEN
⌂ **Alphof Sölden €–€€**
Pitze 182,
tel: 05254 2559,
www.alphofsoelden.com

WENNS (Pitztal)
⌂≉ **Tobadillerhof €**
Ofen 850,
tel: 05414 87458.

TOUR 3
STAMS
⛺ **Eichenwald**
Schiessstandweg 10,
tel: 05263 6159.

EHRWALD
⌂ **Sport-Hotel Schönruh €–€€**
Innsbrucker Strasse 25,
tel: 05673 23220,
www.hotel-scheonruh.com
⌂ **Zum Grünen Baum €–€€**
Innsbrucker Strasse 2,
tel: 05673 2302,
www.gruenerbaum.com

REUTTE
〼〼 **Gasthof zum Mohren €–€€**
Untermarkt 26,
tel: 05672 62345.
Excellent Tirolean food.

IMST
⌂ **Hirschen Gasthof €**
Thomas-Walch-Strasse,
tel: 05412 6901,
www.hirschen-imst.com

TOUR 4
INNSBRUCK
⌂ **Bierwirt €**
Bichlweg 2,
tel: 0512 342143,
www.bierwirt.com
⌂ **Romantik Hotel Schwarzer Adler €€**
Kaiserjägerstrasse 2,
tel: 0512 587109,
www.deradler.com

🏕 **Innsbruck Kranebitten**
Kranebitten Allee 214,
tel: 0512 284180,
www.tiscover.com/campinnsbruck

🏠♣ **Nockhof €**
a Mutters, Nockhofweg 47,
tel: 0512 548582,
www.geocities.com/nockhof

🍴 **Ottoburg €–€€**
Herzog-Friedrich-Strasse 1,
tel: 0512 584338.
Austrian food. Closed Mon.

TOUR 5
IGLS
🏨 **Sporthotel Igls €–€€**
Hilber Strasse 17,
tel: 0512 377241,
www.sporthotel-igls.com

BRESSANONE
🏨 **Stadthotel Goldene Krone €**
Via Fienili 4,
tel: 0472 835154,
www.goldenekrone.com

MATREI IN OSTTIROL
🏨 **Goldried €**
Goldriedstrasse 15,
tel: 04875 61130,
www.goldried.at

🏠♣ **Johann Rainer €**
Berg 21,
tel: 04875 6145.

ZELL AM ZILLER
🏨 **Tirolerhof €**
Dorfplatz 8,
tel: 05282 2227.

🏕 **Hofer**
Gerlosstrasse 33,
tel: 05282 2248,
www.tiscover.com/camping-hofer

MAYRHOFEN
🍴 **Alpenhof Kristall €€–€€€**
Marktplatz 218
tel: 05285 62428.
Good Austrian food.

TOUR 6
KITZBÜHEL
🏨 **Sporthotel Reisch €€–€€€**
Franz-Reisch-Strasse 3,
tel: 05356 633660,
www.sporthotelreish.at

🏕 **Schwarzsee**
Reither Strasse 24,
tel: 05356 62806,
www.bruggerhof-camping.at

🍴 **Chizzo €**
Josef-Herold-Strasse 2,
tel: 05356 62475.
Good Tirolean food.

ST JOHANN IN TIROL
🏨 **Gruber €**
Gasteiger Strasse 18,
tel: 05352 61461,
www.hotelgruber.at

WALCHSEE
🏨 **Schick €€**
Johannestrasse 1,
tel: 05374 5331,
www.hotelschick.com

TOUR 7
KÖTSCHACH/MAUTHEN
🏨 **Schlank-Schlemmer-Hotel Kürschner €–€€**
Schlanke Gasse 74,
tel: 04715 259,
www.hotel-kuerschner.at

🏠♣ **Alois Hohenwarter €**
Near Wegscheider,
Mandorf 3,
tel: 04715 8730,
www.urlaubambauernhof.com/Wegscheider.htm

HERMAGOR
🏨 **Alpen Adria Hotel €**
Presseggersee,
tel: 04282 2666,

GMÜND
🍴 **Werner Pauser €€**
Bahnhofstrasse 44
tel: 02582 53860.
Local carp a speciality.

TOUR 8
EBERNDORF
🏕 **Sonnencamp Gösselsdorfersee**
Seestrasse 21–25,
tel: 04236 2168.

KLAGENFURT
🏨 **Geyer €**
Priesterhausgasse 5,
tel: 0463 57886,
www.hotelgeyer.com

🏠♣ **Gundersdorf Schloss €**
Gundersdorf 1 (8km from Klagenfurt),
tel: 0463 43215.

🍴 **Schlosswirt €€**
Schlossstrasse 26
tel: 0463 35300.
Carinthian fusion cooking.

MARIA WORTH
🏨 **San Michele €–€€**
Süduferstrasse 149,
tel: 04273 2282.

TOUR 9
SAALFELDEN
🏨 **Hindenburg €–€€**
Bahnhofstrasse 6,
tel: 06582 793.

🏠♣ **Obenaufhof €**
Uttenhofen 3,
tel: 06582 73395.

GOLDEGG
🏨 **Zur Post €**
tel: 06415 81030,
www.hotelpost-goldegg.at

BAD HOFGASTEIN
🏨 **Klammer's Kärnten €€**
Dr Zimmermannstrasse 9,
tel: 06432 67110,
www.hotel-kaernten.com

BADGASTEIN
🏨 **Haus Hirt €**
Kaiserhofstrasse 14,
tel: 06434 2797,
www.haus-hirt.com

🏨 **Vital Hotel Lindenhof €**
Poserstrasse 2,
tel: 06434 26140,
www.lindenhof-vital.com

🍴 **Fischerwirt €€**
Karl-Heinz-Waggerl-Strasse 32
tel: 06434 27550.
Specialises in fish and pizza.

TOUR 10
BAD KLEINKIRCHHEIM
🏨 **Harmony Hotel Felsenhof €€**
Mozartweg 6, tel: 04240 6810.

🏨 **Trattlerhof €€**
Gegentalerwag 1,
tel: 04240 8172,
www.trattlerhof.at

MAUTERNDORF
🏨 **Vitalhotel Elisabeth €€**
Ledermoos 274,
tel: 06472 7365.

SCHLADMING
🏨 **Alte Post €–€€**
Hauptplatz 10,
tel: 03687 22571,
www.alte-post.at

🏠♣ **Feldlhof €**
Untere Klaus 26,
tel: 03687 22142.

Kirchenwirt €–€€
Salzburgerstrasse 27,
tel: 03687 22435.
Good plain cooking.

ST VEIT AN DER GLAN
Ernst Fuchs Palast €€
Prof Ernst Fuchs Platz 1,
tel: 04212 46600,
www.fuchspalast.com

TOUR 11
GRAZ
**Best Western Hotel
Pfeifer Kirchenwirt €€**
Kirchplatz 9, tel: 0316 3911120,
www.kirchenwirtgraz.com
**Romantik Parkhotel
Graz €€**
Leonhardstrasse 8,
tel: 0316 36300,
www.romantik-parkhotel.at
Gambrinuskeller €€
Färbergasse 6–8,
tel: 0316 810181.
Balkan specialities.

SPITAL AM PHYRN
Niessersriegel €
Mitterweng 6,
tel: 07562 8768.

BRUCK AN DER MUR
Arcotel Landskron €
Am Schiffertor 3,
tel: 03862 58458,
www.arcotel.at

TOUR 12
ST PAUL IM LAVANTTAL
Logge €
Hauptstrasse 19,
tel: 04357 2056,
www.loigge.com

BAD RADKERSBURG
Triest €€
Alfred Merlini-Allee 5,
tel: 03476 41040,
www.hoteltriest.at

TOUR 13
SALZBURG
Auersperg €€
Auerspergstrasse 61,
tel: 0662 88944,
www.auersperg.at
**Best Western Hotel Zum
Hirschen €€**
St Julien Strasse 21–23,
tel: 0662 889030,
www.zumhirschen.at

Panorama Stadtblick
Rauchenbichlerstrasse 21,
tel: 0662 450652.
Kolmbauer €
Moosstrasse 156,
tel: 0662 826298.
Krimpelstätter €€
Müllner-Hauptstrasse 31,
tel: 0662 432274.
*Austrian cuisine; Augustiner beer
on tap. Closed Mon.*

TOUR 14
**ST JOHANN IM
PONGAU**
Tannenhof €€
Alpendorf 3,
tel: 06412 52310,
www.hotel-tannenhof.at
Ötzmoos €
Ober Alpendorf 76,
tel: 06412 7832,
www.oetzmooshof.at

HALLSTATT
Bräugasthof €
Seestrasse 120,
tel: 06134 8221.
Klausner-Höll
Lahn 201,
tel: 06134 8322.
**Berggasthof Rudolfsturm
€€€**
Salzberg 1,
tel: 06134 8253.
*Regional specialities; panoramic
views.*

ST WOLFGANG
**Romantik Hotel 'Im
Weissen Rössl' €€**
Markt 74,
tel: 06138 23060,
www.weissesroessl.at

FUSCHL
Mohrenwirt €
Dorfplatz 3,
tel: 06226 8228,
www.mohrenwirt.at

TOUR 15
LINZ
**Best Western Spitz
Hotel €€**
Fiedlerstrasse 6,
tel: 0732 7364410,
www.spitz.at
City Hotel €€
Schillerstrasse 52,
tel: 0732 652622,
www.cityhotel.at

Pichlingersee
Wiener Strasse 937,
tel: 070 305314.
**Kremsmünster Stuben
€€–€€€**
Altstadt 10,
tel: 0732 782111.
Austrian dishes.

FREISTADT
Jonihöh €
Sonnberg 7,
tel: 07942 76616.

TOUR 16
STEYR
Mader €
Stadtplatz 36,
tel: 07252 533580,
Parkhotel Styria €
Eisenstrasse 18,
tel: 0752 47831,
www.styriahotel.at
Forelle
Kematmüllerstrasse 1a,
tel: 07252 78008,
www.forellesteyr.com
**Zu den 3 Goldenen Rosen
€–€€**
Hotel Mader, Stadtplatz 36,
tel: 07252 53358.
Set menu particularly good value.

ENNS
**Austria Classic Hotel
Lauriacum €**
Wiener Strasse 5–7,
tel: 07223 82315,
www.austria-classic-hotels.at/
lauriacum

TOUR 17
EFERDING
**Fischrestaurant
Dannerbauer €–€€**
Brandstatt-Pupping 5,
tel: 07272 2471.
Fish specialities.

SCHÄRDING
Biedermeier-Hof €
Passauer Strasse 8,
tel: 07712 3064.
Gugerbauer €
Kurhausstrasse 4,
tel: 07712 3191,
www.hotel-gugerbauer.at

RIED
Kaiser Hotel €
F Thurnerstrasse 4,
tel: 07752 82488.

BRAUNAU AM INN
🏕 **Freizeitzentrum**
Industriezeile 50 Quellenweg,
tel: 07722 84268136.

TOUR 18
ST PÖLTEN
🏨 **Seeland €**
Goldegger Strasse 114,
tel: 02742 3624610.
🏨 **Stadthotel Hauser-Eck €**
Schulgasse 2, tel: 02742 73336,
www.hausereck.at
🏕 **Freizeitpark**
Am Ratzersdorfer See,
tel: 02742 251510.

MARIAZELL
🏨 **Feichtegger €**
Wiener Strasse 6,
tel: 03882 24160.
🏠⚘ **Bauernhof Stockreiter €**
Sandbühel 14,
tel: 03882 4875.
🍽 **Zum Alten Brauhaus €**
Wiener Strasse 5,
tel: 03882 2523.
Styrian specialities.

TOUR 19
GMÜND
🏨 **Goldener Stern €€**
Stadtplatz 15,
tel: 02852 545450.

MELK
🏨 **Zur Post €**
Linzer Strasse 1,
tel: 02752 52345.

DÜRNSTEIN
🏨 **Romantikhotel Richard
Löwenherz €€**
No 8,
tel: 02711 222,
www.richardloewenherz.at
🍽 **Loibnerhof €€**
Unterloiben 7,
tel: 02732 82890.
Variations on Austrian food. Closed Tue.

TOUR 20
VIENNA
🏨 **Sacher Wien €€€**
Philarmonikerstrasse 4,
tel: 01 51456,
www.sacher.com
🏨 **City Central €€**
Taborstrasse 8,
tel: 01 211050,
www.schick-hotels.com

🏨 **Carlton Opera €**
Schkanedergasse 4,
tel: 01 58753020,
www.ping.at/carlton
🍽 **Demel €–€€**
Kohlmarkt 14,
tel: 01 535 1717.
Celebrated café; bewildering array of desserts.
🍽 **Schweizerhaus €€**
Prater 116,
tel: 01 728 0152.
Atmospheric garden restaurant in the Prater.
🍽 **Gulaschmuseum €–€€**
Schulerstrasse 20,
tel: 01 512 1017.
Goulash dishes.

TOUR 21
TULLN
🍽 **Ratsstüberl €–€€**
Hauptplatz 19,
tel: 02272 62696.
Austrian food. Closed Sun.

HORN
🏨 **Zum Weissen Rössel €**
Hauptplatz 16,
tel: 02982 2398.
🏨 **Zur Stadt Horn €**
Hamerlingstrasse 17,
tel: 02982 2257.

WAIDHOFEN AN DER
🏨 **Thayatal Hotel €€**
Am Golfplatz 1,
tel: 02842 502.

TOUR 22
**MISTELBACH AN DER
ZAYA**
🏨 **Weisses Rössl €**
Hafnerstrasse 8,
tel: 02572 2431.
🍽 **Zur Linde €–€€**
Bahnstrasse 49,
tel: 02572 2409.
Austrian food.

ORTH AN DER DONAU
🏨 **Danubius €**
Am Markt 6,
tel: 02212 2400.
🏨 **Orther Schlosshof €**
Am Markt 6, tel: 02212 2282.

TOUR 23
NEUSIEDL AM SEE
🏨 **Wende €€**
Seestrasse 40–42,
tel: 02167 8111.

🏨 **Leiner €**
Seestrasse 15,
tel: 02167 2489.
🏠⚘ **Maria Königshofer €**
Kalvarienbergstrasse 37,
tel: 02167 2110.

EISENSTADT
🏨 **Burgenland €€**
Franz Schubert-Platz 1,
tel: 02682 696.
🏨 **Parkhotel Eisenstadt €**
Haydngasse 38,
tel: 092682 75325.
🍽 **Haydnbräu €€**
Pfarrgasse 22,
tel: 02682 61561.
Typical Austrian dishes.

TOUR 24
SEMMERING
🏨 **Grand Hotel Panhans €**
Hochstrasse 32,
tel: 02664 8181,
www.panhans.at
🏨 **Belvedere €**
Hochstrasse 60,
tel: 02664 2270,
www.semmering.com/
belvedere

BADEN BEI WIEN
🏨 **Mercure Parkhotel
Baden €€**
Kaiser-Franz-Ring 5,
tel: 02252 44386,
www.mercure.at
🏨 **Helenental €**
Karlsgasse 1-5,
tel: 02252 43128.
🍽 **Rauhenstein €€–€€€**
Weilburgstrasse 11,
tel: 02252 412510.
Best dining in town; jazz brunches.

TOUR 25
LOCKENHAUS
🏨 **Burghotel Lockenhaus €**
Günserstrasse 5,
tel: 02616 2394.

BERNSTEIN
🍽 **Pannonia €–€€**
Hauptstrasse 58,
tel: 03354 6543.
Kaffeehaus.

STADTSCHLAINING
🏨 **Burg Schlaining €**
Klingergasse 2–4,
tel: 03355 2600,
www.hotel.burg.co.at

TOUR INFORMATION

The addresses, telephone numbers, websites where applicable and opening times of the attractions mentioned in the tours, including the telephone numbers of the tourist information offices, are listed below tour by tour.

TOUR 1

⌐i⌐ Bahnhofstrasse 14, Bregenz
tel: 05574 49590,
www.bregenz.at

⌐i⌐ Kulturhaus, Dornbirn
tel: 05572 22188.

⌐i⌐ Hof 454, Schwarzenberg
tel: 05512 3570.

⌐i⌐ Platz 39, Bezau
tel: 05514 2295.

⌐i⌐ Dorf 2, Lech am Arlberg
tel: 05583 2161,
www.lech-zuers.at

⌐i⌐ Alberhaus, St Anton am Arlberg
tel: 05446 22690,
www.stantonamarlberg.com

⌐i⌐ Silvrettastrasse 6, Schruns
tel: 05556 72166,
www.schruns.at

⌐i⌐ Werdenberger-strasse 42, Bludenz
tel: 05552 62170,
www.bludenz.at

⌐i⌐ Kirchdorf 138, Damüls
tel: 05510 6200.

⌐i⌐ Rathaus am Marktplatz, Rankweil
tel: 05522 405105.

⌐i⌐ Herrengasse 12, Feldkirch
tel: 05522 73467,
www.feldkirch.at

⌐i⌐ Schweizer Strasse 10, Hohenems
tel: 05576 42780.

◻2◻ Dornbirn
Vorarlberger Naturschau
Marktstrasse 1,
tel: 05572 23235.
Open 9–12, 2–5. Closed Mon except Jul–Aug.
Rolls-Royce Museum
Gütle, tel: 05572 52652.
Open Nov–Mar 10–5; Apr–Oct 10–6. Closed Mon; mid-Jan to mid-Feb.

◻6◻ St Anton am Arlberg
Ski und Heimatmuseum
Ferienpark,
tel: 05446 2475.
Open mid-Jun to mid-Sep 10–6; Dec to mid-Apr 3–10pm. Closed Sun.

◻9◻ Bludenz
Stadtmuseum
Altstadt/Herzog-Friedrichs-Tor.
Open Jun–Sep 3–5pm. Closed Sun.

◻12◻ Feldkirch
Schattenburg
Burggasse 1,
tel: 05522 72444.
Open 9–12, 1–5. Closed Mon and Nov.

◻13◻ Hohenems
Stoffels Säge-Mühle
Sägerstrasse 11,
tel: 05576 72434.
Open May–Oct 9–6.

TOUR 2

⌐i⌐ Alberhaus, St Anton am Arlberg
tel: 05446 22690,
www.stantonamarlberg.com

⌐i⌐ Malserstrasse 10, Landeck
tel: 05442 65600.

⌐i⌐ Dorf 89, Fliess
tel: 05449 5224.

⌐i⌐ No 27, Ladis
tel: 05472 6601,
www.ladis.at

⌐i⌐ Untere Dorfstrasse 13, Serfaus
tel: 05476 62390,
www.serfaus.com

⌐i⌐ Dr-Tschiggfrey-Strasse 66, Nauders
tel: 05473 87220,
www.nauders.com

⌐i⌐ At Resia, Via Principale 22, Passo di Resia
tel: 0473 633101,
www.reschenpass-suedtirol.it

⌐i⌐ Piazza Glückh 3, Malles Venosta
tel: 0473 831190.

⌐i⌐ Via Capuccini 10, Silandro
tel: 0473 730155.

⌐i⌐ Corso della Libertà 45, Merano
tel: 0473 272000,
www.meraninfo.it

⌐i⌐ Hauptstrasse 108, Obergurgl
tel: 05256 6466,
www.obergurgl.com

⌐i⌐ Rettenbach 466, Sölden
tel: 05254 5100,
www.soelden.com

⌐i⌐ Dorf 3, Umhausen
tel: 05255 5209.

⌐i⌐ Ortsinformation-sstelle, St Leonhard imPitztal
tel: 05414 869990,
www.pitzal.com

◻1◻ Landeck
Schloss Landeck
Schlossweg 2,
tel: 05442 63202.
Open mid-May–Oct 10–5. Closed Mon.

◻2◻ Fliess
Archäologisches Museum
Dorfplatz,
tel: 05449 20065.
Open Jun–Oct 10–12, 3–5. Closed Mon.

◻3◻ Ladis
Burg Laudegg
tel: 05472 6601.
Guided tours Jul to mid-Sep, Wed 9.30, 10.30, 11.30.

◻5◻ Nauders
Burg Naudersberg
tel: 05473 87252.
Guided tours (90 min. ca): mid-May to Oct and 26 Easter, Tue and Fri 4.30, Wed 5, Sun and holidays 11.

◻7◻ Malles Venosta/ Mals in Vinschgau
Fürstenburg
c/o Tourist Office
tel: 0473 831422.
Guided tours Jul–Aug, Mon 3.
Churburg
At Sluderno,
tel: 0473 615241.
Open Apr–Oct 10–12, 2–4.30. Closed Mon except holidays.

◻9◻ Merano
Landesfürstliche
Via Galilei,
tel: 0473 250329.
Open 10–5. Closed Mon, Sun and Jan–Feb.
Stadtmuseum
Via delle Corse 42,
tel: 0473 236015.
Open 10–5. Closed Sun–Mon.
Castel Tirolo
Via del Castello 24,
tel: 0473 220221.
Open Apr–Oct 10–5. Closed Mon.

TOUR 3

⌐i⌐ Rathaus, Kloster-strasse 43, Seefeld in Tirol
tel: 05212 2313,
www.seefeld-tirol.com

[i] Kirchplatz 128a,
Leutasch
tel: 05214 6207.

[i] Bahnhofstrasse 1,
Stams
tel: 05263 6748.

[i] Karl-Mayr-Strasse
116a, Fernsteinsee,
Nassereith
tel: 05265 5253.

[i] Kirchplatz 1, Ehrwald
tel: 05673 2395,
www.ehrwald.com

[i] Untermarkt 34,
Reutte
tel: 05672 62336.

[i] Johannesplatz 4,
Imst
tel: 05412 69100,
www.imst.at

[i] Hauptstrasse 66,
Oetz
tel: 05252 6669,
www.oetz.com

2 Stams
Zisterzienserstift
Stiftshof 1,
tel: 05263 56972.
*Guided tours 9, 10, 11, 2,
3 and 4; May–Sep also
at 5.*

5 Reutte
Grünes Haus
Untermarkt 25,
tel: 05672 72304.
*Open 10–12, 2–5.
Closed Mon and
Nov–Mar.*

Special to...
Imster Fasnachtshaus
Streleweg, Imst
tel: 05412 69100.
*Guided tours for groups
by appointment with
Tourist Office.*

TOUR 4

[i] Burggraben 3,
Innsbruck
tel: 0512 59850,
www.innsbruck-
tourismus.com

3 Altes Rathaus and Stadtturm
Herzog-Friedrich-
Strasse 21,
tel: 0512 575962.
*Open 10—8; Oct–May
10–5.*

4 Goldenes Dachl and Maximilianeum
Herzog-Friedrich-
Strasse 15,
tel: 0512 581111.
*Open May–Sep 10–6;
Oct–Apr 10–12.30, 2–5.
Closed Mon.*

6 Hofburg
Rennweg 1,
tel: 0512 587186.
Open 9–4.

7 Hofkirche
Universitätsstrasse 2,
tel: 0512 584302.
*Open 9–5. Free
admission during services
and Sun.*

8 Tiroler Volkskunst-museum
Universitätsstrasse 2,
tel: 0512 584302.
*Open 9–5; Sun and
holidays 9–12.*

9 Tiroler Landesmuseum Ferdinandeum
Museumstrasse 15,
tel: 0512 59489.

Schloss Ambras
Schlossstrasse 20,
tel: 0512 348446.
*Open 10–5; Dec–Mar
2–5. Closed Tue and Nov.*

TOUR 5

[i] Burggraben 3,
Innsbruck
tel: 0512 59850,
www.innsbruck-
tourismus.com

[i] Piazza Principale, Igls
tel: 0512 377101.

[i] Brenner Strasse 104,
Matrei am Brenner
tel: 05273 6278.

[i] Piazza Città 3,
Vipiteno
tel: 0472 765325,
www.infovipiteno.it

[i] Viale Stazione 9,
Bressanone
tel: 0472 836401,
www.brixen.org

[i] Via Europa 24,
Brunico/Bruneck
tel: 0474 555722.

[i] No 81, Anterselva
tel: 0474 492116.

[i] Rauterplatz 1, Matrei
in Osttirol
tel: 04875 6527.
Informazioni Parco
Alti Tauri
tel: 04875 5161,
www.hohetauern.at

[i] Marktplatz 4,
Mittersill
tel: 06562 42920,
www.mittersill-
tourismus.at

[i] Oberkrimml 37,
Krimml
tel: 06564 7239,
www.salzburg.com/
krimml-tourismus

[i] Dorfplatz 3a,
Zell am Ziller
tel: 05282 2281,
www.zell.at

[i] No 300, Fügen
tel: 05288 62262,
www.fuegen.cc

[i] Wallpachgasse 5,
Hall in Tirol
tel: 05223 56269.

4 Vipiteno
Spirito Santo
Piazza Città.
*Open 8.30–12, 2.30–6.
Closed Sat pm, Sun and
holidays.*
Schloss Reifenstein
Campo di Trens,
tel: 0472 765879.
*Guided tours Easter–All
Saints 9.30, 10.30, 2 and
3. Closed Fri.*

5 Bressanone/ Brixen
Museo Diocesano
Piazza Vescovile 2,
tel: 0472 830505.
*Open mid-Mar to Oct
10–5. Closed Mon.
Open for cribs Dec–Jan
2–5, except 24 and 25
Dec.*

6 Brunico/Bruneck
Museo Etnografico
At Teodone, Via Duca
Teodone 24,
tel: 0474 553292.
*Open Apr–Oct
9.30–5.30, Sun and
holidays 2–6; Jul–Aug
9.30–6.30, Sun and
holidays until 7. Closed
Mon.*

9 Mittersill
Schloss Mittersill
tel: 06562 4523.
*Guided tours mid-Jul to
Aug, Wed and Sun 2 and
3.30.*
Felberturmmuseum
Museumsstrasse 2,
tel: 06562 4444.
*Open May–Oct, Sat., Sun
and holidays 1–5; Jun–Sep
also Mon—Fri 10–5.*

10 Krimml
Krimmler Wasserfälle
tel: 06564 7212.
Open May–Oct.
Wasser Wunder Welt
tel: 06564 20113.
*Open May–Oct
10–5; 20 Dec–Easter,
Sun–Wed 3–7.*

11 Zell am Ziller
**Erlebniswanderung
Goldbergau (mine walk)**
Unterberg 109,
tel: 05282 4820.
*Guided tours Zillertaler
Goldschauberwerk,
11.15, 1.15, 3.15;
Hochzeller Käsealm,
open 9–6; Tierpark
Hainzenberg all day.*

13 Hall in Tirol
Burg Hasegg
Münzergasse,
tel: 05223 6269.

Castle open by appointment with Tourist Office.
Museum der Stadt, open Jul–Sep 10–3.
Alte Münze open Apr–Oct 10–12, 2–5; Nov–Mar, Mon–Thu 10–12, 2–5, Fri 10–12.

Special to...
Swarovski Kristallwelten
Kristallweltenstrasse 1,
Wattens
tel: 05224 51080.
Open daily 9–6.

TOUR 6

ℹ Unterer Stadtplatz 8,
Kufstein
tel: 05372 62207,
www.kufstein.at

ℹ Franz-Josef-Strasse 2,
Schwaz
tel: 05242 632400,
www.schwaz-pill.at

ℹ Unterdorf 62, Stans
tel: 05242 63579,
www.stans.tirol.gv.at

ℹ Hnr 53d, Pertisau
am Achensee
tel: 05243 4307,
www.achensee.com/
pertisau

ℹ Römerstrasse 1,
Brixlegg
tel: 05337 62581,
www.tvb-brixlegg.at

ℹ Klostergasse 94,
Rattenberg
tel: 05337 63321,
www.rattenberg.at

ℹ Hinterstadt 18,
Kitzbühel
tel: 05356 621550,
www.kitzbuehel.com

ℹ Poststrasse 2,
St Johann in Tirol
tel: 05352 63335,
www.st.johann.tirol.at

ℹ Dorfplatz 1,
Fieberbrunn

tel: 05354 56304,
www.pillerseetal.at

ℹ No 310, Lofer
tel: 06588 83210.

1 Schwaz
Franziskanerkirche
Gilmstrasse 1,
tel: 05242 632650.
Guided tours 8–8.

2 Stans
Stift Fiecht
At Vomp,
tel: 05242 63276.
Open by appointment.
Schloss Tratzberg
tel: 05242 6356620.
Guided tours Apr–Oct 10–4.

4 Brixlegg
Heimatmuseum
At Reith, Schloss Matzen,
tel: 05337 62674.
Open Wed and Fri 2–6.
Museum Tiroler Bauernhöfe
At Kramsach, Angerberg 10, tel: 05337 62636.
Open Apr–Oct 9–6.

5 Rattenberg
Augustinermuseum
Pfarrgasse 8,
tel: 05337 64831.
Open May to mid-Oct 10–5.

9 Lofer
Seisenbergklamm
At Weissbach,
tel: 06582 83524.
Open May–Oct 8.30–6.30.
Lamprechtsofenhöhle
At Weissbach
tel: 06582 8343.
Guided tours (approximately 40 minutes): 9–6; Nov–Easter 10–4.

Special to...
Schwazer Silberwerk
Alte Landstrasse 3a,
Schwaz,
tel: 05242 72372.
Guided tours (approximately 90

minutes): 9.30–4; May–Oct 8.30–5.

TOUR 7

ℹ No 86, Sillian
tel: 04842 66660,
www.hochpustertal.com

ℹ No 29, at Liesing,
Maria Luggau
tel: 04716 24212,
www.lesachtal.com

ℹ Rathaus, No 390,
Kötschach-Mauthen
tel: 04715 8516.

ℹ Gösseringlände 7,
Hermagor
tel: 04282 20430.

ℹ Marktplatz 14,
Millstatt
tel: 04766 37000,
www.millsee.info

ℹ Rathaus, Gmünd
tel: 04732 221514.

ℹ Gemeindeamt,
Greifenburg
tel: 04712 21614.

ℹ No 32, Lavant
tel: 04852 68216.

4 Kötschach-Mauthen
Museum 1915–1918
Rathaus, No 390.
Open mid-May to mid-Oct 10–1, 3–6; Sat–Sun and holidays 2–6.

5 Hermagor
Schloss Möderndorf
Möderndorf 1, at Möderndorf
tel: 04282 3060.
Open May to mid-Oct 10–5. Closed Sat, Sun, Mon; Jul–Aug Mon only.

7 Gmünd
Porsche Automuseum Pfeifhofer
Riesertrasse 4a,
tel: 04732 2471.
Open mid-May to mid-Oct 9–6; mid-Oct to mid-May 10–4.

Scenic routes
Schloss Anras
At Anras, No 27,
tel: 04846 6595.
Open in summer, 10–12, 2–4, Sun 3.30–5.30; in winter, 4.30–6.30, Sun 3.30–5.30. Closed Sat.

For history buffs
Aguntum
On the B100 road,
tel: 04852 61550.
Open May to mid-Sep 9–4, in summer until 6; mid-Sep to mid-Oct, Sat–Sun 9–4.

TOUR 8

ℹ Rathausplatz 1,
Villach
tel: 04242 2052900.

ℹ Dietrichsteiner Strasse 2, Faaker See
tel: 04254 21100.

ℹ Kirchgasse 5, Ferlach
tel: 04227 5119.

ℹ Hauptplatz 7,
Bad Eisenkappel
tel: 04238 8686.

ℹ Kirchplatz 1,
Eberndorf
tel: 04236 2221.

ℹ Hauptplatz 1,
Völkermarkt
tel: 04232 257147,
www.stadtgemeinde-voelkermarkt.at

ℹ Rathaus, Neuer Platz,
Klagenfurt
tel: 0463 5372223.

ℹ Freisinger Platz, Maria Wörth
tel: 04273 25570.

ℹ Villacher Strasse 19,
Velden am Wörther See
tel: 04274 2103,
www.velden.at

ℹ Amthofgasse 3,
Feldkirchen in Kärntner
tel: 04276 2176.

ⓘ No 8, Ossiach
tel: 04243 497,
www.ossiach.com

2 Ferlach
Carnica Bienenmuseum
No 6, Kirschentheuer,
tel: 04227 2328.
*Open mid-May to mid-
Sep, Sat–Sun and
holidays 3–6; Jul–Aug
also Tue, Thu–Fri 3–6,
Wed 3–9.*
Büchsenmacher and
Jagdmuseum
Sponheimer Platz 1,
tel: 04227 4920.
*Open mid-May to mid-
Oct 10–6; mid-Oct to
mid-May, Tue–Fri 2–6.*

6 Klagenfurt
Landhaus and
Wappensaal
tel: 0463 57757.
*Open Apr–Oct 9–1,
2–5. Closed Sun and
holidays.*
Landesmuseum für
Kärnten
Museumgasse 2,
tel: 0463 53630552.
*Open Tue–Sat 9–4, Sun
and holidays 10–1.*

10 Ossiach
Stiftskirche
No 1,
tel: 04243 2280.
*Open May, Jun, Sep
9.30–5; Jul–Aug 9–12,
1.30–6.*

For children
Minimundus
Villacher Strasse 241,
Klagenfurt,
tel: 0463 211940.
*Open Apr and Oct 9–5;
May, Jun, Sep 9-6; Jul–Aug
9–9.*

Special to...
Pyramidenkogel
At Keutschach.
*Open Apr, Oct 10–6;
May, Sep 10–5; Jun 9–8;
Jul–Aug 9–9.*
Zauberwald
At Rauchele See, No 3,
tel: 04273 2325.
Open May–Oct 10–6.

Back to nature
Schloss Rosegg
At Rosegg, Rosegg 1,
tel: 04274 3009.
*Castle open May–Oct
10–6. Closed Mon
except Jul–Aug.
Park open Apr–Nov 9–5.*

TOUR 9

ⓘ Burgplatz 1, Spittal an
der Drau
tel: 04762 5650220,
www.spittal-drau.at

ⓘ No 99, Flattach
tel: 04785 615,
www.flattach.at

ⓘ Döllach 47,
Grosskirchheim
tel: 04825 52121.
Hohe Tauern Park
information
Döllach 14,
tel: 04825 6161,
www.hohetauern.at

ⓘ Hof 4, Heiligenblut
tel: 04824 2001.

ⓘ Grohag, Heiligenblut,
Grossglockner
Hochalpenstrasse
tel: 04824 2212.

ⓘ Brucker Bundesstrasse
1a, Zell am See
tel: 06542 770,
www.zellamsee.com

ⓘ Bahnhofstrasse 10,
Saalfelden am
Steinernen Meer
tel: 06582 70660,
www.leogang-
saalfelden.at

ⓘ Hofmark 18, Goldegg
tel: 06415 8131,
www.goldegg.org

ⓘ No 11, Dorfgastein
tel: 06433 7277.

ⓘ Tauernplatz 1, Bad
Hofgastein
tel: 06432 71100,
www.badhofgastein.
co.at

ⓘ Kaiser-Franz-Josef-
Strasse 27, Badgastein
tel: 06434 25310,
www.badgastein.at

ⓘ No 11, Mallnitz
tel: 04784 290,
www.malnitz.at

1 Flattach
Naturdenkmal
Raggaschlucht
No 99,
tel: 04785 615.
*Open mid-May to Oct
9–6.*

2 Grosskirchheim
Goldbergbau- und
Heimatmuseum
Döllach 36,
tel: 04825 226.
*Guided tours Jun–Sep
1.30. Closed Wed, Sun.*

**6 Saalfelden am
Steinernen Meer**
Pinzgauer
Heimatmuseum
Schloss Ritzen,
tel: 06582 72759.
*Open Jul–Sep 10–12,
2–5, Sat–Sun and
holidays 12–5. Closed
Mon, Nov and Apr.*

8 Dorfgastein
Entrische Kirche
tel: 06433 7695.
*Guided tours Jul–Aug
10–5; Easter–Oct, 11,
12, 2 and 3, except
Mon.*

11 Mallnitz
BIOS Erlebniswelt
No 36,
tel: 04784 200020.
*Open mid-May to Oct
10–6; Christmas–Easter
Sun–Thu. 1–7.*

Back to nature
Wildpark and
Kindererlebnisland
At Ferleiten,
tel: 06546 220.
*Open May–Nov
8–sunset.*

TOUR 10

ⓘ Rathausplatz 1, Villach
tel: 04242 2052900.

ⓘ Dorfstrasse 30, Bad
Kleinkirchheim
tel: 04240 8212.

ⓘ Raikaplatz 242,
St Michael im Lungau
tel: 06477 8913.

ⓘ Marktplatz 134,
Tamsweg
tel: 06474 2145,
www.tamsweg.at

ⓘ No 7, Mauterndorf
tel: 06472 7949.

ⓘ Stadtplatz 17,
Radstadt
tel: 06452 7472,
www.radstadt.com

ⓘ Erzherzog-Johann-
Strasse 213, Schladming:
tel: 03687 222680,
www.schladming.com

ⓘ Bundesstrasse 13a,
Murau
tel: 03532 27200,
www.murau.at

ⓘ Hauptstrasse 1,
St Lambrecht
tel: 03585 2345.

ⓘ Hauptplatz 1,
Friesach
tel: 04268 4300,
www.friesach.at

ⓘ Dr Schnerichstrasse
12, Gurk
tel: 04266 812527.

ⓘ Hauptplatz 1,
Strassburg
tel: 04266 223613.

ⓘ Hauptplatz 1, St Veit
an der Glan
tel: 04212 5555668.

ⓘ Längseestrasse 6, St
Georgen am Längsee
tel: 04213 4192,
www.hochosterwitz.or.at

i Am Platz 7, Maria Saal
tel: 04223 2214.

4 Mauterndorf
Burg Mauterndorf and Lungauer Landschaftsmuseum
tel: 06472 7425.
Open May–Oct 10–5.30.

7 Murau
Schloss Obermurau
Guided tours mid-Jun to Sep, Wed, Fri. 3.
Stadt- und Heimatmuseum
Grazerstrasse,
tel: 03532 2720.
Guided tours Jul to mid-Sep, Thu–Sat 4.
Brauereimuseum
Raffaltplatz,
tel: 03532 326637.
Open May–Sep 3–5. Closed Mon, Sat–Sun.

8 St Lambrecht
Benediktinerstift
tel: 03585 230529.
Guided tours mid-May to mid-Oct 10.45, 2.30; Sun and holidays 2.30.

9 Friesach
Virtuelle Mythenwelt
Getreidespeicher.
Open May–Sep 9–6.

10 Gurk
Dom
Domplatz 11,
tel: 04266 823612.
Open 9–5, in winter 10–4. Guided tours 10.30, 1.30 and 3, in summer 10.30 and 2.

12 St Veit an der Glan
Verkehrsmuseum
Hauptplatz 29,
tel: 04212 555564.
Open May to mid-Oct 9–12, 2–6; mid-Jul to mid-Sep, Mon–Fri 9–6.

13 St Georgen am Längsee
Burg Hochosterwitz
At Launsdorf,
tel: 04213 2010.

Open Apr–Oct 9–5; May–Sep 8–6.

Back to nature
Holzmuseum
At St. Ruprecht ob Murau,
tel: 03534 2202.
Open Apr–Oct 9–4; Jul–Aug 9–5.

TOUR 11

i Herrengasse 16, Graz
tel: 0316 80750,
www.graztourismus.at

i Peter Rosegger Gasse 1, Köflach
tel: 03144 2519750.

i Hauptplatz 15a, Knittelfeld
tel: 03512 864640.

i Hauptplatz 1, Judenburg
tel: 03572 85000,
www.judenburg-online.at

i No 350, Spital am Pyhrn
tel: 07563 249,
www.pyhrn-priel.net

i Hauptstrasse 36, Admont
tel: 03613 2164.

i Freiheitsplatz 7, Eisenerz
tel: 03848 3700,
www.eisenerz.steiermark.at

i Peter-Tunner-Strasse 2, Leoben
tel: 03842 48148.

i Koloman-Wallisch-Platz 1, Bruck an der Mur
tel: 03862 890120,
www.bruckmur-tourismus.at

i Brückenkopf 1, Frohnleiten
tel: 03126 2374,
www.frohnleiten.at

1 Graz
Landeszeughaus
Herrengasse 16,
tel: 0316 80179810.
Open Mar–Oct 9–5; Nov–Jan 10–3. Closed Mon.

3 Knittelfeld
Benediktinerabtei
At Seckau,
tel: 03514 52340.
Guided tours May–Oct, Sun 12 and 2 or by appointment.

4 Judenburg
Stadtmuseum
Kaserngasse 27,
tel: 03572 85053.
Open Jul–Aug, Mon–Fri 9–12, 3–5, Sat 9–noon; Sep–Jun, Mon–Fri 9–noon.
Stadtturm
Hauptplatz.
Open May–Oct, Fri–Sun 10–6; Jul–Aug daily.

6 Admont
Benediktinerstift
Kulturressort,
tel: 03613 2312601.
Open Apr–Oct 10–12, 2–5; Christmas school holidays 10–12; rest of year by appointment.

7 Eisenerz
Erzberg
c/o VOEST Alpine Erzberg GmbH,
tel: 03848 3200.
Guided tours May–Oct 10, 12.30 and 3.

Special to...
Heimatmuseum
At Trofaiach, Rebenburggasse 2,
tel: 03847 2255262.
Open Sat 10–12, 3–5, Sun 10.30–12.

Back to nature
Lurgrotte
At Peggau, Lurgrottenstrasse 2,
tel: 03127 2580.
Open Apr–Oct daily 9–4.

TOUR 12

i Herrengasse 16, Graz
tel: 0316 80750,
www.graztourismus.at

i Minoritenplatz 1, Wolfsberg
tel: 04352 3340,
www.wolfsberg.at

i Rathaus, No 5, Griffen
tel: 04233 22470,
www.griffen.cc

i Hauptstrasse 10, St Paul im Lavanttal
tel: 04357 201722,
www.region-lavanttal.at

i Hauptplatz 37, Deutschlandsberg
tel: 03462 7520,
www.deutschlandsberg.at

i Sparkassenplatz 40, Leibnitz
tel: 03452 76811,
www.leibnitz.or.at

i Hauptplatz 14, Bad Radkersburg
tel: 03476 2545,
www.bad-radkersburg-online.at

i Hauptplatz 1, Feldbach
tel: 03152 30790,
www.feldbach.at

2 Griffen
Tropfsteinhöhle
tel: 04233 2029.
Guided tours May–Sep 9–11, 1–5; Jul–Aug 9–5; Oct 10–11, 1–4.

3 St Paul im Lavanttal
Stift
Hauptstrasse 1,
tel: 04357 201922.
Open May–Oct 9–5.

5 Leibnitz
Schloss Seggau
Seggauberg 1,
tel: 03452 82435.
Guided tours May–Oct, Sat 3, Sun 11.

Scenic routes
Weinmuseum
At Gamlitz, Eckberger
Weinstrasse 32,
tel: 03453 2363.
*Open Mar to mid–Nov
9–7.*

Back to nature
Schloss Herberstein
At St Johann bei
Herberstein, Buchberg
2,
tel: 03176 8825.
Open Apr–Oct 10–4.

TOUR 13

i Mozartplatz 5,
Salzburg
tel: 0662 889870,
www.salzburginfo.at

❸ Residenz
Residenzplatz 1,
tel: 0662 80422690.
Open 10–5.
Residenzgalerie
Residenzplatz 1,
tel: 0662 840451.
*Open 10–5. Closed Wed
Oct–Mar.*

**❻ Festung
Hohensalzburg**
Mönchsberg 34,
tel: 0662 84243011.
*Open mid-Mar to mid-
Jun 9–6; mid-Jun to mid-
Sep 8.30–8; mid-Sep to
mid-Mar 9–5. Guided
tours with audio-tape in
7 languages:
Fürstenzimmer and
Burgmuseum, mid-Mar to
mid-Jun 9.30–5; mid-Jun
to mid-Sep 9–5.30;
mid-Sep to mid-Mar
9.30–4.30.
Rainermuseum open only
May to mid-Oct.*

❼ Mozart Geburtshaus
Getreidegasse 9,
tel: 0662 844313.
*Open 9–5.30; Jul–Aug
9–6.30.*

Schloss Hellbrunn
Fürstenweg 37,
tel: 0662 8203720.
Open Apr–Oct 9–4.30;

*May, Jun and Sep
9–5.30; Jul–Aug 9–10.*

Back to nature
**Zoo Salzburg in
Hellbrunn**
At Anif,
tel: 0662 8201760.
*Open Nov–Feb 8.30–4;
Mar–Apr 8.30–4.30;
May to mid-Sep
8.30–6.30; mid-Jun to
mid-Sep, Fri–Sat
8.30am–9.30pm; mid-
to end Sep 8.30–5.30;
Oct 8.30–4.*

Special to…
**Mozart Ton- und Film-
Sammlung**
Makartplatz 8,
tel: 0662 883454.
*Open Mon, Tue, Fri. 9–1,
Wed, Thu 1–5. Closed
Sat–Sun.*

For children
Spielzeugmuseum
Bürgerspitalgasse 2,
tel: 0662 620808300.
Open 9–5.

Special to…
Mozart-Wohnhaus
Makartplatz 8,
tel: 0662 87422740.
*Open 9–5.30; Jul–Aug
9–6.30.*

TOUR 14

i Mozartplatz 5,
Salzburg
tel: 0662 889870.

i Pernerinsel, Hallein
tel: 06245 85394,
www.hallein.com

i Markt 51, Golling an
der Salzach
tel: 06244 4356.

i Markt 35, Werfen
tel: 06468 5388,
www.werfen.at

i Salzburger Strasse 1,
Bischofshofen
tel: 06462 2471.

i Hauptplatz, Ing-
Ludwig-Pech-Strasse 1,
St Johann im Pongau
tel: 06412 6036,
www.stjohann.co.at

i Seestrasse 169,
Hallstatt
tel: 06134 8208,
www.hallstatt.net

i Kolloman Wallisch
Platz, Bad Aussee
tel: 03622 52323,
www.badaussee.at

i Bahnhofstrasse 6, Bad
Ischl
tel: 06132 277570,
www.badischl.at

i Graben 2, Gmunden,
tel: 097612 64305,
www.traunsee.at

i Nussdorfer Strasse
15, Attersee
tel: 07666 7719,
www.attersee.at

i Dr-Franz-Müller-
Strasse 3, Mondsee
tel: 06232 2270.

i Au 140, St Wolfgang
im Salzkammergut
tel: 06138 8003,
www.wolfgangsee.at

i Dorfstrasse 65,
Fuschl
tel: 06226 82500,
www.fuschlseeregion.com

❶ Hallein
Keltenmuseum
Pfegerplatz 5,
tel: 06245 80783.
Open Apr–Oct 9–5.
Salzbergwerk
At Bad Dürrnberg,
Zatloukalstrasse 3,
tel: 06345 80737.
*Guided tours
(approximately 2 hours):
Apr–Oct 9–5; Nov–Mar
11–3.*
Keltendorf
Ramsaustrasse 3,
tel: 06245 8528515.
*Open Apr–Oct 9–5;
Nov–Mar 11–3.*

❸ Werfen
Eisriesenwelt
tel: 06468 5248.
*Guided tours May–Oct
9.30–3.30; Jul–Aug 4.30.*
Burg Hohenwerfen
Burgstrasse 2,
tel: 06468 7603.
*Guided tours Apr–Oct
9–4.30; Jul–Aug 9–6.
Closed Mon Apr. Bird
displays11 and 15.*

❺ St Johann im
Pongau
Liechtensteinklamm
At Plankenau,
tel: 06412 8572.
Open May–Oct 8–5.

❻ Hallstatt
**Salzbergwerk
Hallstatt**
tel: 06134 8400.
*Guided tours May–Sep
9.30–4.30; Oct 9.30–3.*

❼ Bad Aussee
Salzbergwerke
At Altausse,
tel: 06132 2002490.
*Guided tours May–Oct
10–4.*

❽ Bad Ischl
Kaiservilla
Jainzen 38,
tel: 06132 23241.
*Open May to mid-Oct
9–11.45, 1–5.15. Guided
tours for groups by
appointment in winter.*
Franz-Lehár-Museum
Leharkai 8,
tel: 06132 26992.
*Guided tours May–Sep
9–12, 2–5.*

❾ Traunsee
Radmuseum
At Altmünster, Maria-
Theresia-Strasse 3,
tel: 07612 87525.
*Open May–Jun, Sat–Sun
2–5; Jul–Aug 10–12,
2–6; Sep–Oct, Sat–Sun
12–5.*
Seeschloss Ort
At Gmunden,
tel: 07612 794266.
*Guided tours May–Nov
every Sun.*

⓫ Mondsee
Heimat- und
Pfahlbaumuseum
Marschall-Wrede-Platz I,
tel: 06232 2270.
*Open May–1st week Sep
10–6; Sep–Oct 10–5,
2nd, 3rd and 4th week
Oct only Sat, Sun and
holidays.*

For history buffs
Museum Hallstatt
Seestrasse 56,
tel: 06134 8298.
*Open Mar, Nov 10–4;
May–Jun 9–6; Jul–Aug
10–7; Sep–Oct 9–4.
Closed Mon.*

Back to nature
Rieseneishöle
At Obertraun.
*Guided tours May–Oct
9.20–4; Jun to mid-Sep
9.20–4.40.*
Mammuthöle
At Obertraun.
*Guided tours end May to
mid-Sep 9.15–3; mid-Sep
to end Oct 10.20–2.30.*

TOUR 15

ⓘ Hauptplatz I, Linz
tel: 0732 70701777,
www.linz.at

ⓘ Heindlkai 13,
Mauthausen
tel: 07238 2243.

ⓘ Oberer Markt 15,
Kefermarkt
tel: 07947 5910,
www.kefermarkt.at

ⓘ Hauptplatz 14,
Freistadt
tel: 07942 75700.

ⓘ Marktplatz 45,
Haslach an der Mühl
tel: 07289 72300.

ⓘ Hauptstrasse 2,
Aigen-Schlägl
tel: 07281 8051,
www.aigen-schlaegl.at

ⓘ Markt 22, Neufelden
tel: 07282 62550.

❶ Linz
Schlossmuseum
Tummelplatz 10,
tel: 0732 774419.
*Open 9–6, Sat–Sun and
holidays 10–5. Closed
Mon.*
Ars Electronica
Center
Hauptstrasse 2,
tel: 0732 72720.
*Open 10–6. Closed
Mon–Tue.*

❷ Mauthausen
Schloss Pragstein and
Heimatmuseum
Schlossgasse I,
tel: 07238 22550.
*Open May–Oct, Mon,
Tue, Thu 5–7.*
Gedenkstätte
tel: 07238 2269.
*Open Feb–Mar, Oct to
mid-Dec 9–4; Apr–Sep
9–5.*

❹ Freistadt
Mühlviertel
Heimatmuseum
Schlosshof 2,
tel: 07942 72274.
*Open May–Oct 9–12,
2–5, Wed until 7.30.*

❺ Haslach an der
Mühl
Webereimuseum
Kirchenplatz 3,
tel: 07289 71593.
*Open Apr–Oct 9–12.
Closed Mon.*
Kaufmannsmuseum
Windgasse 17,
tel: 07289 72173.
*Open May–Oct 9–1.
Closed Mon.*
Schulmuseum
Kasten,
tel: 07289 71957.
*Open Apr–Oct 8–11,
2–5. Closed Mon.*
Museum für
Mechanische Musik &
Volkskunst
Windgasse 9,
tel: 07289 71379.
Open by appointment.
Ölmühle
Stahlmühle 1–2,
tel: 07289 71216.
Open by appointment.

❻ Aigen-Schlägl
Stift
Schlägl I,
tel: 07281 8801293.
*Open May–Oct 10–12,
1–5. Closed Mon.*

For children
Grottenbahn
Am Pöstlingberg 16,
tel: 0732 34007506.
*Open May–beginning
Sep 10–6; Apr and
Sep–beginning Nov
10–5; Advent Sunday 24
Dec 10–3.*

For history buffs
Pferdeeisenbahn
At Rainbach im
Mühlkreis,
Kerschbaum 61,
Pfarrfeld 12,
tel: 07949 6800.
*Open May–Oct, Sat–Sun
and holidays 10–4;
Jul–Aug also Mon-Fri
2–4.*

TOUR 16

ⓘ Hauptplatz I, Linz
tel: 0732 70701777,
www.linz.at

ⓘ Kaiser-Josef-Platz 22,
Wels
tel: 07242 43495.
www.tiscover.at/wels

ⓘ Rathausplatz I,
Kremsmünster
tel: 07583 7212,
www.kremsmuenster.at

ⓘ Stadtplatz 27, Steyr
tel: 07252 532290,
www.tourism-steyr.at

ⓘ Freisingerberg 2,
Waidhofen an der Ybbs
tel: 07442 511255,
www.waidhofen.at

ⓘ Steyrer Strasse I,
Seitenstetten
tel: 07477 42224,
www.seitenstetten.at

ⓘ Mauthausner Strasse
7, Enns
tel: 07223 82777.

ⓘ Marktplatz 2, Markt
St Florian
tel: 07224 5690.

❶ Wels
Burgmuseum
Burggasse 13,
tel: 07242 235694.
*Open Tue–Fri 10–5, Sat
2–5, Sun and
holidays10–12, 2–4.
Closed Mon.*

❷ Kremsmünster
Benediktinerstift
Burgfried I,
tel: 07583 5275151.
*Guided tours 10, 11, 14,
15 e 16; Nov–Easter only
10 and 2.*

❹ Waidhofen an der
Ybbs
Heimatmuseum
Oberer Stadtplatz 32,
tel: 07442 511247.
*Open Easter–Oct
10–5. Closed Mon.*

❺ Seitenstetten
Benedektinerstift
Am Klosterberg I,
tel: 07477 42300.
*Guided tours Easter–All
Saints 10, 3 or by
appointment. Gardens
open Easter–All Saints
8–8.*

❼ Markt St Florian
Chorherrenstift
Stiftstrasse I,
tel: 07224 890210.
*Guided tours Apr–Oct
10, 11, 2, 3 and 4.*

For children
Puppenmuseum
Stelzhamerstrasse 14,
Wels,
tel: 07242 44631.
*Open Sat 2–4 or by
appointment.*
Tiergarten
Maria-Theresia-Strasse,
Wels,
tel: 07242 235765.
*Open Apr–Oct 7–7.45;
Nov–Mar 7–6.*
Zoologischer Garten
Schmiding 19, Schmiding
tel: 07249 46272.

Open mid-Mar to mid-Nov 9–5.

TOUR 17

[i] Hauptplatz 1, Linz
tel: 0732 70701777,
www.linz.at

[i] Linzer Strasse 14,
Wilhering
tel: 07226 225512,
www.oberoesterreich.at
/wilhering

[i] Stadtplatz 31,
Eferding
tel: 07272 5555160,
www.eferding.at

[i] Marktplatz 61,
Engelhartszell
tel: 07717 805516.

[i] Unterer Stadtplatz
19, Schärding
tel: 07712 43000,
www.schaerding.at

[i] Stadtplatz 2, Braunau
am Inn
tel: 07722 62644.

[i] Kapuzinerberg 8,
Ried im Innkreis
tel: 07752 85180.

[i] Marktplatz 8,
Lambach
tel: 07245 2835514.

6 Ried im Innkreis
Innviertler
Volkskundehaus
Kirchplatz 13,
tel: 07752 901244.
*Open 9–12, 2–5, Sat
2–5. Closed Sun–Mon.*

7 Lambach
Benediktinerstift
Stiftpforte,
tel: 07245 21710.
*Guided tours Easter–All
Saints, daily 2pm.*

For children
Forellenzirkus
Mühlbach 2,
tel: 07717 7552.
Open 10–12, 2–6.

TOUR 18

[i] Rathausplatz 1,
St Pölten
tel: 02742 353354.

[i] Dörflstrasse 4,
Lilienfeld
tel: 02762 52212,
www.lilienfeld.at

[i] Im Markt 1, Gaming
tel: 07485 9730812.

[i] Amonstrasse 16,
Lunz am See
tel: 07486 808115,
www.lunz.at

[i] Hauptplatz 13,
Mariazell
tel: 03882 2366,
www.mariazellerland.at

[i] Rathausplatz 22,
Herzogenburg
tel: 02782 83321,
www.herzogenburg.at

2 Lilienfeld
Zisterzienser Abtei
tel: 02762 52420.
*Open 8–12, 2–6, Sun
and holidays 2–6.*

3 Gaming
Kartause Marienthron
No 1,
tel: 07485 9846649.
*Guided tours May–Oct
11 and 3.*

6 Herzogenburg
Augustiner
Chorherrenstift
Stiftsgasse 3,
tel: 02782 83113.
*Open Ap–Oct 9–11,
1–5.*

For history buffs
Schloss Pottenbrunn
Pottenbrunner
Hauptstrasse 77,
tel: 02785 2337.
*Open Apr–Oct 9–5.
Closed Mon.*

Back to nature
Naturpark Ötscher-
Tormäuer
Ufficio informazioni,

At Lackenhof,
Käferbichlstrasse 14,
tel: 07480 5286.
Ötscher-
Tropfsteinhöhle
tel: 07485 98559.
*Guided tours May–Sep,
Sat–Sun and holidays
9–4.*

For children
Saurierpark
At Traismauer,
Traisenau,
tel: 02783 20020.
*Open fine Mar–Oct
9–18.*

TOUR 19

[i] Undstrasse 6, Krems
an der Donau
tel: 02732 82676.

[i] Gartenstrasse 3,
Zwettl
tel: 02822 503127,
www.zwettl.gv.at

[i] Schremser Strasse 6,
Gmünd
tel: 02852 52506100,
www.gmuend.at

[i] Rathausplatz 1,
Weitra
tel: 02856 2998.

[i] No 39,
Rappottenstein
tel: 02828 8240.

[i] Stadtplatz 7, Grein
tel: 07268 7055.

[i] Hauptplatz 1, Ybbs an
der Donau
tel: 07412 52612.

[i] Babenbergerstrasse
1, Melk
tel: 02752 52307410.

[i] Mittergasse 3a, Spitz
an der Donau
tel: 02713 2363,
www.spitz-wachau.at

[i] No 32,
Weissenkirchen in der
Wachau
tel: 02715 2232.

[i] No 25, Dürnstein
tel: 02711 219,
www.duernstein.at

[i] Untere Landstrasse
1, Göttweig
tel: 02732 84622.

1 Zwettl
Zisterzienserstift
Stift Zwettl 1,
tel: 02822 5500.
*Guided tours May–Oct
10, 11, 2 and 3; Jul–Sep
also 4.*

2 Gmünd
Naturpark Blockheide
tel: 02852 52506.
Open all year round.
Glassmuseum and
Steinmuseum
Stadtplatz 34,
tel: 02852 5250620.
*Open May–Sep,
Mon–Fri 9–12, 1–5,
Sat–Sun and holidays
only 9–12.*

3 Weitra
Schloss
tel: 02856 3311.
*Open May–Oct
10–12.30, 2–5.30.
Closed Tue.*
Museum Alte
Textilfabrik
Brühl 12,
tel: 02856 2973.
*Open May–Oct 10–12,
12–5. Closed Mon.*

4 Rappottenstein
Burg Rappottenstein
No 85,
tel: 02828 82500.
*Guided tours May–Sep,
Tue–Sun 10, 11, 2, 3, 4
and 5; Easter, 15–30 Apr
and Oct only Sat–Sun
and holidays.*

5 Grein
Schloss Greinburg
No 1,
tel: 07268 7007.
*Open Apr–Oct by
appointment.*
Oberösterreichisches
Schiffahrtsmuseum
Schloss Grainburg.
Open Jun–Sep 10–6;

May, Oct 10–12, 1–5.
Closed Mon.

6 Ybbs an der Donau
Schloss Artstetten
At Artstetten,
tel: 07413 8302.
Open Apr–All Saints
9–5.30.

7 Melk
Stift
At Berthold
Dietmayrstrasse 1,
tel: 02752 52312232.
Open Apr–Oct 9–6;
Nov–Easter only guided
tours 11 and 2.

8 Spitz an der Donau
Schiffahrtsmuseum
Auf der Wehr,
tel: 02713 2246.
Open Apr–Oct 10–12,
2–4, Sun and holidays
10–12, 1–5. Closed
Sat.

9 Weissenkirchen in der Wachau
Wachaumuseum
No 32,
tel: 02715 2268.
Open Apr–Oct 10–5.
Closed Mon.

11 Göttweig
Benediktinerstift
At Furth bei Göttweig,
tel: 02732 85581231.
Open Jun–Sep 9–6.

Special to...
Märchenhaus & Puppenmuseum
At Rosenau,
Schloss Rosenau 11,
tel: 02822 51441.
Open Apr–Nov 9–5.
Closed Mon.

Recommended walks
Schloss Schallaburg
At Schollach-Loosdorf,
No 1,
tel: 02754 6317.
Open May–Oct 9–5;
Sat–Sun and holidays
9–6.

TOUR 20

[i] Tourist-Info
Albertinaplatz 1. Vienna
Open 9–7. Personal
callers only.
Wien-Hotels & Info
tel: 01 24555,
www.info.wien.at
Telephone information
and bookings.

1 Stephansdom
Stephansplatz,
tel: 01 515523767.
Guided tours of
cathedral, 10.30 and 3,
Sun and holidays 3;
Jun–Sep also Sat 7.
Catacombs, 10–11.30,
1.30–4.30, Sun and
holidays 1.30–4.30.

3 Hofburg
Kaiserappartaments and
Silberkammer
tel: 01 5537570.
Open 9–4.30.
Burgkapelle
tel: 01 5339927.
Open Jan–Jun, mid-Sep
to Dec, Mon–Thu 11–3,
Fri 11–1. Service with
young choristers Jan–Jun,
mid-Sep to Dec 9.15.
Schatzkammer
tel: 01 525240.
Open 10–6. Closed
Tue.

4 Neue Burg
Ephesos-Museum,
Sammlung alter
Musikinstrumente,
Waffernsammlung and
Museum für
Völkerkunde
Heldenplatz,
tel: 01 525240.
Open 10–6. Closed Tue.

5 Kunsthistorisches Museum
Maria-Theresien-Platz
(entrance Burgring 5),
tel: 01 525240.
Open 10–6. Closed Mon.
Naturhistorisches
Museum
Maria-Theresien-Platz
(entrance on Burgring
7),

tel: 01 521770.
Open 9–6.30, Wed 9–9.
Closed Tue.

6 Kunsthalle
tel: 01 5218914.
Open 10–7, Thu
10–10.
Leopold Museum
tel: 01 52570.
Open 11–7, Fri 11–9.
Closed Tue.
MUMOK
tel: 01 52500.
Open 10–6, Thu10–9.
Closed Mon.

7 Schmetterlinghaus
tel: 01 5338570.
Open Apr–Oct 10–4.45,
Sat–Sun and holidays
10–6.15; Nov–Mar
10–3.45.

8 Albertina
Albertinaplatz 1,
tel: 01 534830.
Open 10–6, Wed 10–9.

9 Nationalbibliothek
Josefsplatz 1.
Prunksaal
tel: 01 0524100.
Open May–Oct, Mon,
Wed, Fri–Sat. 10–4, Thu
10–7, Sun and holidays
10–2; Nov–Apr 10–2
except Sun.
Globenmuseum
tel: 01 53410297.
Open 11–12, Thu 2–3.
Closed Sat–Sun,, holidays
and 1–21 Sep.
Herzgruft der
Habsburger
Augustinerkirche,
Augustinerstrasse 3,
tel: 01 5337099.
Guided tours by
appointment.
Spanische Hofreitschule
Josefplatz.
Open mid-Feb to Jun, end
Aug–beginning Nov.
Lipizzaner Museum
Reitschulgasse 2,
tel: 01 5337811.
Open 9–6.

10 Kapuzinerkirche and Kaisergruft
Neuer Markt/

Tegetthoffstrasse,
tel: 01 512685312.
Open 9.30–4.

Schloss Schönbrunn
Schönbrunner
Schlossstrasse 47,
tel: 01 81113264.
Schauräume
tel: 01 81113239.
Open 8.30–5; Jul–Aug
8.30–7.
Tiergarten
tel: 01 87792940.
Open Mar and Oct
9–5.30; Apr 9–6,
May–Sep 9–6.30;
Nov–Jan 9–4.30; Feb
9–5.

For children
Riesenrad
Prater Funfair
tel: 01 7295430.
Open Nov–Feb 10–8;
Mar–Apr, Oct 10–10;
May–Sep 9am–midnight.

Special to...
Österreichische Galerie
Belvedere
Prinz-Eugen-Strasse 27,
tel: 01 79557261.
Open 9–6.
Barockmuseum and
Museum
Mittelalterlicher Kunst
Rennweg 6a.
Open 9–6.
Alpengarten
Landstrasser Gürtel 1,
tel: 01 7983149.
Open end Mar–beginning
Aug 10–6.

TOUR 21

[i] Tourist-Info
Albertinaplatz 1. Vienna
Open 9–7. Personal
callers only.
www.info.wien.at

[i] Niedermarkt 4,
Klosterneuburg
tel: 02243 34396,
www.klosterneuburg.com

[i] Minoritenplatz 2,
Tulln
tel: 02272 65836,
www.tulln.at

[i] Hauptplatz 83, Gars am Kamp tel: 02985 2276, www.kulturpark-kamptal.at

[i] Hauptstrasse 16, Geras tel: 02912 7050, www.geras.at

[i] Hauptplatz 1, Waidhofen an der Thaya tel: 02842 50350, www.waidhofen-thaya-stadt.at

[i] Litschauer Strasse 18, Heidenreichstein tel: 02862 5250660.

[i] Pleissing 2, Hardegg tel: 02948 8450.

[i] Krahuletzplatz 1, Eggenburg tel: 02984 3400, www.info.eggenburg.com

1 Klosterneuburg
Augustiner-Chorherrenstift
Stiftsplatz 1, tel: 02243 411212.
Guided tours 9–4.30; Sun, holidays and Nov–Mar 10–4.30.

2 Tulln
Egon Schiele Museum
Donaulände 28, tel: 02272 64570.
Open Feb–Nov 10–6. Closed Mon.
Schloss Grafenegg
At Haitzendorf, tel: 02735 220514.
Open Apr–Oct 10–5. Closed Mon.

4 Geras
Prämonstratenser-Chorherrenstift
Hauptstrasse 1, tel: 02912 345.
Guided tours Easter–All Saints 10, 11, 2 and 3, Sun and holidays 11, 2 and 3. Closed Mon.

5 Waidhofen an der Thaya
Erstes Waldviertler Webereimuseum
Moritz Schadekgasse 4, tel: 02842 51500.
Open May–Sep, Sun and holidays 10–12.

6 Heidenreichstein
Wasserburg
tel: 02862 52268.
Guided tours mid-Apr to mid-Oct 9, 10, 11, 2, 3 and 4. Closed Mon.
Haus des Moores
Klein Pertholz 36, tel: 02862 5250660.
Open end Mar–beginning Nov, Fri–Sun and holidays 10–4; Jul–Aug also Wed 7–9pm.

7 Hardegg
Burg Hardegg
No 38, tel: 02916 400.
Open Apr to mid-Nov 9–5; Jul–Aug 9–6.

8 Eggenburg
Krahuletz-Museum
Krahuletzplatz 1, tel: 02984 34003.
Open Easter–Dec 9–5.

For children
Schloss Rosenburg
Rosenburg am Kamp, No 1, tel: 02982 2911.
Open Apr to mid-Nov 9–5.

Special to...
Abenteuerpark Anderswelt
Litschauer Strasse 18, Heidenreichenstein, tel: 02862 52506.

TOUR 22

[i] Tourist-Info Albertinaplatz 1. Vienna Open 9–7. Personal callers only. www.info.wien.at

[i] Hauptplatz 39, Korneuburg tel: 02262 770700.

[i] Hauptplatz 6, Mistelbach an der Zaya tel: 02572 2515.

[i] No 169, Asparn an der Zaya tel: 02577 8240.

[i] Rathausplatz 1, Gänserndorf tel: 02282 265116, www.gaenserndorf.at

[i] Hauptplatz 30, Marchegg tel: 02285 710013.

[i] Am Markt 26, Orth an der Donau tel: 02212 2208, www.orth.at

1 Korneuburg
Burg Kreuzenstein
a Leobendorf, Kreuzensteinerstrasse, tel: 02262 66102.
Open Apr–Oct 10–4.

2 Mistelbach
Heimatmuseum
Barockschlössel.
Open Sat–Sun 2–6.

3 Asparn an der Zaya
Museum für Urgeschichte
Schloss Asparn, tel: 02577 8039.
Open Apr–Oct 9–5. Closed Mon.

4 Gänserndorf
Safari-Park
Siebenbrunnerstrasse 2, tel: 02282 70261.
Open mid-Apr to Oct.

5 Marchegg
Jagdmuseum and Afrikanmuseum
Schloss Marchegg tel: 02285 8224.
Open Easter–mid-Nov 10–12, 1–5. Closed Mon.

6 Orth an der Donau
Schloss
Schlossplatz 1, tel: 02212 2555.
Open mid-Mar to mid-Nov 9–12, 1–5, Sat–Sun 9–5. Closed Mon.

For children
Schulmuseum
At Michelstetten, No 8, tel: 02525 64037.
Open Apr–Oct 9–5.

For history buffs
Heimatmuseum
At Deutsch Wagram, Erzherzog Carl-Strasse 1, tel: 02247 3790.
Open mid-Mar- to Nov, Sun 10–4.

TOUR 23

[i] Tourist-Info Albertinaplatz 1. Vienna Open 9–7. Personal callers only. www.info.wien.at

[i] Kirchengasse 57, Petronell-Carnuntum tel: 02163 2228.

[i] Hauptplatz 23, Hainburg an der Donau tel: 02165 62111.

[i] Hauptplatz 11, Kittsee tel: 02143 2203.

[i] Joseph Haydn-Platz 1, Rohrau tel: 02164 2204.

[i] Hauptplatz 1, Neusiedl am See tel: 02167 2229, www.neusiedlamsee.at

[i] Schloss Esterházy 1, Eisenstadt tel: 02682 67390, www.eisenstadt.co.at

1 Petronell-Carnuntum
Archäologischer Park Carnuntum and Freilichtmuseum Petronell
Hauptstrasse 296, tel: 02163 33770.
Open end Mar–beginning Nov 9–5; Jul–Aug, Sun

and holidays 10–6.
Museum Carnuntinum
At Bad Deutsch-
Altenburg, Badgasse
40–46,
tel: 02163 33770.
*Open end Mar–beginning
Nov 10–5; Nov–Dec,
Sat–Sun 10–5. Closed
Mon.*

❸ Kittsee
**Schloss Kittsee and
Ethnographisches
Museum**
Dr Ladislaus
Batthyányplatz 1,
tel: 02143 2304.
*Open 10–5, in winter
10–4. Closed mid-Dec
to Jan.*

❹ Rohrau
**Geburtshaus Joseph
und Michael Haydn**
Obere Hauptstrasse 25,
tel: 02164 2268.
Open 10–5. Closed Mon.
Schloss Harrach
tel: 02164 22536.
*Open Apr–Oct 10–5.
Closed Mon.*

❺ Neusiedler See
**Pannonische
Heimatmuseum**
At Neusiedl an See,
Kalvarienbergstrasse 40,
tel: 02167 8173.
*Open May–Oct
2.30–6.30, Sat–Sun and
holidays also 10–12.*

❻ Eisenstadt
Schloss Esterházy
Esterházyplatz 5,
tel: 02682 7193000.
*Open 9–6; Nov–Mar
9–5.*
Haydnmuseum
Johan-Hayden-Gasse
21,
tel: 02682 7193900.
*Open end Mar–beginning
Nov 9–5.*

TOUR 24

[i] Tourist-Info
Albertinaplatz 1. Vienna
Open 9–7. Personal
callers only.

[i] K Elisabethstrasse 2,
Mödling
tel: 02236 26727.

[i] c/o Gemeindeamt
(Municipio),
Heiligenkreuz
tel: 02258 8720,
www.heiligenkreuz.at

[i] Markt 21, Gutenstein
tel: 02634 7220,
www.gutenstein.at

[i] Passhöhe 248,
Semmering
tel: 02664 20025,
www.semmering.at

[i] Schlossplatz 1,
Bad Vöslau
tel: 02252 70743.

[i] Brusattiplatz 3,
Baden bei Wien
tel: 02252 22600,
www.badenbeiwien.at

❶ Mödling
Seegrotte
At Hinterbrühl,
Grutschgasse 2a,
tel: 02236 26364.
Open 9–5.
Burg Liechtenstein
At Maria Enzersdorf,
tel: 02236 44294.
*Open Apr–Oct 9.30–5.
Closed Mon except
holidays.*

❷ Heiligenkreuz
Zisterzienserabtei
tel: 02258 8703.
*Guided tours 10, 11, 2,
3 and 4, Sun 11, 2, 3
and 4.*

TOUR 25

[i] Hauptplatz 1–3,
Wiener Neustadt
tel: 02622 373468,
www.wiener-neustadt.at

[i] Hauptstrasse 54,
Forchtenstein
tel: 02626 63125.

[i] Hauptstrasse 38,
Kobersdorf
tel: 02618 8200.

[i] Hauptplatz 10,
Lockenhaus
tel: 02616 2202.

[i] Alois Wesselyplatz 6,
Bernstein
tel: 03354 6502.

[i] Baumkircher Gasse 1,
Stadtschlaining
tel: 03355 220130.

[i] Hauptplatz 7,
Güssing
tel: 03322 44003.
[i] Schlossweg 296,
Burgau
tel: 03383 2325.

[i] Markt 63, Kirchberg
am Wechsel
tel: 02641 2460.

❶ Forchtenstein
Burg Forchtenstein
Melinda Esterházy-
Platz 1,
tel: 02626 81212.
Open Apr–Oct 9–4.

❸ Lockenhaus
Burg Lockenhaus
Günsertrasse 5,
tel: 02616 2394.
Open 8–5; Dec–Feb 8–4.

❹ Bernstein
Burg Bernstein
tel: 03354 6382.
*Open 9–12, 1–5 by
appointment.*

❺ Stadtschlaining
Burg Schlaining
Rochusplatz 1,
tel: 03355 220130.
*Open 9–12, 1–5. Closed
Mon.*

❻ Güssing
Burg Güssing
Batthyánystrasse 10,
tel: 03322 43400.
*Open Apr–Oct 10–5.
Closed Mon.*

❼ Burgau
Schloss Burgau
tel: 03383 2325.
*Open 8–12, 1–6. Closed
Sat–Sun.*

**❽ Kirchberg am
Wechsel**
Hermannshöhle
Ramsstrasse,
tel: 02641 2326.
*Guided tours Apr–Oct,
Sat–Sun and holidays
9.30, 11, 1.30, 3 and 4.*

Special to…
Stift
At Pöllau,
tel: 03335 2253
(parrocchiale),
tel: 03335 4210
(tourist office).
*Guided tours by
appointment.*
Chorherrenstift
At Vorau,
tel: 03337 23510.
*Guided tours Mon–Fri
10, 11, 2 and 3; Sat10
and 11; Sun and holidays
11, 2 and 3.*

For history buffs
Liszthaus
At Raiding.
*Open Palm Sunday–Oct
9–12, 1–5.*

A

Abentauerpark Anderswelt 143
Abtenau 101
accommodation 159–162
Admont 81
Aguntum 53
Aigen-Schlägl 112
Alpbach 42
Alpenpark Karwendel 24
Alpenwild 9
Altenfelden Wildpark 112
Anterselva/Antholz 35
Asparn an der Zaya 146
Attersee 106
automobile clubs 158

B

Bad Aussee 104
Bad Bleiberg 69
Bad Eisenkappel 55–56
Bad Hofgastein 66
Bad Ischl 104–105
Bad Kleinkirchheim 69–70
Bad Radkersburg 88–89
Bad Vöslau 154
Baden bei Wien 154
Badgastein 66–67
Bärenstein 112
Bernstein 157
Bezau 10
Bielerhöhe 11–12
Bischofshofen 102
Bludenz 12
Bodensdorf 60
Brand 12
Braunau am Inn 119
breakdowns and accidents 158
Bregenz 9
Bressanone/Brixen 34–35
Brixlegg 42
Bruck an der Mur 83
Brunico/Bruneck 35
Burgau 157
Burgenland 120–121, 155–157
Bürgeralpe 125
Burg Kreuzenstein 146
Burg Stein 88

C

car hire 158
Carinthia 48–49
children 158
credit cards 4
currency 4
customs 4

D

Dachstein caves 105
Damüls 13
Deruta 146
Deutsch Wagram 147
Deutschlandsberg 88
discounts 4
documents 158
Dorfgastein 66
Dornbirn 9
Dörrkeusche 88
drinking and driving 158
driving in Austria 158
Duller-Mühle 88
Dürnstein 130
Dürrnberg 101

E

Ebene Reichenau 69
Eberndorf 56
Eferding 118
Eggenburg 144
Ehrenhausen 87
Ehrwald 25
Eisenerz 82
Eisenstadt 151
Eisenstrasse 82
Eisriesenwelt 102
electricity 4
embassies and consulates 4
emergencies 4–5
Engelhartszell 118
Enns 116
entrance formalities 5
Europa Panoramaweg 36
Europareservat Unterer Inn 119

F

Faaker See 55
Feldbach 89
Feldkirch 14
Feldkirchen in Kärntern 59–60
Ferlach 55
Ferleiten 64
Fernsteinsee 25
Fieberbrunn 44
Flattach 62
Fliess 16
food and wine 46–47
Forchtenstein 156
Freistadt 110–111
Friesach 73–74
Frohnleiten 83
fuel 158
Fügen 38
Fuschl 107

G

Gaming 124
Gamlitz 88
Gänserndorf 146
Gänserndorf Safari-Park 146
Geras 142
Gesäuse (canyon) 82
Gmünd (Carinthia) 53
Gmünd (Lower Austria) 127
Gmunden 105
Goldegg 65–66
Golling an der Salzach 101
Göttweig 130
Graz 78–79
Greifenburg 53
Grein 128
Griffen 87
Grosser Ötscher 124
Grossglockner Hochalpenstrasse 63–64
Grosskirchheim 62–63
Grossraming 114
Gurk 74
Güssing 157
Gutenstein 153

H

Habsburgs 138–139
Hainburg an der Donau 149
Hall in Tirol 39
Hallein 101
Hallstatt 103–1-4
Hardegg 144
Hart 38
Haslach an der Mühl 111
Heidenreichstein 143
Heiligenblut 63
Heiligenkreuz 153
helmets 158
Hemmaberg 56
Hermagor 52
Herzogenburg 125
Hinterer Gosausee 104
Hittisau 10
Hohe Mut 21
Hohe Tauern National Park 36, 64
Hohe Wand 154
Hohenems 14
Horitschon 156
hospitality 5
hot water spas 84–85
Huben 36
Hutterer Höss 81

I

Igls 33
Imst 26
Innerviertel-Hausruckwald 119
Innsbruck 27
Alpenzoo 31
Altes Rathaus 28
Annasäule 28
Dom St Jakob 29
Domplatz 29
Goldenes Dachl 29
Herzog-Friedrich-Strasse 28
Hofburg 29–30
Hofkirche 30
Katzunghaus 29
Maria-Theresien-Strasse 28
Maximilianeum 29
Neuer Hof 29
Neues Stift 31
Schloss Ambras 31
St Laurentius 30
Stadtturm 28
Tiroler Landesmuseum Ferdinandeum 31
Tiroler Volkskunstmuseum 30–31
Triumphpforte 28
Weiten 30

J

Judenburg 80
Jenbach 38

K

Kals 61
Kamptal 142
Käse Strasse 10
Kaunergrat Park 22

Index

Kaunertaler Gletscher-Panoramastrasse 16
Kefermarkt 110
Keutschacher See 58
Kirchberg am Wechsel 157
Kittsee 149
Kitzbühel 43–44
Klagenfurt 57–58
Kleinarl 103
Klosterneuburg 141
Knittelfeld 79
Kobersdorf 156
Köflach 79
Kolbnitz 62
Korneuburg 146
Kötschach/Mauthen 52
Kremsmünster 114
Krimml 37

L

Ladis 17
Lambach 119
Lammeröfen 101
Landeck 16
language 5
Lavant 53
Laxenburg 149
Lech 10–11
Leibnitz 88
Leoben 82–83
Leobendorf 146
Leutasch 24
Lienz 51
lights 158
Lilienfeld 124
Linz 109
Lockenhaus 156
Lofer 44–45
Lower Austria 120–121
Lunz am See 124–125
Lurgrotte 83

M

Magdalensberg 76
Maishofen 65
Malles Venosta/Mals in Vinschgau 19
Mallnitz 67
Marchegg 146–147
Marchenschlossstrasse 127
Märchenwald Steiermark theme park 80
Maria Luggau 52
Maria Saal 76
Maria Wörth 58–59
Mariazell 125
Markt St Florian 116
Matrei am Brenner 33

Matrei in Osttirol 36
Matzen 147
Mauterndorf 71
Mauthausen 110
Mayerling 153
Mayrhofen 38
medical assistance 5
Melk 129
Merano/Meran 20–21
Michelstetten 146
Millstatt 52–53
Mistelbach 146
Mittelberg 22
Mittersill 36–37
Mödling 153
Mönchhof 151
Mondsee 106
Mönichkirchen 157
Mörbisch am See 150
motoring in Austria 5
Mühl 25
Mühlviertler Museumstrasse 110
Mühlviertel Weberstrasse 112
Murau 72
music 98–99
Muttekopf 26

N

Naturpark Grebenzen 73
Naturpark Leiserberge 146
Naturpark Ötscher-Tormäuer 124
Nauders 18
Neufelden 112
Neusiedl am See 150
Neusiedler See 150
Niedernfritz St Martin 103
Northern Salzburg 90–91

O

Obergurgl 21
Obertraun 105
Obir caves 56
Oetz 26
opening times 5
Orth an der Donau 147
Ossiach 60
Ossiacher See 60

P

Passo del Brennero/Brennerpass 33
Passo di Resia/Reschenpass 18–19
Patscherkofel 33

Peggau 83
Pertisau am Achensee 42
Petronell-Carnuntum 149
Pfänder 9
Pitztal 22
Plansee 25
public holidays 5
Pyramidenkogel 58

R

Radstadt 71–72
Rainbach im Mühlkreis 111
Rankweil 14
Rappottenstein 128
Rattenberg 42–43
Rauris 66
Reichenau 154
Reifnitz 58
Reith 42
Rennweg 70
restaurants 159–162
Reutte 25–26
Ried im Innkreis 119
roads 158
Rohrau 149–150
Rust 150

S

Saalfelden am Steinernen Meer 65
safety belts 158
Salzachöfen 101
Salzkammergut 100–107
Salzburg 92–97
  Alter Markt 96
  Burgmuseum 95
  Dom 94
  Domplatz 94–95
  Festung Hohensalzburg 95
  Getreidegasse 96
  Glockenspiel 94
  Hellbrunner Berg 96, 97
  Hettwer Bastei 97
  Hohensalzburg 93
  Kapitelplatz 95
  Kapuzinerberg 96–97
  Kapuzinerkloster 97
  Kuenburg-Bastei 95
  Mönchsberg 93
  Mozart Geburtshaus 96
  Mozartplatz 94–95
  Mozart-Wohnhaus 94
  Petersfriedhof 95
  Rainermuseum 95
  Residenz 94
  Residenzbrunnen 94
  Residenz-Neugebäude 94
  Residenzplatz 94

Schloss Hellbrunn 97
Schloss Mirabell 93
Spielzeugmuseum 95
St. Peter Erzabtei 95
St Aegidi 118
St Andrä 151
St Anton am Arlberg 11
St Corona 157
St Georgen am Längsee 75
St Georgen ob Judenburg 80
St Johann im Pongau 102–103
St Johann in Tirol 44
St Lambrecht 72–73
St Margarethen 150
St Michael im Lungau 70
St Paul im Lavanttal 88
St Peter in Holz 62
St Pölten 123–124
St Ruprecht 73
St Veit an der Glan 75
St Wolfgang im Salzkammergut 106–107
Schärding 119
Schladming 72
Schlögen 118
Schloss Eggenberg 78
Schloss Rosegg 59
Schloss Rosenburg 142
Schloss Shallaberg 129
Schruns 12
Schwarzenberg 9–10
Schwaz 41
Seewinkel National Park 151
Seitenstetten Markt 115–116
Semmering 154
Semriach 83
Serfaus 17
Shattenberg 65
Silandro/Schlanders 19–20
Sillian 51
Silvretta Hochalpenstrasse 11
Sölden 21
speed limits 158–159
Spital am Pyhrn 81
Spitz an der Donau 129
Spitzelofen 88
Stadtschlaining 157
Stams 24
Stans 41
Stausee Gespatch 16
Steyr 114–115
Strassburg 74–75
Stuibenfall 25
Stübing 87
Styria 48–49

T

Tamsweg 71
telephones 5
Thaytal National Park 144
Tierpark Herberstein 89
time 5
Tirol 6–7
tolls 159
Toplitzsee 104
tourist information 5
traffic rules 159
Traismauer 125
Traunkirchen 105
Traunsee 105–106
Trofaiach 82
Tulln 141

U

Umhausen 22–23
Upper Austria 90–91

V

Velden am Wörther See 59
Via Claudia Augusta 17
Vienna 131–137
  Albertina 135
  Alpengarten 137
  Augustinerkirche 136
  Burggarten 135
  Burgtor 133
  Donauinsel 134
  Donaukanal 134
  Donnerbrunnen 136
  Ephesos-Museum 134
  Globenmuseum 136
  Graben 132
  Heldenplatz 133
  Hofburg 133
  In der Burg 133
  Josefsplatz 135–136
  Kapuzinerkirche 136
  Katakomben 132
  Kohlmarkt 133
  Kunsthalle 134–135
  Kunsthistorisches Museum 134
  Leopold Museum 135
  Leopoldinischer Trakt 133
  Lippizaner Museum 136
  Michaelerplatz 133
  Museum für Völkerkunde 134
  Museum moderner Kunst Stiftung Ludwig 135
  MuseumsQuartier 134–135
  Nationalbibliothek 136
  Naturhistorisches Museum 134
  Neue Burg 133–134
  Neuer Markt 136
  Oberes Belvedere 137
  Palmenhaus 135
  Prunksaal 136
  Pummerin 132
  Riesenrad 133
  Sammlung alter Musikinstrumente 134
  Schloss Schönbrunn 137
  Schweizerhof 133
  Stallburg 136
  Stephansdom 132
  Stephansplatz 132
  Tiergarten 135
  UNO-City 134
  Unteres Belvedere 137
  Waffernsammlung 134
Vipiteno/Sterzing 34
Vorarlberg 6–7
Vordernberg 82
Vorderer Gosausee 104
Völkermarkt 56–57

W

Waidhofen an der Thaya 143
Waidhofen an der Ybbs 115
Walchsee 45
Wattens 39
Weissenkirchen in der Wachau 129–130
Weitra 127
Wels 114
Wenns 22
Werfen 101–102
Wiedersberger Horn 42
Wienerwald 146
Wildpark Assling 51
Wildspitze 22
Wilhering 118
Wolfsberg 87

Y

Ybbs an der Donau 128

Z

Zauberwald 58
Zeinisjoch 11
Zell am See 64–65
Zell am Ziller 38
Zibern 18
Zisterdorf 147
Zürs 10
Zwettl 127

Picture acknowledgements

ARCHIV SCHUBERTIADE/P. MATHIS 10; F. ARDITO 26, 27, 29, 91a, 96, 101; AUSTRIAN NATIONAL TOURIST OFFICE/BARTL 122; AUSTRIAN NATIONAL TOURIST OFFICE/BOHNACKER 12, 73, 87; G. CIGOLINI 90; AUSTRIAN NATIONAL TOURIST OFFICE/DIEJUN 107a; ENTE NAZIONALE AUSTRIACO PER IL TURISMO 17, 22, 23, 34-34, 35, 40, 45, 48, 55, 58-59, 59, 60, 61, 63, 70, 84, 92, 93, 98, 100, 102, 103, 123a, 129, 142, 152, 153, 154; AUSTRIAN NATIONAL TOURIST OFFICE/FANKHAUSER 145; FARABOLAFOTO/P. PESCALI 46-47, 127; /P. SCHOLEY 47a; /STRUMMER 66, 82, 123b; AUSTRIAN NATIONAL TOURIST OFFICE/H.P. GRANER 144b; AUSTRIAN NATIONAL TOURIST OFFICE/GRUENERT 113; AUSTRIAN NATIONAL TOURIST OFFICE/HERZBERGER 156-157; AUSTRIAN NATIONAL TOURIST OFFICE/JEZIERZANSKI 114-115, 115, 144a; AUSTRIAN NATIONAL TOURIST OFFICE/KHS/REINHARD 89; AUSTRIAN NATIONAL TOURIST OFFICE/LAMM 105; M. LANFRANCHI 24; AUSTRIAN NATIONAL TOURIST OFFICE/MALLAUN 16b; M.E. SMITH 9, 15, 16a, 18, 20a, 21, 25, 50, 54, 69a, 69b, 71, 74, 75, 80, 81, 84a, 84b, 86, 91b, 109, 117, 118, 119, 120; AUSTRIAN NATIONAL TOURIST OFFICE/MARKOWITSCH 4-5, 13a, 72, 140; AUSTRIAN NATIONAL TOURIST OFFICE/MAYER 156; OVERSEAS 52-53, 67, 128; M. PEDONE 38, 39; AUSTRIAN NATIONAL TOURIST OFFICE/PIGNETER 20; AUSTRIAN NATIONAL TOURIST OFFICE/G. POPP 36-37; AUSTRIAN NATIONAL TOURIST OFFICE/RAMSTORFER 155; G. ROLI 30, 32, 37, 41, 43, 47b, 51, 64, 64-65; AUSTRIAN NATIONAL TOURIST OFFICE/ROSENFELD 14; AUSTRIAN NATIONAL TOURIST OFFICE/SIMONER 125; G. SOSIO 7, 28, 31, 33, 49b, 56, 57, 76, 78, 79, 83, 94, 95, 97, 104, 108, 110, 116, 121, 126; THE IMAGE BANK/G. CRALLE 99a; /E. FREA 46; /J.R. RAMEY 99b; /S. SCATÀ 77; /P. AUSTRIAN NATIONAL TOURIST OFFICE/TRUMLER 44-45; /S. WILKINSON 11; / H. WOLF 18-19; TRUMLER 88, 107b, 111, 112, 124, 139; VORARLBERG TOURISMUS/C. BRANZ 13b; /P. MATHIS 6, 49a; /R. HORNER 8; AUSTRIAN NATIONAL TOURIST OFFICE/W. WEINHAEUPL 68, 106.